The Regulation of Madness

Robert Castel

The Regulation of Madness

The Origins of Incarceration
in France

Translated by
W. D. Halls

University of California Press
Berkeley and Los Angeles

University of California Press
Berkeley and Los Angeles

© 1988 by Polity Press
in association with Basil Blackwell
First published as *L'Ordre psychiatrique* by
Les Editions de Minuit
© 1976 by Les Editions de Minuit
English translation first published in 1988 by Polity Press
in association with Basil Blackwell
U.S. edition published in 1988 by the University of California Press

Printed in Great Britain

1 2 3 4 5 6 7 8 9

Library of Congress Cataloging-in-Publication Data

Castel, Robert.
   The regulation of madness.
   (Medicine and Society; v. 1)
   Translation of: L'Ordre psychiatrique.
   1. Psychiatry—France—History—19th century.
I. Title. II. Series.
RC450.F7C3713 1988   616.89′00944   87-35856
ISBN 0-520-06306-6

Contents

Introduction

On 27 March 1790 the Constituent Assembly decreed, in Article 9 of the law concerning the abolition of *lettres de cachet*, as follows:

> Persons detained because of a state of insanity within three months dating from the publication of the present decree, and upon the order of our prosecutors, will be interrogated by judges in the customary form and, by virtue of the latter's instructions, will be examined by doctors who, under the supervision of the district directors, will enquire into the true situation of those sick so that, in accordance with the decision taken about their condition, they are either freed or cared for in hospitals that will be designated for this purpose.[1]

This decision of the first Revolutionary assembly encompasses the whole modern problem of madness. For the first time all the elements that, right up to the present day, were to constitute the bases for the assumption of social responsibility for madness, and its anthropological status, are set out together. But, although they are all cited, the definitive articulation between the various parts had not yet been found. These elements are four in number:

1 *The political context of the advent of legal intervention* The modern question of madness arises from the break-up of the traditional balance of powers, and precisely because of the collapse of the ancient foundations of political legitimacy. Under the *Ancien Régime* the royal administration, the judicial apparatus and the family shared control over deviant forms of behaviour, according to procedures regulated by tradition. With the abolition of the *lettres de cachet*, an essential piece of the framework abruptly went

missing, ruining the construction as a whole. Because the repression of madness still appeared to be just as necessary, direct
recourse to the political authority in order to bring this about was
blocked, since that authority was disqualified, as being a
manifestation of royal tyranny.

2 *The appearance of new agents* The authorities entrusted to fill this
gap are appointed without difficulty: justice (prosecutors and
judges), local authorities ('district directors') and medicine. It is
apparently merely a matter of calling upon those authorities
already in operation to establish fresh relationships with one
another. But, as they are, they cannot immediately fill the gap
left by the one missing authority. A long process of transformation of their practices and a renegotiation of their relationships will be needed before they are able to assume their new
task. A stable equilibrium will be found only when medicine is
able to constitute its cornerstone.

3 *The attribution of patient status to the insane person* In so far as
procedures for the assumption of responsibility for insanity are
no longer destined to be consistent with those that control
criminals, vagabonds, beggars and other social 'marginals', the
insane person is recognized as different. But such a system of
classification at first poses more problems than it resolves. The
medical code is not yet finely enough adjusted to endow this
identification with a scientific status. Medicine has as yet no
specific techniques for dealing with insanity. Its place for medical
specialization on both the theoretical and practical plane, is
indicated through this new political mandate, but as yet it
remains unfilled.

4 *The constitution of a new institutional structure* The privileged
installation of these practices in 'hospitals that will be designated
for this purpose' is also anticipated. But this is the very moment
when such institutions are tainted by discredit. This discredit
was attached to those places of segregation which the royal
administration and the Church had made the instruments of
their policy for neutralizing those they considered undesirable or
their enemies. It is also the moment when a general move to
break up institutions of public assistance had destabilized the
former institutional hospital complex, at the same time as it did
the strongholds of political absolutism. The imposing of a
'special institution' (or asylum) as a 'therapeutic environment'

thus presupposes the reconquest by the new medicine of a part of
the old hospital organization that was the object of popular
hatred and the scorn of enlightened minds.

Condemnation of political arbitrariness in 1790; and the passing of
the law, still in force, governing regulations for the insane in 1838.
This lapse of time of nearly fifty years between two legislative events
is in fact filled by a slow progress in practices relating to the insane.
What the Constituent Assembly had put forward as a formal
solution – although it may have been a means of escape from a
critical situation – became institutionalized as a new structure of
domination. The insane person, who surfaced as a problem in the
rupture caused by the Revolution, will at the end of the process
come under the aegis of a complete statute for the insane. He will
have become completely a medical matter, that is to say wholly
defined as a social person and human type by the authority that had
gained for itself a monopoly in assuming legitimate responsibility for
him. This is the first history that must be traced, for it is that of the
reciprocal constitution of a new form of medicine and a new social
relationship of guardianship.

An old story, it will be said, and sufficiently well known. In fact, a
somewhat glib inclination to symmetry would draw a contrast
between a kind of totalitarian Utopia, a paradigm of nineteenth-
century psychiatry, and one that might be said to be capillary, the
main escape route for present-day mental health medicine: shutting
away / release; segregation of the people concerned / treatment in
an everyday environment; enclosure / 'deinstitutionalization';
asylum / hospital section; normal and pathological dualism / fluidity
of present-day psycho-pathological categories; harsh stigmatization
through nosographic labels / universalist application of new
psychiatric and psycho-analytical codes; treatments limited to well-
defined areas (patent pathological and criminal states) / initiatives
embracing every type of behaviour and even cutting across the traditional cleavages between the psychological, the cultural, the social
and the political; specialized expertise / generalized expertise;
authoritarianism, paternalism and directiveness / permissiveness, a
welcome and listening; the solitary exercise of power / the circulation of information among a team and, at the margin, reversibility
of the roles of 'carers' and 'patients', etc.

All is not false in these pairs of opposites, provided that one looks closely at how, why and for whom they function. A system is said to be outmoded when there is hardly anyone left to defend it. Yet this is often because those that used to operate it have simply moved on and begun to do something else, which, all things being equal, might not be so very different. For example, there are no longer many who practise shutting away the insane: the 'therapeutic isolation' of the nineteenth century appears crude enough for the social segregation it effects to be detectable without too much difficulty – above all by those who have ceased to practice it. On the contrary, the adoption of psychoanalysis or behaviourist conditioning will find more defenders. The latter will not assent to such a hypothesis: it is because those same professionals who used to segregate now integrate the insane that those who used to exclude them now subject them to norms. However, one cannot set a rendezvous for some date within a century in order to see how things will turn out.

Hence the proposal made here to try to render axiomiatic the data system that constitutes a 'policy of mental health', and to follow its transformations. Such a policy, irrespective of the rationalizations behind which it shelters, links together a limited number of elements: a theoretical code (for example, in the nineteenth century, the classical categories of illness); a technology of intervention (for example, 'moral treatment'); an institutional set-up (for example, the asylum); a body of professionals (senior consultants); a statute for the 'user' (for example, the insane person, defined in the 1838 law as being a non-adult assisted person). I am simplifying: there are also those that make payment, the intermediaries, the promoters, and those that make demands, etc. This group of variables forms a relatively stable complex, whose content is relatively fixed. Thus, as we shall see, the synthesis of elements relating to asylums presented an extraordinary coherence, since each one of its parts had been constructed in relation to all the others, on the basis of the common pattern of internment.

This is not a functionalist hypothesis. On the one hand, these dimensions do not constitute the elements of a structure, but the crystallization of practices worked out in a precise historical context in relation to a complex of concrete social problems. On the other hand, the relative stability of the whole does not rule out conflicts, tensions, crises, course deviations, readjustments of equilibrium, or changes. But one must draw a distinction between a change, however important, in a series, and the transformation of the entire set of mechanisms. For instance, in relation to the initial classifications of insanity, the discovery of monomania by Esquirol, and then that of the degenerative process by Morel, shook the belief in the rationality of the classifications that had been constituted on the basis of the grouping of symptoms (see chapter 4). However, this crisis was surmountable within the framework of the system. The interest shown in agricultural settlements about 1860 opened up a breach in the absolute supremacy of the asylum within the institutional framework. As much might also be said concerning legislation, therapeutic remedies, the status of staff, etc. Nevertheless, almost a century later the structure was still standing. Processes of evolution, and crises, however important they may be, can give rise to rather lame compromises, and more or less chance restructurings. They can even signal a new departure, by imparting a fresh impetus to a tired-out organization. Thus the triumph of organicism at the end of the nineteenth century established once more the permanence of the asylum.

In contrast to a series of changes, I term the transformation of all the elements in the system a *metamorphosis*. It denotes the transition to another kind of cohesion; it is the expression of a different policy. It can no longer be interpreted on the basis of an internal restructuring of the medical mechanisms. It is the outcome of a global renegotiation of the distribution of power with the other controlling authorities: justice, the central administration, the local communities, the school, families, etc. From the 1860s onwards there were criticisms of the asylum, the law of 1838, psychiatric knowledge, and medical treatments. These were as violent and lucid as those of modern anti-psychiatric critics. But it has only been a few decades since a global alternative model has begun to emerge, positing the replacement of the former system by taking over all the previous functions, and adding some others. Thus we are living through the first metamorphosis of mental medicine since the endorsement through the law of 1838 of the synthesis based upon the asylum.

Thus, a decisive transformation. But the choice of the term 'metamorphosis' implies no value judgement on the meaning and ultimate outcomes of the change. It is precisely the purpose of this analysis to attempt such an assessment. Let us therefore not prejudge the result. Is it a mutation, a revolution? This is not self-evident.

According to the Petit Robert dictionary, 'metamorphosis' means: 'Change in nature, form or structure that is so considerable that the being or thing that is its object *is no longer recognizable.*' Thus everything can be different. Nevertheless, Zeus changed into a bull is still Zeus. He is – and is not – Zeus, and one has to be more skilful in recognizing him. The same functions can be realized through practices that have been entirely renewed, monopolies of the same type can be perpetuated, and identical interests worm their way in. This remains to be seen.

Following the same line of logic, rather than be so bold as to claim that mental medicine has carried out its revolution (if the psychiatrists are to be believed, it is already undergoing its third or fourth one), more prudently, I shall formulate the hypothesis that its *aggiornamento* is proceeding. In the first place, metaphor for metaphor, religious symbolism is better suited for the type of respectability attached to the medical profession. But above all because, at least up to the present, the high priests of psychiatry have done their utmost to keep control of the changes.

A council of the Church is a rendezvous with history, in the course of which the clerics themselves carry out the diagnosis of the crisis, call upon the faithful to espouse once more their century, to transform the ritual, and yet remain faithful to the spirit of the doctrine. External changes are welcomed, but on condition that one can re-interpret them within the logic of the dogma and under the authority of its qualified interpreters. Modern French psychiatry has held its councils (the Journées de Sainte-Anne in 1945, a certain colloquium at Bonneval, Bonnafé-Ey-Lacan, and that of Sèvres in 1958 . . .). Marxists, psychoanalysts and progressives have shaken the old-style mental health specialists who called a sick person a madman and practised exclusion from society with a clear conscience. That was important. We must take seriously the new strategies that they have defined (the hospital sector, institutional psychotherapy, listening to the patient, serving the 'user', etc.) for they concern, or will concern, many people: they are ambitious strategies. But let us also realize that such specialists do not possess papal infallibility when they decree that we have entered a totally new era. If *each one of the dimensions* of the complex of problems relating to mental health has been profoundly shaken up (or is in the process of transformation), *their interrelationship* continues fairly adequately to circumscribe almost everything done in this field. Let us concede as much as possible to the apostles of change. Professionals, who have become extremely numerous, continue to work in institutions that have exploded the theoretical codes, which themselves have become more subtle; technologies that have been diversified continue to meet populations whose numbers have increased and whose characteristics have become more subtly defined. These constitute many innovations. Yet they do not invalidate the hypothesis that the same apparatus of domination was able, during the course of its modernization, to renew its prestigious nature, to tighten its grip and multiply its powers.

Thus it may well be that the present psychiatric and psychoanalytic mode of discourse represents the sticking point for 'spiritualists' considering a profound transformation in the forms through which the dominant authority imposes its will. The actors could be the instruments for the installation of new mechanisms of control, with manipulators and manipulated in a general renegotiation among those authorities responsible for the codification of norms. In any case, the ultimate goal of an evaluation of present-day mental medicine should be to help draw this new map of constraints through the reorganization of public assistance, of social work, of the assumption of responsibility and committal into guardianship.

Yet it is also the field for which we are the least equipped, as we are swept along in a current that takes everybody along with it. If the nineteenth century put out more reliable benchmarks, it is not only because it allowed axiomatic expression of the form of the asylum system that is now moribund. The relationships between the medical machinery for mental health and the judicial and administrative mechanisms, the state of the labour market, the policy towards the poor, towards deviants and 'marginals', at that time also appeared to be less confused. Because the issues have shifted, we are today less linked to the categories of the nineteenth century. Because the old strategies were deployed right to the very end, until they had worn threadbare, they exhibit a perfect coherence when we read of them. The proposal to use these models in order to help unravel the more confused situation in which the analyst finds himself caught today is the 'methodological' justification for this long detour.

Thus there will be close solidarity between the two wings of this diptych: the *golden age*, or the installation and triumph of a new official authority that gains a monopoly in the legitimate treatment of madness (through strategies, at the expense of other authorities, with the help of others, and for whom, etc.); and the *aggiornamento*, or the present modification of practices and the displacement of functions (on the basis of a certain plan, through certain conflicts, in relationship to certain issues at stake, etc.). The analysis of the transformation in the same constellations of objects – in schematic form: codes, technologies, institutional mechanisms, professional and political actors, the status of the 'users' – these will weave a net-work of relationships between the two eras which each time will attempt to fit the medicine of mental health into its specific social context. There is a first metamorphosis, at the moment when mental health medicine is constituted, amid the revolutionary destruction of the traditional equilibrium existing between authorities, one which served to rectify their deficiencies, in harmony with the new bourgeois conception of legitimacy. The second metamorphosis is the moment when the mechanisms of control transform their authoritarian and coercive techniques into treatments that are manipulatory and persuasive.

Here I set out only the first 'wing' of this study, the *golden age*, as the realization in part of a long-standing project. Such an intention does not weave a course through events and men without contracting debts at every encounter. I can name only those that appear essential to me. I first conceived of this project within the framework of the research programme of the Centre de Sociologie Européenne concerning relationships of symbolic inculcation. The works of Pierre Bourdieu and Jean-Claude Passeron, in particular, open the way to a taxonomy for the interpretation of the mechanisms of domination whose relevance goes far beyond the interpretation of the education system. In this work are to be found much more than traces of this. The reader will also perceive all that the study owes to the works of Michel Foucault. *L'histoire de la folie* marks a cut-off point in medical ethnocentricity in whose wake any undertaking of this nature can only follow. But there is no question of this basis being a mythical one. I have taken for granted a number of analyses made in the book, and borrowed from the other works of Michel Foucault certain of the categories that henceforth control access to a materialist theory of power.

The contemporary part will make plainer what the French and foreign members of the 'alternative to psychiatry' network have helped me to understand, and particularly those of the group once constituted with Franco Basaglia, at the time when these hypotheses were taking shape. But already their friendship allows me to hope that the critical difference I have held *vis-à-vis* the viewpoint of the technocratic professionals in the medicine of mental health is not at odds with the position of all those working in this sector. This distance in relation to the dominant model of psychiatry seeks to be, in its theoretical range, the same as others try to impose in their practice.

Finally, I should like to thank those who have kindly read the manuscript, and whose vigilance has not been lulled to sleep by our community of views, strengthened by lengthy exchanges.

A word in conclusion about the pace of the exposition, another about its tone, and a last one about its level.

The pace will be slow. This is a calculated risk. A few years ago, the fact of demonstrating that the asylum is not a wholly therapeutic environment, that the mandate entrusted to the psychiatrist is not entirely medical, or that the psychoanalyst does not deal solely with the unconscious, might have made an impact. Today, when certain elements in this criticism have become part of the atmosphere of the times, the threshold must be heightened. Not in order to create better theory, but as a function of the practical stance that is imperative nowadays. To fight against the process of constraint and dispossession deployed by mental health medicine demands an exact consciousness of the *modus operandi* of these new 'soft' technologies. Thus it is necessary to build and rebuild, and to dismantle their concrete workings. It has perhaps been said often enough that psychiatric knowledge is not 'serious' and that the procedures of psychoanalysis are monotonous. Nevertheless their operators are neither naïve jesters nor impudent usurpers. They are sophisticated technicians whose jurisdiction is becoming more extensive and whose power is increasing. Today one would run the risk of being led astray if one took short cuts out of impatience, even if that were boiling over.

As for the tone of such a criticism regarding the agents who propagate such techniques, everyone will interpret it as he deems fit, but I reject any note of moral condemnation as well as the position of the sermonizer. The modern slogan of 'cop-psychiatrist', taken literally, is nonsense. If the psychiatrist and the policeman performed precisely the same function and did exactly the same work, why would they have been duplicated? The first specialists in mental health were well-intentioned young men, ambitious and often poor, with 'social' ideas. Having completed their medical studies, they 'went up' to Paris (they often came from the South). They went to the Salpêtrière Hospital, following assiduously the course taught by the maestro of the age, Esquirol. They were won over by this kind of teaching, which linked the apparent rigour of science, the broad aspirations of philanthropy and the prestige of being 'Parisian'. There is nothing machiavellian or dishonourable about that. Just look at the present day.

For advocates of all parties, let us consider the history of one of them, Ulysse Trélat. Trélat has the career profile of the best specialists in mental health: one-time houseman at the Salpêtrière, a disciple of Esquirol, he went into peaceful retirement after a long time as the senior consultant at the Salpêtrière. But, from the foundation of the French *Carbonari* movement in 1821, he had been a *carbonaro*, a representative in the central Vente lodge, a titular member of the Haute Vente lodge in Paris. Up to 1848 he had been involved in every plot, organizing the *Carbonari* movement in the French *départements*, mounting the barricades in 1830, then opposing the reinstallation of the monarchy, and being brought to justice several times. Before the Chamber of Peers he pronounced these proud words, which earned him three years in prison: 'What need have you of justice? . . . Tyranny has its bayonets, its judges and your embroidered collars; liberty has truth on its side. Sentence me, but you will not judge me.' He was not to serve his sentence, but was placed in forced residence at Troyes because of ill-health, after the intervention of his best friend, François Leuret.

Trélat was the close friend of one of the four sergeants of La Rochelle, and of Leuret, who represents the most 'muscular' form of paternalism among mental health specialists. The revolution of 1848 rewarded his intransigent opposition by making him a minister, but in 1861 he wrote *La folie lucide* to warn families against those insane who are even more dangerous because they appear to be inoffensive: 'Not only has nothing been done for the improvement of the human race, but it is left absolutely free, and, we may say also, absolutely ignorant and blind, to deteriorate without ever having been given any warning . . . Do not allow ourselves to mix poison with blood that can be passed on noble and pure.'[2]

I have not chosen this picture from a storybook to illustrate the eternal contradiction between intentions and actions (moreover, what meaning should be read into it?). But it can help to trace the bounds of the political dimension with which this book has to deal.

The range of the analysis has little to do with the subjective intentions of the actors. Nor does it claim either to denounce machiavellian programmes that smack of political fiction. There is no Leviathan State, no abstract class domination allegedly imposing from on high its authority through ideological or other mechanisms worked by cynical operators. At the very most one might say that mental health medicine *became*, fairly late on and then only partially, one piece in a centralized apparatus of power. But this is because it had already been constituted as a specific technology, had carved out privileged paths for itself and had laid siege to strategic strongpoints. Before its adoption into the official scheme of power distribution, and even afterwards, it won its place in the sun by taking risky initiatives, proceeding by trial and error. Wide-ranging practices progress slowly, meet up with and confront one another, before flowing into one another and pursuing a systematic course.

This coherent order is difficult to define. Yet it is this that characterizes the political effectiveness that is peculiar to mental health medicine. Let us state – it will be the object of the analysis to demonstrate it – what promotes a new type of technical management of social antagonisms. Psychiatry is indeed a political science, for it answered a problem of government. It allowed madness to be 'administered'. But it displaced the direct political impact of the problem, proposing a solution for it by turning it into a 'purely' technical question. If there is repression, it is contained in this: through medicine, madness became capable of being administered.

Thus it is this constitution of the 'administered' madman (if I dared I would say, 'the administratively manageable' madman), in order to administer madness, in the sense of *actively* reducing its entire reality to the conditions of its management in a technical framework – this is what we must unravel. A lengthy exchange of places, in numerous episodes, between doctor and administrator dominates the whole history of mental health medicine. The successive states of equilibrium arrived at in these exchanges impart concretely a content to what must be understood as a strategy of social control: not the brutal imposition of an apparatus of coercion, but the setting up of practical arrangements by the well-intentioned people responsible. The other partners – above all the judge and the policeman – supervise the negotiation, standing somewhat in the background. They also have become marginal: to the extent that where administration and medicine set their machine in motion, and when that works well, they lose all jurisdiction. As for the madman himself, let us leave him out. In this order of logic there is really not much to say, and even less to let *him* say.

Why this complicity between medicine and the administration? Why, correlatively, the dispossession of justice and the police in their role of *direct* intervention?

Against the backcloth of the contractual society that is installed by the French Revolution, the madman stands out. Unreasonable, he is not amenable to the law; irresponsible, he cannot be the object of punishment; incapable of working or 'being useful', he does not enter the regulated round of exchanges, that 'free' circulation of goods and men for which the new bourgeois legality serves as the blueprint. A focus of disorder, more than ever he must be repressed, but according to a system of punishments different from that laid down by the legal codes for those who have wittingly transgressed against the laws. A little island of irrationality, he must be administered, but in accordance with norms that are different from those that assign to their station and submit to their tasks 'normal' subjects in a rational society.

These contradictions have introduced a practice of expertise into the very heart of the functioning of modern societies. An assessment based upon technical competence imposes on certain 'marginal' groups a *statute* that will have legal validity, although constituted on the basis of technical and scientific criteria, and not on juridical precepts laid down in the legal codes. A process of nibbling away at the law by a form of knowledge (or pseudo-knowledge – but that is not the main question), the progressive subversion of legal process by activities requiring expertise – these constitute one of the great trends that, since the coming of bourgeois society, is at work in the process of deciding the destinies of men. The trend is one that proceeds from contract to guardianship.

Mental health medicine was an essential actor in that transformation. As we shall see, the machine was set in motion by the question of madness. The great success of its golden age was the medical, juridical and administrative statute of the *insane person*, legitimized by the law of 30 June 1838. Modest and open beginnings: this first stage involved a few thousand mad persons duly labelled and handed over to a few hundred highly expert professionals. A brutal placing into guardianship, total, implying the entire status of an under-age person, and total sequestration. But the distinction made between the normal and the pathological, on which such an operation relied, must be read both ways: the 'mad' were completely mad, and the 'normal' were completely normal.

This was certainly not an ideal state. Perhaps, however, we are beginning to suspect that there were not solely advantages in breaking up this rigid dichotomy. Today, this form of activity by experts, having been generalized, is on the way to becoming the true magistracy of our age. An increasing number of decisions in sectors of social and personal life that are ever more numerous are being taken on the basis of technical and scientific assessments produced by the competent experts. There is doubtless no limit that can be assigned to this process. But at the very least one should dare to ask: 'Who has made you king?' of the one who has made *you* the subject and the subjected.

1

The Challenge of Madness

In the Revolutionary era there were several thousand insane. Even in 1834, Ferrus reckons there were hardly 10,000.[1] This is very few in comparison with some two million poor, 300,000 beggars, roughly 100,000 'travellers', and 300,000 foundlings.[2] Yet most of these acute 'social problems' remained without legal solution right up to the first 'social laws' of the Third Republic. The Law of 30 June 1838 concerning the insane was the first great legislative measure that recognized a *right of assistance and treatment* for a category of the sick or those in need. It was the first one to set up a complete mechanism of assistance, with the invention of a new 'space', the asylum, the creation of the first body of medically qualified civil servants, the constitution of a 'special knowledge', etc. Why did legislation concerning the insane precede by half a century all the other measures of public assistance, going beyond them in its systematic approach? One cannot speak of the need to 'win back some of the labour force' at a time when hundreds of thousands of the poor, less unproductive, were without a job. Nor can one adduce the pathos aroused by madness when families idling away their Sunday afternoons slipped a tip into the hand of the warder at the Bicêtre Hospital so they could gawp at the contortions of the demented.

Madness posed a challenge to the society that had arisen as a result of the convulsions of the fall of the *Ancien Régime*. And in that collapse the challenge was picked up because what was at stake was the credibility of its principles and the balance of powers. There were grave bourgeois matters concerning order, justice, the administration, finance, discipline, the police, and government, where the pathos of madness would be literally out of place. Discussions of the madman's fate have only ever involved those entrusted with the task of controlling him. Thus we shall begin by analysing this distribution of responsibility, and by questioning the responsibility for this distribution at the moment when it begins, during the crisis of the Revolution.[3]

The State, Justice and the Family

Before the Revolution the judicial and executive powers shared the responsibility for the detention of the mentally deranged. Their complex, inadequately harmonized procedures gave rise to conflicts of jurisdiction, but these did not call into question the legal foundation for repressive official modes of conduct.

'Justice orders' consisted of decrees or sentences of detention, generally for an unlimited period, handed down by numerous legally empowered jurisdictions (*parlements*, baileywick tribunals, provost jurisdictions, the tribunal of the Châtelet in Paris, etc.). Occasionally, detention was decided on a 'special order' issued by a magistrate, but this measure, suspected of running the risk of being arbitrary, was tending to fall into disuse at the close of the *Ancien Régime*. The most elaborately worked out judicial procedure was that of *interdiction*, which the Napoleonic Code was to adopt practically in its entirety. Upon a demand presented by the family (and, exceptionally, by the royal prosecutor), the judge gave his decision, after marshalling the evidence, summoning the parties involved to appear, and questioning the insane person. The person declared to be mentally deranged could then be detained (but there was no obligation to do this) in a prison, and his goods taken into custodial guardianship.[4] The complexity of this procedure, its high cost, the publicity of discussions that was so feared because of 'family honour', made it a measure to which relatively little recourse was had. By adding up the number of interdictions and other modes of confinement by judicial process, one can assess that by the end of the *Ancien Régime*, roughly one-quarter of detentions of the mad originated through 'justice orders'.[5]

Other forms of detention order, namely, the majority, were taken on the strength of a 'royal order' or *lettre de cachet*. The former was issued through the minister of the king's household, either on the initiative of the public authorities or on that of the family. Thus, when a mental defective disturbed the public order, the services of the Paris Lieutenant of Police, or in the provinces the *Intendants*, could request the king to issue an order for confinement. They could even take the insane person into custody, but provisional detention only became legal after the obtaining of the *lettre de cachet*.

A 'royal order' could also be obtained upon a request by the family. Through a *placet* the family then justified the reasons for which it sought the confinement of the mentally deranged person (or more generally, the disturber of family order: a prodigal, a libertine or a debauched person, etc.) If the king, through the minister of his household, granted the order, the insane person became one of those 'family prisoners' who made up roughly nine-tenths of those detained under *lettres de cachet* issued under the *Ancien Régime*.[6]

Thus royal power played a double role. Armed with the prerogatives of the executive, it intervened to safeguard public order against disturbances caused by the insane. Yet it was more often a staging point and a regulator in the exercise of the power of punishment appertaining to families. It was the royal power that legitimized and in the last resort evaluated the grounds for the family request. Occasionally the order was not granted despite the 'very humble supplications' of the family. The king's agents could then ask for additional enquiries to be made, or advise the family to set in motion an interdiction procedure.[7]

Such a system was certainly not simple. Yet it was not arbitrary either. It expressed a balance – one that was not without its tensions – between three authorities: royal, judicial and family. These gave mutual support to one another, with various possibilities of negotiation, compromise and graduation. Thus there can be observed a significant evolution in their relationships in the several decades that precede the collapse of the *Ancien Régime*.

In its struggle against the *parlements*, the royal authority at first attempted to impose its hegemony both upon justice and upon the religious orders, which were suspected of occasionally negotiating directly with families about the detention of their mentally defective members, or others deserving punishment. Thus in 1757 the minister of the royal household wanted to abolish the 'special orders issued by magistrates', suspected of being of an arbitrary nature. In 1767 the royal authorities created a new area of detention – the workhouses, placed in the direct charge of the *Intendants*, without any judicial control, despite the vigorous opposition of the *parlements*. The workhouses inherited in part the functions fulfilled by the general 'hospitals' (for beggars) that had been increasingly swamped by numbers of the aged poor, and it became the custom to admit the insane to them in ever-greater numbers.[8] In 1765 the royal authorities imposed Draconian regulations upon the numerous 'charities' (in reality, places of detention) of the Frères de Saint-Jean-de-Dieu, who ran Charenton, among other places. Article I laid down that 'under no pretext whatsoever will there be taken into the places of detention of the Charity any persons save those that are committed there by order of the King or of the judiciary'.[9] Thus there was no stable equilibrium, between the executive power and the judicial power in the control over the legitimacy of confinement.

Yet from 1770 onwards the opposition to *lettres de cachet* became stronger. Malesherbes, one of the main protagonists in the campaign against them, had become minister of the royal household in 1775. He set up family tribunals in order to give a judicial guarantee to the largest possible number of detentions. At the very end of the *Ancien Régime* the count of Breteuil, the minister of the royal household, in a circular of 1784 addressed to the *Intendants*, decreed detailed directives for the issue of *lettres de cachet* and distinguished meticulously between the categories to which they could be applied:

> Concerning persons whose detention is requested because of mental derangement, justice and prudence require that you do not submit orders save when there is an interdiction pronounced after judgement; unless the families are utterly incapable of paying the costs of the procedure that precedes the interdiction. But in that case the madness must be public knowledge and founded upon very precise explanations.[10]

The new tendency was then, even before the collapse of the *Ancien Régime*, to let the maximum possible number of practices relating to sequestration pass from royal jurisdiction to the judicial authorities, a trend that opened the way for the attempt to ensure that all sequestrations of the insane were backed by interdiction. But these freshly required guarantees depended upon whether a procedure for interdiction could be set in train, and therefore upon the wealth of families. The rules summarized by Essarts in his *Dictionnaire universel de police* applied to all-comers:

> Those who have the misfortune to be attacked by these kinds of illness must be maintained by their relatives, or at the latters' expense, so that the public peace is not disturbed by these unfortunate people.

When families are not capable of paying for their board and lodging, the officers entrusted with the maintenance of order must ensure that these categories of the sick are taken to hospitals or other places intended by the government to receive them. Relatives may be prosecuted in order to make good the damage wrought by persons who are mad, furibund or demented; but the action against them can only be a civil one.[11]

Thus the legitimization of sequestration did indeed waver between royal and judicial authority, with the preponderance tending to pass from the former to the latter. Yet on the one hand they remained complementary, with the beginnings of a division of labour: guarantees for the rich provided by justice, repression for the poor by the agents of the executive. And above all, beneath these changes, the general tenor of the legislation concerning madness under the *Ancien Régime* continued, so far as possible, to make it a 'family matter'. It was only when, negatively, there was absence, default or inability to cope on the part of the family, or, positively, at its own request, that an external authority intervened. In fact, three cases could occur.

First case: the family assumed the entire burden of the maintenance and 'neutralization' of the insane person. In that case he fell in advance into the later category of the 'unassisted insane' that the psychiatrists were to constitute when a unified system of assistance was set up during the first half of the nineteenth century. At that time, however, it was an anachronism: these 'unassisted insane' were in fact assisted normally, or at the very least tolerated by the primary groupings to which they belonged – the family and neighbours. They best avoided an external 'assumption of responsibility' for them when the family was either better off and/or better integrated, and when there existed around it client networks and a means of connivance. Hence this decisive implication: by claiming to put forward, in the form of a public service, a *global* and 'democratic' policy of assistance, mental health medicine in fact aimed as a priority at special categories of the population: the poor rather than the rich, the nomadic rather than the integrated, the town-dwellers rather than country folk.

Second case: the family did not want or could not assume the supervisory function, either because the presence of the insane persons posed too difficult problems of control (the case of the 'furibund', for example), or because the irresponsible actions of the madman threatened the family inheritance. It then had a choice between two possibilities, which were in fact two ways of delegating its authority, but through procedures whereby it *retained the initiative*. It could turn to the judicial authority in order to obtain a confinement order, and even request interdiction. This procedure led to a clear-cut situation where the insane person was placed into guardianship, and the management of his property fell to his family. This was the preferred solution chosen by the wealthiest families. It was even the necessary one when the purpose was to obtain a civil commitment into guardianship without sequestration, for interdiction did not stipulate the placing of the insane person outside the family. A second possibility was the 'royal order', which allowed sequestration to be obtained by the swiftest procedure. In its request the family generally suggested the place of confinement, which depended above all on the amount it was prepared to pay for board and lodging. Through this procedure the family was spared the 'dishonour' (and the expense) of a suit for interdiction. But the *lettre de cachet* represented the opposite of any arbitrary act, since it was solicited by the relatives, the natural judges of the family interests.

Third case: the insane person completely eluded family control, either because he had no family, or because he was caught straying outside his fixed surveillance area. To take repressive measures was then a matter for those authorities responsible for the maintenance of public order. These (in Paris and in the large towns they were the superintendency of police, elsewhere of the *Intendants*) could themselves take steps to obtain a 'royal order'. Most frequently they took action first and afterwards requested the order that made their intervention legal. This was how it was in principle. In reality, the legalization of these premature detentions on higher authority, by resorting directly to the king's authority, does not seem to have been the rule. For example, Piersin, 'lunacy superintendent' at the Bicêtre Hospital, in a letter to the Commission of Civil Administrations and Tribunals (on the 10th Frimaire, Year III) enquiring into the conditions upon which the mentally deranged had been detained ever since the *Ancien Régime*, only singled out 23 cases, of 207, who had been admitted upon 'the tyrant's order' (and only five by 'decree of the one-time

Parlement').[12] Most of the other mental cases were interned on the initiative of police or hospital administrators. Yet this was in no way scandalous: under the *Ancien Régime* the agents of the executive frequently assumed, by an implicit delegation of powers, the prerogatives of royal authority. What is important is the legitimacy that these interventions drew from the former synthesis of administrative and judicial authority. Des Essarts stated it plainly: 'In the person of the Lieutenant of Police one must distinguish between the magistrate and the administrator. The first is the man of the law, the second that of the government.'[13] Until the Revolution saw in this juxtaposition the scandal of despotism, and denounced it, it formed the legal basis for the practices relating to the shutting away of mad people under the *Ancien Régime*.[14]

Thus there is no reason to be astonished that the same arrangements were equally valid for the insane as for the other categories of prisoners: prodigals, libertines, and even spies and Jansenists. The 'orders' were taken out either because of family shortcomings or because of breaches of public security: crimes against the state, military or religious indiscipline, police matters. Thus the problems relating to the mentally deranged only represented one sub-category of the kind of offences that entailed the intervention of the executive. The different types of deviance were therefore less lumped together but rather assembled upon the basis of the common repression that they required.

Likewise we must not be astonished that these different types of prisoner were brought together in the same institutions, since the 'orders' that placed them there were common to all. Rather, there might well be reason for surprise at discovering the beginnings of a differentiation in the internal regulations, whereas the legal measures for admission of detainees gave them the same status. However, the lack of differentiation between those shut away for good was never absolute. In fact by 1660, only four years after the foundation of the General Hospital, the Paris *Parlement* decided that a special area in it would be reserved for 'the detention of the insane, male and female'.[15] From the beginning of the eighteenth century ever finer distinctions began to be operated within the general category of the demented.[16] But such a differentiation can be ascribed to managerial and internal disciplinary needs rather than to any inclination to carry out diagnoses or treatment.

Some perception of a medical nature of madness is not strictly incompatible with the system for its repression under the *Ancien Régime*. But the results and the internal equilibrium of the system do not depend upon how far madness is a medical matter. The goals and tensions of the system are of a social, juridical and political order. It is when the political cornerstone of the edifice is decapitated that the co-existence of its elements becomes contra-dictory. The medical reference will then take on a completely different meaning: from being subordinate it will become preponderant, for it will constitute the axis of the new equilibrium.

Schematically, three potential focuses for an explosion, inherent in the previous synthesis, can be identified.

1 *The dual nature of the authorities responsible for sequestration*

The executive and the judiciary shared the right to take out 'orders' legitimizing detention. The rivalry that pitted them against each other towards the end of the *Ancien Régime* also gave rise to innumerable conflicts about madness. But the antagonism did not reveal any contradiction of principle so long as there remained at the pinnacle of the power pyramid a sovereign authority capable in the last resort of arbitrating. 'All justice flows from the king', even if he delegated his prerogatives to his 'officers'. Thus Loiseau, in his *Traité des seigneuries* (1613), placed as the foremost of the four sovereign rights of the monarch (the *regulia*) that of 'being the fount of justice of last resort' (the other three are: 'making laws', 'appointing officers' and 'arbitrating between peace and war'[17]) For instance, when in 1757 the minister of the royal household wished to abolish the 'special magistrates' orders' that allowed families to negotiate directly with the judges about the seques-tration of one of their number, without any control by the executive, he justified the measure in these terms: 'His Majesty deems that liberty is far too precious an attribute for any of his subjects to be able to be deprived of it without judicial process, unless he himself has weighed up the reasons.'[18] The royal *imperium* could therefore in the last resort 'weigh up the causes' for any dispensation from the law, which by this action ceased to be illegal. The *Parlements* protested and even disregarded this. But, so long as the principle of the absolute monarchy subsisted, the conflict was not yet one of open contradiction.

2 *The dual nature of the types of institution in which the insane and other prisoners are sequestrated*

At the end of the *Ancien Régime*, besides the hospitals such as the Hôtel-Dieu dispensing treatment, there can be identified four or five types of institution that took in the insane: religious foundations (the numerous 'Charities' of the Frères de Saint-Jean-de-Dieu, and also the convents of the Cordeliers, the Bons-Fils, the Frères des Ecoles chrétiennes, the house of Saint-Lazare, founded by Saint Vincent de Paul, etc., plus a dozen female convents that accepted at the same time prisoners, the female insane and 'penitent prostitutes'); state prisons such as the Bastille or the fortress of Hâ; the General Hospitals, particularly those of Bicêtre and Salpêtrière, in which were shut away almost half the insane in the kingdom; finally, lodgings run by lay people, a score being in Paris, including the famous Pension Belhomme, where Pinel was to try out his first treatments.[19]

However, there existed a basic division between them, which did not relate in any way to whether they were of a more or less medical character, but to whether their management or control was more or less public or private. Certain state prisons, the General Hospitals and the workhouses for the poor were royal foundations, managed by a lay staff. The other institutions were generally founded and managed by religious orders, which submitted with bad grace to the various conditions of control imposed by the *Parlements* and the services of the *Intendants* or of the Lieutenant of Police. This institutional dualism legitimized different policies, particularly regarding the degree of initiative left to families. The state power was already tending to standardize both procedures for admission and those of surveillance. But disparities would exist for a long time, raising conflicts from which the debates on the Law of 1838 would identify the modern issues.

3 *The dual nature of the 'surfaces of emergence' in madness*

The madman is a disturber of the peace through whom scandal occurs, either in the family domain or the social domain. This is the origin of two very different policies with regard to insanity. The latter poses a problem of *public order* because the mentally deranged 'stray' into a social no man's land. Wandering in this way is dangerous, and occasions an often physically violent intervention, a sanction taken in the name of people's security, and the safeguarding of property and decorum, etc. But it poses also a problem of *private repression*, the effectiveness of which might spare costly remedies in the face of disorder that has already occurred. Hence the question of the installation of family controls and of the control of family controls. The crudest form of the relationships between these two 'surfaces' is the one whereby the family, unable to act as its own watchdog, takes steps to delegate its power to an external authority, which may be administrative or judicial. By bringing medicine to bear upon the problem, an introduction was made to a much more stable dialectic regarding what was the prerogative of those closest to the mad person and what should fall to the state in its task of preserving and reproducing social and family order. The concept of *prevention*, as will be seen, gave rise to the hope that medicine would intervene before public repression became necessary and before the family divested itself of its power. This same conception of prevention also ruled out the intervention of justice, which was formally required to punish acts that had already taken place. Thus the whole system was to swing from the repression of acts committed to the anticipation of acts to be committed, and from the redressing of an objective disorder to the assumption of responsibility for subjective structures that were in process of modification. A long road to travel, whose goal would imply the subordination to medical authority of these three powers, the juridical, the administrative and the family, which previously shared the responsibility for neutralizing madness. But it was at this point that the process was set in motion: at the moment when this fourth power insinuated itself into the breach opened up by the political disequilibrium of the three others.

Sovereignty, Contract and Guardianship

Thus the mechanisms for the control of madness in the eighteenth century only appear crude if they are measured according to the yardstick of medical monopoly. But they were precarious because responsibilities were shared between competitive systems, through complex and disparate procedures. This baroque synthesis would therefore be broken up when the arbitrating authority, the royal power, was condemned as tyrannical. There is a fundamental point here: at first it is less the *practices* that are called upon to change than the *principle* of their legitimation. And it was the impossibility of legitimizing the former practices that was to bring forth new ones – or impose at the centre of the system ancient procedures that had played only a subordinate part – thus ensuring, by a long diversion, the triumph of the medical approach to madness.

Pressed to abolish the *lettres de cachet*, Louis XVI addressed himself as follows to the States–General on 23 June 1789:

> The King, desirous of assuring the personal liberty of all citizens in solid and lasting fashion, invites the States-General to search out and procure for him the most fitting means of reconciling the abolition of the orders known under the name of *lettres de cachet*, with the maintenance of public safety and with the necessary precautions, either, in certain cases, to satisfy the honour of families, or to repress with despatch the beginnings of sedition, or to safeguard the State against the ill-effects of criminal dealings with foreign powers.[20]

Thus the problem was clearly posed: not to suppress the whole of the repressive *practices* that the royal power covered with the cloak of legitimacy, but to get round the sustained suspicion that the *forms* employed were tyrannical. Hence Article I of the law decreeing the abolition of *lettres de cachet* continued to restrict the categories of 'victims of despotism', which it purely and simply set free:

> In the space of six weeks after the publication of the present decree, all persons detained in fortresses, religious houses, prisons, police stations or any other prisons of whatever kind under *lettres de cachet* or upon the order of agents of the executive power, unless they have been legally condemned or their bodily seizure decreed, or because a legal complaint has been made against them by reason of crimes that carry with them punishment of the person, or unless their father, mothers, grandparents or other relatives duly assembled have solicited and obtained their detention according to memorials and requests supported by serious facts, *or finally unless they have been shut away because of insanity*, shall be set free.[21]

Thus only sequestrations made for affairs of state, i.e., cases very few in number, were directly annulled. For example, out of some thousand *lettres de cachet* issued in Paris in 1751, Funck-Brentano hardly counted more than one or two classifiable under this heading.

Essentially, the 'royal orders' were the legal basis for interventions whose necessity, in the eyes of contemporaries, remained just as pressing, even when they had lost their legal justification. If the abolition of *lettres de cachet* set free a few innocent 'victims of the tyrant', above all it posed the difficult problem of legally justifying the continuance of the majority of sequestrations.

Thus, hardly had the decree of 27 March 1790 been made than Bailly, the mayor of Paris, wrote to the Constituent Assembly to ask at the very least for its application to be deferred: 'Would it not be dangerous in this moment to return unthinkingly to society men who have been snatched from it, illegally, it is true, but almost always for sound reasons?'[22] The lack of haste with which the mad were set free was at least as evident. In January 1790, according to a list communicated to the National Assembly by the Prior, there were at Charenton 92 detainees committed by 'royal order' and labelled as 'imbeciles', 'madmen', 'sporadically mad', 'dangerously mad', 'maliciously mad', 'furibund madmen', 'demented' and 'mentally deranged'. Only one was detained for 'misconduct' and another for 'unknown causes'. The ninety-third was the Marquis de Sade; the Prior had previously 'petitioned the Assembly to be so good as to rid him of such a person'. In November 1790 there remained 89 detainees. Sade had been freed on 27 March. A commission went to Charenton on a tour of inspection, following a complaint by the Committee of *lettres de cachet* attached to the municipality of Paris, which was drawing up a list of arbitrary internments. Chaired by a doctor, it picked out only one suspect case, whom it demanded should be freed: the one who had been categorized under 'unknown causes'. In fact he was an Italian by origin, suspected of complicity in a counterfeit money case, who had been held for four years without being tried. Thus at Charenton, out of 93 persons placed by royal order in the section for the insane, the decree of March 1790 set free de Sade (although not for long), one accused of swindling, and perhaps two other detainees, who might have died in the meantime.

Thus quantitatively the problem was ridiculously small, even if the objection is made that the Charenton institution was particularly well run. But it is a crucial problem, because it questions the bases of the new social order. In its solution there is at stake the possibility of passing from an equilibrium of powers, relying in the last resort upon royal sovereignty, to a contractual society. For this reason the question of madness took on prime importance at the end of the eighteenth and the beginning of the nineteenth centuries. It was at the very heart of an insoluble contradiction for the new juridical order. At first sight madness should only have posed a minor social problem, exceeded in importance and urgency by several others: indigence, homelessness, pauperism, foundlings, the sick poor, etc. – these concern, it has been said, groups of people infinitely more numerous, and for the most part at least as dangerous. Yet the insane 'benefited' from this first assumption of responsibility, acknowledged as a right and backed by a law that anticipated by more than 50 years all the 'social legislation' that was to come. The originality of this might not be understood were it not the pivot of a fundamental matter for the rising bourgeois society. Through the medical approach adopted, the question of madness was invested with *a new status of guardianship* essential for the functioning of a contractual society.

A political revolution overthrowing the past does not wipe the slate clean. The restructuring of state power, consecrated by the new bourgeois order, had been progressively marked out from the Middle Ages onwards. Under relationships of allegiance of subjects to sovereign, a centralized administrative structure that obeyed technical criteria of rationality had been gradually installed. In this way increasingly preponderant sectors of activity succeeded in becoming autonomous: the creaming off of wealth through taxation, the circulation of goods through trade, the collection of information by means of the wide-scale enquiries inspired by the central authority. At the margin state power would not constitute more than the guarantor for these exchanges bound by contract. It was the liberal myth of the complete separation of the social from the economic which would allegedly ensure the free interplay of the laws of the market.

To this autonomy of the laws regulating the exchange of wealth and the production of goods there corresponds the rationalization of the mechanisms governing the movement of people, the technical organization of their activities and the control of their initiatives. There is the myth of the perfect establishment of citizens within a given area, which is parallel to that of the perfect circulation of goods, and which the Napoleonic State attempted to realize by installing a vast administrative structure divided up into as many sectors as the person had social activities. Thus in his life as a citizen an individual would find himself boxed in by geographical frameworks administered by others responsible to and depending upon the central authority, and permanently supervised in the accomplishment of the whole of his social duties.

The legal and administrative fiction on which this whole construction rested is, as is well known, that of the *contract*. Each citizen was both subject and sovereign: he was assigned to each of his duties, obligatory under threat of punishment by the state, and at the same time a subject acting under the law, deriving his rights from these practices, the performance of which defined his freedom. Thus the perfect citizen would never encounter state authority in its repressive form. By assuming his duties, he manifested his own sovereignty and reinforced that of the state. It would miss the essential point if one said that this was a mere matter of an 'ideology' through which the rising bourgeois society attempted to justify in law the way it functioned in fact – the fiction of formal liberties, the reality of economic exploitation.

Firstly, if fiction there was, it was not just any kind of fiction, but one that made available an autonomous space that was necessary for the free unfolding of a market economy. By intervening in the framework of contracts in order to underwrite them, the state in fact guaranteed private property and the circulation of wealth and goods, the basis for a trading economy.

Secondly, individuals were administered in objective frameworks whose interchangeability contrasted with the territorial allocation underpinning the former relationship between sovereignty and its clients. The state thus contrived a 'free' circulation of people that paralleled the 'free' circulation of goods and was necessary to sustain it. Yet, since this freedom was regulated by laws, the state could at the same time assume its tasks of surveillance and policing on the basis of a rational pattern that was technically manageable at the least cost.

Thirdly, in this way the 'non-interventionism' of the liberal theorists took on its precise meaning, which in no way signified the weakening of the coercive power of the state apparatus. Instead it firmly demarcated the situations where it could and must intervene, and this more pitilessly because in this way it eliminated all that was arbitrary and enunciated what was the law. The state had to respect the liberty of the citizen, the contracts he made that were founded upon private property, his free exchanges, according to the laws of the market. Conversely, the state could and must punish any transgression of this juridical and economic order. It carried out its functions of social preservation and political repression by inculcating respect for society's contractual structure. This structure was not the legal order within which sovereign individuals might experience the possibilities of exchange. It was the juridical matrix through which state violence was exerted and economic exploitation was imposed.

However, despite its formal character, all citizens did not enter this contractual framework without problems arising. The truly specific nature of the mad resisted this repression to such an extent that, for them to submit to it, it would prove necessary to impose upon them a different statute, one complementary to the contractual statute, that regulated citizens as a whole.

Criminal, Child, Beggar, Poor Wage-earner and Mad Person

In relation to this conception of the law five groups of individuals present special problems.

1 *Criminals*

Michel Foucault has shown how the transformation of the right to punish at the beginning of the nineteenth century was carried out around the birth of the prison.[24] The novelty of the prison form must not however hide the fact that the juridical innovations proceeded from the evolution of the bases of law, which preceded the revolutionary era. This evolution brought personal responsibility to the forefront.[25] The criminal act is the result of a calculation whereby an individual opts for his personal interest against the rights of others. A miscalculation if the criminal is caught, but a rational calculation for which he is entirely responsible. The punishment that he incurs therefore has a legal basis, attacking the breaking of contracts whose function is guaranteed by law. The abolition of *lettres de cachet* thus posed no problem of principle in transferring the share in criminal repression still exercised by the executive to the judiciary. Thus under the *Ancien Régime* a 'royal order' occasionally saved the scandal of a law-suit by allowing an individual (generally from a good family) to be shut away without trial, whereas the case was really one for the courts. By taking matters in hand themselves alone from this point onwards, the courts were only exercising once more their full prerogatives.

The new problems posed by the restructuring of the right to punish were connected with the difficulties experienced in setting up an effective technology of punishment, and not in finding a legal basis for it. They were: how to detain, supervise, reform and re-educate the criminal – or even to adopt a medical approach to him. This last aspiration appeared very early on, as Cabanis testifies:

> You are aware that the nature of several kinds of prisons makes them closer to that of hospitals: for instance, such are the places termed reformatories, where the task is undertaken of subjecting to regular treatment the evil dispositions of the young: such will one day be the prisons for those individuals sentenced by the criminal courts to a more or less lengthy period of imprisonment. Indeed, *these prisons may easily become veritable infirmaries for crime:* this kind of sickness will be treated there with the same sureness of method and the same hope of success as other derangements of the mind.[26]

This is a remarkable text for an era when the medicine of mental health did not yet officially exist. However, it must not lead us astray. The logic that leads to the adoption of a medical approach to the criminal is very different in principle from that which will cause a medical approach to be adopted in the case of the mad person. Although the right to punish claims to become humane, a matter of instruction, or a medical affair, it deals with as many variations in relation to a right to correct error, a right that is wholly soundly based upon the axioms that are its starting-point: the balance between offences and punishments is contained within a rational system, because the criminal is responsible for his acts. The madman poses a different problem. No rational link directly unites the transgression that he commits and the repression he undergoes. He cannot be punished, but he will have to be treated.

Doubtless the treatment will often be a kind of punishment. But even if it were always so, repression of the insane can only continue in a disguised form. It must be justified by the rationalization of therapy.

It is the medical diagnosis that is deemed to impose this, i.e. that provides the condition making it possible. There is an essential difference: *in a contractual system, a medical foundation for the repression of the mad person will have to be constructed, whereas the repression of the criminal has from the outset a juridical basis.* The medical approach to the mad was first imposed in the form of a statute for the insane as distinct from the criminal, and was towards the end of the nineteenth century becoming more general by making ever more varied facets of human behaviour a pathological matter. Much later, the medical approach to the criminal, in its turn, was to change in meaning. It would no longer be a form of intervention after the event in order better to apply the punishment, but an attempt to base the legitimacy of the punishment on a psycho-pathological evaluation of the criminal's responsibility (see chapter 4). At this time, however, it was the lawyers who blocked the path to the discovery of the new solution. By wishing to give pride of place to the judicial apparatus (cf. *infra,* the discussions on the need to deprive the insane of civil rights before their sequestration) the lawyers were in fact fighting a rearguard action, and would be progressively overcome through the development of new practices, legitimized through medicine, for dealing with madness. The analogy between institutions (prison and asylum) and the techniques for imposing a discipline (penal re-education and ethical treatment) must not therefore mask the contradiction of principle between the right to punish and the duty to help. The solution to the social problem of madness could not be found in the extension that which was to prevail for criminal behaviour – *quite the opposite.* This is not to say that the correspondences between the solutions arrived at were accidental. But, as we shall see, they were to take on meaning after a form of medical legitimacy different from that of justice had been constituted. Then psychiatry was able to perform its part in the great concert of supervisory and disciplinary procedures that at the time reshaped every kind of institution. Yet it would first have to win ground for its intervention, side by side with, and in certain respects, *against* that of justice.

2 *Families*

The second category for which the abolition of the *lettres de cachet* posed specific problems was that which related to the judicial regime for families. During the discussion of the Law of 16–27 March 1790 in the Constituent Assembly, representative Pétion declared: 'You will not force families to receive in their midst rogues that might cause disturbance in them.'[27] The direct complicity between the executive power and family power, whereby the royal authority gave its assistance to family authority, broke down because henceforth it depended upon royal 'tyranny'. It was necessary to reconstitute a balance between judicial and family power, a formula for which was difficult to discover. The setting up (or rather the revival) during the revolutionary period of family tribunals, which handed over to parents very wide prerogatives, with a possibility of appeal to the normal jurisdiction, was a long-drawn out process. The nineteenth century progressively sought to encroach upon the privileges of the family, until the law of 1889 stripping the father of his powers, and through which the judge could remove a part of the traditional power of the family.

We shall come back later to this evolution. When a certain medical threshold is reached the treatment of certain family conflicts as pathological widens the breach that has been opened up in the law relating to families: the medical specialist becomes the arbiter of decisions that formerly were entrusted to the guardianship of the family. That guardianship breaks down, and on the one hand the judge (the judges for guardianship and for the children), and on the other hand the doctor (above all the psychiatrist and the psychoanalyst) become the heirs of certain family prerogatives.[28] But this intrusion of the doctor into the intimacy of the family, the royal road to psychiatric intervention later, supposes a stage of development in psychiatric techniques that only appeared at the end of the nineteenth century, blossoming with psychoanalysis. Initially psychiatry did not face up squarely to the problem of childhood, unless, from Esquirol onwards, it were along the byway of lack of development (idiocy), and not of insanity. There are a number of theoretical and practical reasons for this, but the control of the child does not pose thorny juridical questions because he is already under guardianship (of the family), whilst the mad person is *like* a child (see below), but has not yet found his guardian legally. It would be the doctor who would act as a substitute for this.

3 *The offences of vagrancy and begging*

Under the *Ancien Régime*, the 'neutralization' of the masses of vagrants was a prerogative of the sovereign power, the guardian of public order. In order to found the General Hospital, or to sentence vagrants to the galleys, a royal ordinance sufficed (the problem that caused the royal power to fail was connected with its lack of ability to *apply* such measures, which were constantly re-enacted and each time circumvented).[29] But here also the instal-lation of a generalized contractual structure brought out a contradiction that had been concealed by the royal *imperium*. Henceforth if every punishment had only to be inflicted upon transgressions entailing responsibility, punishment could only apply to a person who was not obliged to commit the offence for which he could be sentenced. If misery, equivalent to his destiny, forced the vagrant to take to the road and obliged the luckless wretch without work to beg, under what law should they be condemned?

Undoubtedly the Constituent Assembly Committee on Begging undertook its task in order to assist the poor, but also to establish reciprocity between the right to punish and the possibility of not transgressing the law. Only the right to assistance and work could impose duties upon those living in misery, rendering their asocial acts criminal: 'Where there exists a class of men without the means of subsistence, there exists a violation of human rights; there the social equilibrium is disturbed.'[30] Cabanis clarified this contra-diction in the repression of misery, which would strike at the innocent if the minimum number of objective possibilities for escaping punishment were not doled out to them:

> *Begging forms the lowest level, I will not say of crime, but, if it may be expressed in this way, of inclination to acts that disturb the social order:* this is the first premise that must be considered in the question of repression, which in turn must be regarded as the first purpose of penal legislation. But the repression of begging is so closely linked to the organization of public assistance that it is doubtless impossible to separate the two. How – how indeed – can one pronounce begging to be a crime *if the public authorities have*

not established, in the name of the nation, sufficient means of assistance to prevent or assuage misery; if they have not provided work for any individual who lacks it, or says he does?[31]

Acting upon this logic, the Constituent Assembly proclaimed that it 'places on the level of the most sacred duties of the nation assistance to the poor of all ages and in all circumstances of life'. In this it did no more than follow the recommendations of the Committee on Begging, whose legalist line of argument – a somewhat embarrassed one – deserves attention: 'Equality of rights is the fundamental principle of your Constitution. Can this principle, common to all citizens, cease to be applicable to those who, knowing only misfortune and need, have the right to demand help from society, which itself has a duty only to give them what is strictly necessary?' The Convention goes even farther by writing article 23 into the Declaration of the Rights of Man in 1793: 'Subsistence is a sacred debt of society; it is for the law to determine its extent and how it is applied.'[32]

These are noble principles, but they remain a dead letter: the revolutionary assemblies had neither the time nor the means to ensure their realization. However, the need was so imperative that the Napoleonic State took it up again with renewed vigour. The imperial administration put together in generous proportions a generalized right of the poor to public assistance, but laid the emphasis on what could justify the right to repress them. Thus the Law of 5 July 1808, concerning 'the eradication of begging' significantly coupled together two measures: the prohibition of begging throughout the imperial territory, and the establishment in every department of a refuge for beggars where

the indigent will find asylum, subsistence, and work, paternalist institutions where good works moderate behaviour by kindness, sustain discipline by affection, and stimulate once more the desire to work by awakening a salutary feeling of shame. As a reward for its efforts the government is confident that in a few years France will offer the solution, so often sought in vain up to now, to the problem of how to wipe out begging in a great State.

There is the same gap between the principles and their realization. Even in 1890, 32,822 condemnations for vagrancy would be pronounced, whereas for the whole of France only 33 refuges for beggars existed.[33] Even worse, the penal code (article 274) laid down punishments of three to six months in prison for beggars arrested in places where a refuge for beggars existed, but it also prescribed punishment, reduced by half (article 275), where no institution for assistance existed. Here bourgeois law was on the very verge of abusing its own legal position: it dispensed the minimum juridical protection against injustice by establishing a purely formal reciprocity between the letter of the law and the existence on paper of assistance that would allow well-intentioned wretches to escape its harshness. If this fiction, hardly standing up juridically, nevertheless worked, it was because it was replaced by a conception of 'philanthropy' to which we shall have to return. The right to assistance loses its effectiveness when one can impute to faults of the individual (laziness, debauchery, fecklessness etc. . .) the responsibility for a situation where he is almost obliged to find himself at odds with the law. Unfortunate people can be assisted, but with no obligation to do so, according to their merits or the extent to which their condition deserves pity. They can also be, if not punished, at least held in check (this is the 'moralization of the masses') according to their defects or the danger to order that they represent. It is political prudence that will duly apportion repression and charity: not to call into question again, by the recognition of rights to the poor, the foundations of a liberal society, but to intervene before the weight of misery leaves the victims of the system no other alternative than revolt. The call to public good works, less fickle than private charity but less obligatory than justice, systematized as a veritable policy for those in material distress, is thus the necessary counterweight to the legalism of a class society, at least for the most 'enlightened' minds.

4 *The proletarian class*

To these first groups that caused a problem in relation to contractual legality might be added the proletarian class in its entirety. In a social structure founded upon private property and the 'freedom' of economic exchange, only the possessors were citizens in the full sense of the word, as the system of voting by capacity to pay taxes reflected at the political level. Fortunately an escape route existed. For the worker lacking resources (the 'healthy poor' but possessing an occupation), the fiction of the contract could still apply, since there was a 'labour market' on which his abilities could be freely 'sold'. Thus there was exchange, a regulated reciprocity, a contract (or pseudo-contract) between exploiter and exploited. The proletarian was still the object of law because he *belonged to himself.* He was neither a slave nor *alienus* (alienated to another). The owner of himself, he could *acquire* things. Since salary was private property, it allowed the accumulation of goods and access to them: it was a matter of zeal, of saving, and of morality.

Thus if the ideal pattern of equality of persons is belied by the facts, the responsibility for this can be laid upon the individual, who is indeed in part responsible for his misfortune, even if he is not legally guilty. One can then fall back in good conscience upon the policy of assistance, which wipes away the extreme manifestations of distress, without having for that matter to fulfil a formal obligation. In fact this construct is a little overdrawn. It corresponds to the euphoric era at the onset of all liberalism, when its theorists still imagine that it is sufficient to free the conditions for access to employment in order to resolve in principle the 'social question'. The discovery of the necessity for *pauperism* as a structural condition for the functioning of capitalism, coming to replace the moral condemnation of *begging*, leads to the transformation of the problem of specialized assistance into a generalized policy of subjection of the popular classes. This is the second stage of the process, in which the medicine of mental health, then representing the vanguard of philanthropy, is an essential partner (see chapter 3). But here we are still at the point when this problem is emerging, when legalism is both perfectly assured of its own legitimacy, and convinced that it is contributing principles capable of universal validation, upon which can be built and defended a rational social order.[34]

5 *The insane*

Public assistance for madness is included in this contractual logic, but it pushes it to breaking-point. Thus it requires the discovery of a more rigorous solution.

At the end of the eighteenth century madness was perceived in a dual and contradictory way. The insane person was the generalized image of asociability. He did not transgress explicitly any law, as did the criminal; he could break them all. The insane person reactivated the picture of the nomad wandering in a social no-man's-land, threatening all the rules that governed the organization of society. Such 'wanderings' were assimilated to those of wild animals, even by as 'progressive' a body as the Constituent Assembly, which, by the Law of 16–24 August, 1790, entrusted 'to the vigilance of municipal bodies those untoward happenings that might be occasioned by the insane and furious left at liberty and by evil and ferocious animals.'[35] Article 479 of the penal code again brackets together 'the effect of the wanderings of the mad and the violently insane, or of evil or ferocious animals, the excessive pace, bad driving or overloading of vehicles, dray-, pack- or riding-animals'. The absolute necessity to repress madness was included among an order of nature where all bounds had burst, tending to class the insane with the animal kingdom, and even the blind destructiveness of things that, like the careering of a chariot launched down a slope, obeyed no longer anything but the law of gravity.

Yet such images that summon up fanciful or real fears are just as much ones of irresponsibility. Just as he is dangerous, the insane person is also an object of pity. He is wretched, an 'unfortunate person' who has lost the most precious attribute of man: reason. Thus he represents an inordinate polarity lacking any compensating force, one to whom the rationality of punishment cannot be applied. No longer 'belonging to himself', he is not capable of participating in the process of production and acquisition of goods. Contractual logic, which fully justifies the repression of the criminal and invents an acceptable compromise to punish begging and vagrancy, here comes up against something that is specific and insurmountable.

In the face of the ambivalence of horror and pity that the insane person arouses, the medicine of mental health plays a game of benevolence. By so doing it controls the pole marked 'danger'. Since the madman, who is both frightening and guiltless, escapes the juridical classifications of a contractual society, philanthropy will assume charge of him. But philanthropic humanism is merely the auxiliary of legalism, which is its ultimate recourse in marginal situations where the formal universality of the right to punish comes up against a brick wall. Thus compassion has been the constant attitude of the movement for the treatment of the insane who, 'far from being guilty people who must be punished, are sick people whose dire state is worthy of all the care owed to suffering humanity, and whose wandering reason one must seek to re-establish by the simplest means.'[36] It was only after Morel and Magnan, when the notions of degeneration and diathesis highlighted the 'perversion' of the mentally ill, that psychiatry tended towards a kind of racialism directed against the insane. Up to about 1860 a form of paternalism prevailed. In it benevolence was illuminated by knowledge and was exercised in an institutional relationship of domination.

Yet there is no contradiction between compassion and science, or between benevolence and authority. Pity is not purely an impulsion of the heart. For Jean-Jacques Rousseau it 'tends to bring us unreflectingly to the help of those we see are suffering'. But this spontaneity is not the effect of blind instinct, 'it is this which, in the state of nature, takes the place of law, morality and virtue, with the advantage that none are tempted to disobey its gentle voice.'[37] Pity indicates the place of the law in the spot where the law cannot be made manifest in its proper form. It is the analogy of the law, its metaphor, supplementing it.[33] It is both supplement and substitute. Compassion for the 'unfortunate', which forms the basis of the philanthropic attitude, for them makes up for the deficiencies of the law. Among those who lie outside the ambit of the law compassion establishes a new relationship, one which is no longer that of formal reciprocity but of regulated subordination – *a relationship of guardianship*. This is the matrix for every policy of assistance. Doubtless it is a relationship of domination, but one which still shares in the Utopia of a general rational exchange and imitates it even when one of the poles of reciprocity is missing. Thus the violence exerted shares in the good conscience enjoyed by reason: it is unleashed for the good of those subjected to it. Contemporaries – at least the most clear-sighted among them – perceived this intermediary function, one of placing under guardianship, in relationship to contractualization. It is entirely significant that, in a report made to the Paris Council on 6 August 1791 concerning the state of the insane in the Salpêtrière Hospital, Cabanis, at least by implication, elaborated the conception of *social non-adulthood* that is shared by both children and the insane:

When men have reached an age where their strength suffices for their existence, nature desires that they should no longer be subject

to any coercive authority. Society must respect and fulfil this wise
arrangement so long as men enjoy their rational faculties, namely,
so long as these are not deformed to a point where they compromise the safety and tranquillity of others, or expose the men
themselves to real dangers. Nobody has the right, not even society
as a whole, to infringe their independence to the slightest degree.[39]

Either the individual is an autonomous entity, since he is capable
as such of carrying out rational exchanges, or his inability to enter
a system of reciprocity renders him not responsible, and he must
be assisted. The contractual basis of liberalism necessitates the
comparison of the insane person with the child.[40] This is the great
pedagogical analogy of the medicine of mental health within
whose framework its whole history develops. Either the family
relationship or guardianship by official mandate: for medicine
there is no other alternative.

Judge, Administrator, Father of the Family and Doctor

This transferral to medicine of the essential part of the prerogatives of assuming responsibility for madness is nevertheless very
far from being self-evident at the fall of the *Ancien Régime*. This is
because the embryonic stage of the development in medical practices
rendered them unfit to assume such a mandate overnight. Instead,
the medical solution appeared as a last resort after more traditional
authorities have failed to share out among themselves the former
attributions of the royal executive power. Thus, right up to the very
last years of the eighteenth century and even a little beyond, we are
in the presence of a proliferation of divergent attempts.

1 *The judiciary*

A first tendency – one that already inspired the circular of Breteuil
in 1784 – consisted in making the judicial authority the exclusive
guarantor of the whole process of 'neutralization' of madness.
This is a model that, if it were realizable, would present a dual
advantage: it would offer the solution closest to that already
applied to the problem of criminality; it could adopt the procedure
of interdiction already practically achieved under the *Ancien*

Régime. At the expense of a minimal readjustment in the judicial machine, one could therefore make the assumption of responsibility for insanity a legal matter. It is this solution that Article 489 of the Civil Code appears to validate: 'The adult person whose habitual state is one of imbecility, dementia or violent insanity must be deprived of civil rights, even when this condition is interspersed with intervals of lucidity'. Hence legal guardianship, one whose status is perfectly defined in the Civil Code and the guarantees for which are perfectly vouchsafed by the judicial machinery.

In fact, up to the passing of the law of 1838, interdiction constituted the sole truly legal procedure for the sequestration of the insane. Thus the need to have recourse to it was continually recalled, especially by the various ministers of justice. But it was always in a manner that proved that it went constantly unheeded:

I have noticed in the various analytical reports of the Prefects that several of them have, on their own authority, caused the insane to be arrested in order that, upon their order, they may be shut away in prisons. To guard against these abuses, I deem it necessary to remind you of the principles and rules governing this matter. According to the Law of 22 July 1791, and in conformity in this respect with former regulations, the relatives of the insane must watch over them, preventing them from wandering away and taking care that they do not commit any disorderly act. The municipal authority, in accordance with the same law, must take steps against any ill-effects that may result from the negligence with which individuals carry out these duties. The violently insane must be put in a place of safety, but they can only be detained by virtue of a judgement that the family must set in motion. The Civil Code indicates in great detail the manner in which one must proceed to the interdiction of individuals who have fallen into a state of dementia and violent insanity. It is to the courts alone that it entrusts the task of certifying to their condition. The laws that have laid down the consequences of this sad infirmity have taken steps to see that an individual cannot be arbitrarily presumed to be stricken by it; they willed that his state should be established by positive proof in a precise and rigorous form . . . I request you to conform to these principles. You must watch carefully to see that the authorities under you never depart from them.[41]

Thus in practice the administrative authority frequently substituted itself for the judicial authority. The insane posed problems of public order that had to be resolved as a matter of urgency. Intervention by the administration short-circuited the slowness of the judicial machine. It was also more 'democratic', in the sense that it required no expenditure or any move to be made by the family. Finally, it was surer, since it led necessarily to sequestration, whereas interdiction without imprisonment could leave a dangerous individual to the uncertain control of the family. Interdiction was not only difficult to apply, but did not determine completely the fate of the madman in society, as recalled in a letter of the minister of justice dated 1 November 1821: 'the justice minister must set in train the interdiction of a violently insane person, but, since this measure does not automatically entail the sequestration of the person in question, the administrative authority can and should detain him in prison so long as he is not claimed by his family and so long as his liberation could present a danger.'[42]

In short, the legal procedure immediately available was not applicable to all the problems posed by the insane. Thus Georget could state in 1825: 'Almost all the insane are shut away, without being placed under interdiction, by virtue of the Law of 24 August 1790.'[43] In 1835, an average year, for the whole of France only 29 judgments of interdiction were pronounced.[44]

2 *The Administration*

Since it was the administrative authority that assumed most of the practical tasks of the sequestration of the insane, why should not its procedures be legalized? This second tendency found legislative backing in the Law of 16–24 August 1790, which entrusted to the vigilance of municipal bodies 'the task of preventing or remedying untoward events that might be occasioned by insane persons, including the violently insane left at liberty'.[45] These administrative functions, at first delegated to local authorities, were soon taken over by the central authorities – the Ministry of the Interior and the prefects. The direct representatives of state power quite naturally became the advocates of such a move. The preliminary draft of the Law of 1838 was thus conceived by the Minister of the Interior as the means of making legal these administrative prerogatives:

> Already this attribute is his in principle, according to the Law of
> 16–24 August 1790 . . . Essentially the matter concerns measures of

public safety and public order. Moreover, the precautionary measures relating to the isolation [of the insane] ordinarily require the utmost speed, prudence and discretion. These are only reconcilable with difficulty with the slowness and the solemnity of the judicial forms, but are easy and natural in administrative operations.[46]

To give the repression of madness its maximum effectiveness, it was therefore sufficient to legalize administrative internment. But in his reply to the minister an Opposition deputy denounced such a move as a return to the 'principle . . . of the *lettres de cachet*, the one in all laws in these calamitous times that have suspended more or less for a long time individual liberty.'[47] Article 7 of the Declaration of the Rights of Man and the Citizen proclaimed that 'no man may be arrested or detained save in cases determined by the law, and according to the forms that it has laid down' – namely, when he has committed an *offence*. Madness is not an offence. It places justice in a position of insurmountable dubiousness, but prevents also the executive from assuming responsibility, unless one is to fall once more into the tyranny of 'royal orders'.

3 The Family

There might indeed be a third option: to throw back upon the family responsibility for the control of the actions of the insane. This tendency could also rely upon a legal prop, the Law of 19–21 July 1791, which prescribed penalties of imprisonment for those who let their mad people 'stray', a clause adopted in article 475 and 479 of the penal Code. By making those closest to him legally responsible for the behaviour of the mad person, the latter was kept dependent upon his family, at the risk of legalizing, by requesting interdiction, this minority status of the insane person. From the guardianship of the family to that of the law, the mad person finds, without overthrowing the law, the basis for a status that relieves him of responsibility.

Yet the family solution is no more general than the two preceding ones. It has been seen that the family can only control one of the planes on which madness may manifest itself, that of pathological domestic behaviour. Control is in reality removed when madness takes on a social aspect. The family could not legally discharge itself of responsibility save by an interdiction, which was very often inapplicable and which, even at best, could not cover all the practical problems posed by insanity. In short, the recourse to 'royal orders' was not available at the historical juncture when their need was most felt: when the transition from a rural civilization to an urban one increased the number of families that had broken up and the number of isolated individuals, and when the beginnings of industrialization required the setting up of a regulated movement of people that was incompatible with the nomadic character of madness.

Thus the insane person increasingly eluded the control of families and wandered into new social wastelands. Justice, bogged down by the weightiness of its procedures, could not compensate for the shortcomings of the family. Administrative authority dealt with what was most pressing, but its interventions, once covered by royal sovereignty, ran counter to the new legal foundations of the social order. A double imperative began to make itself felt. First, to make good the insufficiencies of family control and what might be termed local order. Madness, above all when it was associated with extreme poverty (and this was more and more often the case), posed problems of public order whose repression had to be reorganized in a consistent fashion at national level. Second, to make good the inadequacies of legalism, whilst avoiding arbitrariness. The institution of a new mode of dependency sought to find a way between the system of traditional bonds and that of contracts freely entered into (with its counterpart in punishments that were justly merited). It was aimed at the category of social deviants who are not responsible, in contrast to that of criminals deserving punishment. However, this new relationship, that became as indispensable to the functioning of a contractual society as juridical sanctions, could, unlike the latter, rely upon a mechanism that had already been run in. The new relationship of guardianship was defined and modified through the installation and the transformation of the mechanism of mental health medicine.

   Let us say again, at the risk of being accused of legalism, or even of juridical idealism: in understanding the ascendance of the authority of psychiatric control, the essential does not lie in what occurred on the plane of the concrete problems posed by the insane. It is true that madness is in itself very worrying. Unproductive, dangerous, unfitting, disturbing as it is, the institutional and legislative vacuum that confronted it at the end of the eighteenth century – or the disparity of the laws and the diversity of the institutions that were indirectly concerned with it – raised daily a host of questions: what authority would assume responsibility for putting a stop to the disturber of order? In what institution would that authority place such a person? What administration would assume the expense of his upkeep if he was poverty-stricken? Who would be responsible for extending or breaking off his detention? Etc., etc. But, in these troubled periods, it was fairly easy to improvise solutions or expedients that in terms of numbers have often more importance than sealing the fate of 5,000–10,000 individuals. In addition, the economic fall-out from the lack of productivity of these few thousands of people was almost nil at a time when vagrants and beggars, less unfit for work, could be counted by hundreds of thousands.

On the other hand, if there is one principle with which a liberal society cannot trifle, it is respect for the juridical foundation that has instituted that society and justifies its injustice. The exception is in the violations allowed for in its own formal legal system, something at which legalism excels. If today this way of posing the problem can give rise to reservations, it is because 'advanced' liberalism, this legalism, has collapsed. But why is this so? Because more generalized and more subtle procedures for control have been diffused throughout society as a whole, most frequently allowing recourse to the legal sanction to be sparing; because new techniques for restraint can render useless the exercise of a repression prescribed in the legal codes. In short, because legitimized modes of guardianship have multiplied, gradually reducing the contrasting dichotomy between the contact 'freely' entered into and the penal sanction, the 'fair' quid pro quo for breaking it. In all, because the medicine of mental health has now become part of our social landscape.

The crucial importance of the question of madness at the moment when bourgois society was installed lies firstly in the fact that it revealed in concrete form a gap in the contractual order: juridical formalism could control everything, and there existed at least one category of individuals which had to be neutralized by other means than those available to the apparatus of the law and the police. But the importance also lies in the fact that the new mechanism installed to remedy these deficiencies would develop a new manipulatory model of almost infinite flexibility. The majority of the new modes of control, the new techniques of constraint, and the new relationships of guardianship, would be linked to a medical index (and then one medical and psychological, medical and psycho-analytical, etc.) Thus the crisis invoked by the problem of madness among those authorities traditionally most firmly rooted, and above all, that of justice, revealed three things.

First, it fell to justice, even if refurbished, and administration, even if modernized, to assume the legacy of the royal power in order to undertake the technical control of madness. Second, another authority had to be called upon to weave new relationships between these mechanisms. Third, and above all, through the resolution of the crisis the new medical authority would give proof (still a local affair, to start with) of its flexibility. Faced with the rigidity of justice and the administration, it hinted at its capacity to develop a model for the exercise of power that is an alternative to that of a coercive authority.

The complex of problems embarked upon in this chapter thus in no way implies that in the assumption of responsibility for madness nothing save legal matters is at stake. In certain respects the contrary is true. The process of guardianship of the insane occurred through a series of practical transformations of a very precise nature whose vicissitudes we shall now have to follow: the overturning of institutional arrangements, the organization of theoretical codes, the refinement of disciplinary techniques, the constitution of new professional roles, etc. It is indeed these that are the most important, but on condition that one sees that the constitution of these practices first installed and then 'geared down' the powers of a new relationship of domination that co-existed with the legal order, before supplanting it in part, in order to impose norms on sectors increasingly more important in daily life.

The contradiction that was gnawing at legalism had been formulated with astonishing lucidity by a member of the Legislative Assembly in the revolutionary period:

> We know full well that the law has power only over actions that may concern the order established by it; but we must add that it cannot

view with indifference actions that, without attacking it overtly, nevertheless lead to causing disturbance in society. If society has the right to watch over the physical conduct of its members, it has no less a right of inspection over their moral behaviour.[48]

This 'inspection of their moral behaviour' – this inner control –escapes the formalism of the law, whilst being required for it actually to assume its tasks of preservation of the social order. Short of falling back into the arbitrariness of despotism (yet the condemnation of despotism is not only inspired by moral principles but is the necessary condition for the establishment of the new bourgeois society) legalism, its pomp and works, its verbose declamations and its deceits, its ridiculous or bloodthirsty ceremonial, must operate its discrete counterpart in the form of 'soft' techniques and down-to-earth recipes for subjection: the clandestine disciplinary measures operated backstage in the theatre of justice. The apparatus of mental health medicine will supply them. Such an apparatus was conceived in the shadow of legalism. It fed first of all upon its contradictions, in order to win for itself its own area of intervention. Then it developed by entertaining a relationship with justice that was in appearance polemical, but in reality dialectical. The shifting equilibrium between the two institutions conspires to effect the same end. Whether it relates to justice or medicine, the same arrangement is involved. The one imposes its influence through the objectivity of laws, by combatting its infringement by sanctions. The other detects in each individual a gap in relation to its norms, which it attempts to wipe out through its remedies.

2

The Rescue of the Totalitarian Institution

The linking of social practices concerning madness to medicine at the end of the eighteenth century appeared to be both natural and paradoxical. It was natural because already for a long time the doctor had laid siege to a part of these practices, and because at the end of the *Ancien Régime* the movement towards making insanity a medical matter was becoming systematized. Yet it was paradoxical because the recourse to medicine here posed more problems than it resolved. Making madness a medical matter does not in fact mean simply mere appropriation of madness by medical supervision. It implies, through the institution of medicine, the definition of a new legal, social and civil status for the madman: that of the *insane* person, whom the law of 1838 placed for more than a century firmly in the condition of being socially wholly a minor.

The determining element that conditions this status is placement in a 'special institution'. Making madness a medical matter is therefore not essentially one of establishing a relationship between the doctor and the sick person, which was the second and for a long while, secondary implication. It is the relationship between medicine and hospitalization, the development of a hospital technology, the exercise of a new kind of power within the institution, the acquiring of a new social mandate from practices based at first upon the bastion of the asylum. Hence we must ask why and how an innovation that passes for being 'progressive' and 'modernist' – which in certain respects it was – the medical treatment of the madman, was fitted into the old totalitarian institution, which it worked strenuously to save from discredit. This rescue of the old 'hospital' system at the

The ambiguity of the adjective 'totalitarian', suggested at the time as the translation for the *total institution* of Goffman (*Asiles*, Paris, 1968), is intended. As we shall see, it expresses the very ambiguousness of the concept, whose structural and political registers are indissociable.

end of the eighteenth century must not be taken for granted, either medically or politically.

The struggle against royal absolutism also took place through the destruction of its hospital citadels; the struggle against religious obscurantism highlighted the dissolution of the religious orders, which shared with royal power the privilege of shutting away criminals, the insane and the poor with all those who, more or less voluntarily, worked out their salvation in it. A reorganization of public assistance occurred based on the allocation of aid through the home. Medicine will be 'liberal' in a 'liberal' society. Under these conditions, how was the burgeoning field of psychiatry induced to link its destiny over such a long period of time to the asylum?

Medicine Installs Itself

Let us turn first to what is most 'natural': the introduction of the doctor into the scenario of madness at the end of the eighteenth century in no way represents a complete innovation. He had already intervened on several grounds and, at the end of the *Ancien Régime*, his roles had become systematized.

First, from the middle of the eighteenth century onwards there appeared numerous medical treatises on insanity, in particular the *Traité des affections vaporeuses des deux sexes ou des maladies nerveuses*, by Pomme (1760), the *Traité de l'épilepsie* (1770), and the *Traité des nerfs et de leurs maladies* (1780), both by Tissot. Various articles in the *Encylopédie* ('démence', 'folie', 'hypocondrie', 'manie', 'mélancolie' and 'phrénésie') insisted upon the curable character of madness. Also, from the point of view of treatment, a whole range of remedies was available to the doctor.[1] Pinel did not build his work upon a therapeutic vacuum. On the contrary, he boasted of his 'delaying medicine', as opposed to the frenzied interventions undertaken by his contemporaries.

Within the framework of detention also, madness became the object of a more medical perception (see chapter 1), and practices that dealt with the insane began to differ from those applied to others that were shut away. Thus the Frères de Saint-Jean-de-Dieu converted some of their number into specialists in the care of the insane, and the Charenton asylum was, at the moment of the Revolution, such a well-organized institution that an inspecting committee, in principle hostile to religious orders, and led by a doctor, found little to cavil at in the way in which the insane were treated.[2]

It has already been noted that the assumption of responsibility for the insane under the *Ancien Régime* was not incompatible with a certain degree of medical attention. It is merely that it was not upon this that the system was based. But more important than such developments in medical theory and practice regarding madness, was a dawning acknowledgement of the doctor's authority to intervene in the social questions thrown up by madness, which on the eve of the Revolution denoted progress towards its becoming a medical matter. Through the role of expert that he began to assume, the doctor bid fair to become a central protagonist *in a complex of problems that were indissolubly both medical and social.*

This expert function has likewise a long history. As early as 1569 Jean Wier had clearly postulated it in principle when he demanded that medical authority should be appealed to in cases of witchcraft:

Firstly and immediately, above all else one perceives in it an ill that is engendered against the natural order: in accordance with God's ordinance one must have recourse to the one who, renowned through his learning, profession and practices, understands sicknesses extremely well, the differences between them, their signs and causes: namely, to the doctor who is of a good conscience.[3]

Such recourse had extended beyond the category of religious trials, since a medical certificate was often presented during the procedure for detention.[4] But a much more official role as expert prevailed at the end of the *Ancien Régime*. In 1785 Neckar set up a General Inspectorate of Hospitals and Prisons of the realm, and entrusted its direction to Colombier. The latter drew up, with Doublet, a report on the position of the insane that was widely distributed throughout all the Generalities of the kingdom through the central administration.[5] This was the first acknowledgement by state authority of a specialized competence, one which great specialists in insanity such as Esquirol and Ferrus would systematically exploit.[6] Colombier and Doublet took advantage of this official mandate to advocate a general organization for assisting the insane. It was also an affirmation that the solution to the problem was linked to making it a medical matter. The insane person was officially seen as sick. 'By merely shutting away from society those unfortunates who are out of their mind, the viewpoint that one should adopt would not be entirely met, and it should be demonstrated that in every case it is first essential to treat those ill, especially when the madness is in its infancy.'[7]

Colombier and Doublet dovetailed this plan for 'medicalization' with a reordering of the places of detention. They inveighed against the presence of the insane in prisons and suggested that special quarters should be set aside for them in institutions for beggars: 'Already a large number of asylums have made ready for their treatment by establishing a department reserved exclusively for them in each beggary, where it is proposed to treat without distinction all kinds of madness.'[8]

The creation of beggaries by royal ordinance in 1767 had been the answer to the near-saturation of the Hôpitaux Généraux by the aged and the poor. These institutions sought to settle together the more mobile populations of beggars and vagrants. 'Their real vocation is to hold all those that the hospitals throw out and that the prisons cannot contain.'[9] In 1785 there appeared a royal decree, comprising 135 articles, which reorganized the internal regulations and conditions for admission into these workhouses by laying down that as well as vagrants, beggars, girls and women of ill repute, should be taken in 'fourthly, individuals who may be sent there by order of the King because of their dementia or behavioural defects.'[10]

Colombier and Doublet were not content with making this section of the place of detention independent in order that the doctor could carve out a niche for himself in it. They proposed dividing up this special area according to types of pathological behaviour, thus laying down the basic principle for asylum techniques:

> It is no less essential to arrange fittingly the places designed to receive these unfortunate persons; these places are of two kinds: the one kind is designed for treatment, and the other to hold those not undergoing it. For the former category, it is indispensable to have wards for the different types of insane, namely, the violent, those who are passive, and those who are convalescing.[11]

Tenon defended the same positions. Also, he was invested with a sort of official mandate, since he was entrusted with preparing a complete reform of the Hôtel-Dieu in Paris, which was universally denigrated. He carried out a systematic enquiry into the hospital institutions of Paris and went to England to study recent innovations (it is one of the originals of the English model that also inspired the work of the Committee on Begging in the Constituent Assembly). In particular, Tenon visited St Luke's, where 139 insane were treated and Bedlam, in London, which held 300 insane. Attracted by these, Tenon planned the construction of an institution at Sainte-Anne where, alongside a thousand of those suffering from fever or injuries, would be special quarters for 200 insane persons.[12] The Revolution prevented the project from being realized, but Tenon continued to propound it to the Committee of Public Assistance, which, under the Legislative Assembly, succeeded the Committee on Begging, and over which he presided.[13] It was moreover in the same spirit that the Committee on Begging, under the Constituent Assembly, had already planned the building in every large town of a hospital for those poor not domiciled there, those suffering from contagious or venereal disease, and those curable insane affected 'by the greatest, the most fearful of human miseries that can befall such unfortunate persons, degraded in the most noble part of themselves.'[14] The Committee, whilst deploring their tardiness as compared with the English, launched a veritable appeal to French doctors, asking them to devote to madness all the attention that it deserved:

> This sickness, the most afflicting, the most humiliating for humanity, the one whose cure affords heart and mind the most entire satisfaction, has as yet not aroused in France the practical attention of doctors. A great number of works, doubtless very learned, have been published on this interesting subject; but no profit or solace has as yet resulted from their teachings for that unfortunate group, which is unfortunately too numerous. The proportion of cures has not been increased by them. However, experience in neighbouring countries demonstrates that a large number of the insane can be restored to the use of reason by appropriate forms of treatment, a suitable regime, and even merely by being cared for in a kind, attentive and soothing fashion, whereas the harshness with which they are only too often treated in France renders them both incurable and unhappy. The great learning of French doctors will make their care, in the treatment of this illness, as rewarding as that of English doctors, when forms of treatment in these institutions, which will be entirely suitable for the care the insane require, have become more frequent.[15]

In this way were strengthened both the permanence of the pattern of 'major detention' and the attempt to abolish the lack of differentiation on which this was based, deriving from the joint effect of the humanism of the philanthropists and medical ideology. Tenon went far along this road when he declared:

> It is impossible to sort out the insane that one intends to treat for madness in the same way as one differentiates between normal cases of sickness or pregnant women. A hospital is in some respects an instrument that facilitates treatment. Yet a striking difference exists between a hospital for fever patients or those suffering from injuries, and one for the curable insane: the former offers only a means of treatment, with greater or less advantage according to the degree to which it is differentiated, whilst the latter acts as a remedy in itself.[16]

This is more than a harbinger of the famous mental health axiom formulated by Esquirol: 'An institution for the insane is an instrument in their cure; in the hands of a skilful doctor it is the most powerful therapeutic agent against mental illnesses.'[17]

It might be objected that these were more pious wishes than concrete realizations. For the city of Paris – and for almost the whole of France – in 1788 there were 42 male and 34 female insane huddled together in two insalubrious wards of the Hôtel-Dieu. If they resisted treatment more than twice in six weeks they were transferred to the Bicêtre and Salpêtrière institutions, and were purely and simply shut away. A survey carried out in 1790 at the Bicêtre institution through the offices of M. de Jussieu, the deputy overseer for the governance of hospitals, enquired 'whether there is a method of healing used in the treatment of madness'. The reply was: 'No, all the insane sent to Bicêtre remain as they were until it pleases nature to favour them'[18] (which did not prevent one in five from getting better, or at least from being let out). Innovations and plans in France, as in England, were only concerned with the 'curable insane', namely those whose illness was recent. At St Luke's for example, doubtless the first of the 'special institutions' in which medical treatment was systematically provided, insane persons who had never previously undergone treatment were admitted for a maximum of one year. Tenon's plan to build a new hospital at Sainte-Anne for two hundred of the insane was also only concerned with those curable: it was conceived within the framework of the reform of the Hôtel-Dieu, without challenging its selection principles. In 1792, just before Pinel made his entry into the hagiography of psychiatry, the Legislative Assembly decreed that 'those who are at present shut away at the expense of the nation because of dementia will be transferred to the new houses of detention'. The Convention's decree of 24 Vendémiaire Year II, Title III, described the organization of such houses. Warders armed with gun and sabre stood on guard at the door day and night. The insane may be admitted 'at the expense of the nation', but most numerous were persistent beggars, who on the average spent one year there.[19] It was apparently a far from therapeutic environment.

Another Model of Assistance

Thus, in the revolutionary era, matters were far from being decided. But difficulties about the medical reordering of an environment for the detention of the poor should not be interpreted as mere delays in the conquest by a new science of its natural space. The medical and charitable mission of the hospital was obscured, at the end of the *Ancien Régime*, by a barrier of hatred and resentment that indeed reflected the great fear felt by the poor about these institutions, in which religion and the power of the state were in alliance or took turns in causing a truly terrifying discipline to reign amidst the huddled mass of bodies. One text, among a hundred others, in its grandiloquence translates exactly this general repulsion, which is also expressed in a number of the Books of Complaints of the three Estates:

> The human race existed no longer save through the sense of hearing when a voice cried: 'Eternal God is merciful, He wishes to give absolution to the children of men and draw them again to Him: Grace to all sinners; one alone is excepted.' The entire human race repeated with shuddering and trembling: One alone is excepted. Parricides, poisoners, homicides and slanderers beat their breast, saying: It is we who stand rebuked. A consternated silence followed, and the waiting troubled every spirit. The same voice was heard, with a sound that caused the universe to quake: One alone is excepted . . . It is a hospital administrator.[20]

It must be remembered that the hospital only became a primarily medical environment during the nineteenth century, if indeed it was completely so by that time. Under the *Ancien Régime* the hospital population was not made up solely of sick people, or of all the sick. It was the result of a very specific selection made from among those indigent reduced to the utmost degree of abandonment, as well as from all those whom it was necessary to uproot from their living environment because of the dangers they presented to the stability of society. These two simple reminders are needed to understand the paradox there was in founding a new policy of public assistance upon the hospital structure.

First, the hospital was only the ultimate stage, and the one that is most disputed, of a more general mechanism of struggle against the social risks that misery and sickness brought in their train. Since 1545 there had existed in Paris the 'Grand Bureau des Pauvres', whose main function was to dole out alms to the sick poor in their own homes, and work to those fit poor resident at home.[21] At the end of the eighteenth century in particular, Turgot and Neckar encouraged the development of charity offices and wanted them to be created in every parish. The project tended to secularize and generalize the numerous previous initiatives of religious origin, such as by the Charity Brothers of St Vincent de Paul or the charity funds set up by parish priests.[22]

> The charity office knows the sick poor and their needs. In every place where its zealousness is more enlightened or better supported by public generosity, it holds in stock a sufficient store of linen, furniture and utensils for the use of both sexes in their infirmities; it pays a decent retainer to doctors and surgeons of acknowledged skill and probity for them to visit and treat all the sick of the parish, it provides all the remedies, broths, and food necessary during illness and convalescence.[23]

Doubtless this system worked very badly. However, hospitalization, far from being the exclusive pattern for assistance to the sick, already appeared to be a last resort for the most sorely tried segments of the population. Thus, according to an anonymous writer of the eighteenth century, the vicar of Saint-Roch boasted of 'not letting go to the Hôtel-Dieu any save the sick without a home, or who are not worthy enough to find a friend or a neighbour desirous of giving them some care'.[24] This trend to 'dehospitalization' became, as we shall see, predominant at precisely the time when the asylum was being instituted.

Secondly, under the *Ancien Régime*, assistance was discretionary, and the means available for it derisory in comparison with the immense misery. The indigent person had therefore to compel attention according to criteria among which sickness was not the most apparent. In the dichotomy of assistance and repression that caused the whole policy of assistance to function, the role of repression predominated in making the hospital responsible, because, through detention, it immediately assumed the role of safeguarding public order. Numerous writings of the period distinguish clearly, within the hospital population, between the 'sick poor' and the 'fit poor'. But in many respects the need not to be left to their own devices was more urgent for the 'fit', in so far as their presence immediately posed problems of public order because of the two social scourges of vagrancy and begging. *A fortiori*, the same was true for the different types of penal inmates.

It might broadly be said that under the *Ancien Régime* the 'good poor', and even the majority of the sick that were socially integrated, were, so far as possible, helped in their own homes. They earned alms and assistance through their good behaviour, for which their religious assiduousness constituted the best indication. The parochial hierarchy, with the vicar and his helpers, the charitable devout, the ladies dispensing good works, constituted a supervisory network in which access to public assistance was gauged on merit. With the exception of a few specific illnesses, it was mainly for those who disrupted social integration that the hospital solution was available, or rather was imperative.

This requirement for the policing of society and for public morality brought together the various categories to be detained. The hospital was therefore not apparent as a specifically therapeutic institution in the mid-eighteenth century, even for those of its inmates that had entered it because of illness. The hospital complex formed a heterogeneous continuum, ranging from prisons to institutions that would most resemble treatment hospitals, such as the various Hôtel-Dieu, with all the diverse intermediate forms. Thus Paris (with 660,000 inhabitants on the eve of the Revolution) numbered 20,000 that were hospitalized, of which 12,000 were at the Hôpital Général, 3,000 at the Invalides, 2,500 at the Hôtel-Dieu and the remainder in some 50 establishments, some of which only possessed a few beds. In the same period there existed in France a good 1,000 institutions of this type, housing more than 100,000 of the infirm, the aged, the poor, foundlings, beggars and delinquents of every kind. Among them, there were some 25,000 sick people.[25] Yet can we speak of sick people properly so-called, when the mixture of inmates, the internal discipline, the discretionary power of the administrators hardly distinguished the conditions of their existence from that of others shut away? The hospital was indeed a totalitarian institution within which reigned the laws of the world of the concentration camp, but one which lacked any specific hospital technology. It was perceived as such by contemporaries. We have numerous testimonies of popular resistance not only to the shutting away of the 'fit poor' in general hospitals and workhouses for beggars, but also to the assumption of responsibility for the sick. Michelet summed up this general sentiment as follows:

> The old-time hospitals were in no way different from prisons. The sick person, the poor person, the prisoner, who were thrown into them were always viewed as sinners stricken by God, who first had to expiate their sins. They underwent cruel treatment. Such terrible charity gave rise to fear . . . The sick hid themselves away to die for fear of being dragged away into them.[26]

Or, for those who might deem Michelet to lack scientific even-handedness, this verdict of a contemporary: 'The terms 'hospital' or 'Hôtel-Dieu' have become the object of vilification and serve only to cause all those who have most need of help and assistance, by a natural sentiment, to shrink from them.'[27]

If there was fear on the part of the poor, there was also the revulsion of 'enlightened minds' against institutions that symbolize at one and the same time political absolutism and economic irrationality: 'Hospitals increase poverty instead of extinguishing it, and torment humanity instead of succouring it.'[28] Behind a general consensus to diminish the role of hospitals, if not to abolish them,[29] a new demand for effectiveness emerged at two levels.

On the one hand, the traditional management of the legacy of the hospitals, and, at the margin, its very existence, appeared to make economic nonsense. Since the property of charitable institutions was inalienable, a considerable part of the national wealth was therefore definitively immobilized. The concern not to hand over to financially motivated speculation the property devoted to the service of the poor seemed to justify the fact that the hospital foundations eluded the network of exchange and jealously defended their exemptions and privileges. But this removed many possibilities for using land to advantage and for stimulating commerce from the laws of the market. What is more, these ancient foundations did not even meet the objectives they were designed to fulfil: located according to the whim of their founders, in certain areas they were totally lacking, whilst other areas were too well provided for. In the same geographical area, one kind of distress was amply met, whilst other kinds were completely uncatered for, etc. The economists were at one with Turgot in denouncing this costly anarchy, whose archaic nature blocked the installation of a more rational economic structure, viz. one that was more productive.[30]

But there was worse: such disorganization did not only drain off wealth. Despite the innumerable declarations of principle according to which the Hôpitaux Généraux and the institutions for beggars had to set those detained to work, their internal system was such that the segments of the population locked up in them were practically unproductive. As for more 'therapeutic' institutions on the lines of the Hôtel-Dieu, they served most frequently as antichambers to death rather than places in which the sick might recover their health.[31] Then, from the second half of the eighteenth century onwards the idea began to gain ground that the population also formed part of the 'wealth of nations'. Such a wastage of the labour force and of human lives appeared an economic crime as well as an attack upon humanity. 'If all social benefit is founded initially upon work', one contemporary states explicitly, 'it is consequently indispensable, in the interest of the class that benefits from it, to look to the preservation of the labouring class.'[32]

Such a realization of the value of work as the origin of social wealth necessitated a complete redesigning of the scenario as regards public assistance, one to which we shall have to return (chapter 3). But from the pre-revolutionary era onwards, the conjunction of political criticism of a bastion of absolutism and of economic criticism of the exorbitant cost of its management entailed the discrediting of the hospital sector and the search for an alternative, through development of home assistance: 'In the eighteenth century statesmen and writers dealing with economic questions have a marked tendency to propose home assistance and to place this far above hospital assistance.'[33] As early as 1765, the die appeared to be cast for the Abbé Baudeau:

We no longer hesitate utterly to proscribe public infirmaries. Their income and buildings will be handed over to the common funds of the general almonry in each diocese, under the direction of the General Charity Bureau. The sick poor will no longer be constrained to seek out assistance that is humiliating, painful and often maleficent. Patriotic charity will bring them assistance in their very homes, in the bosom of their nearest and dearest, in accordance with the system of charity bureaux, preferable for a host of reasons to that of the hospitals.[34]

Following this logic, the Committee on Begging of the Constituent Assembly put at the top of its vast programme of aid a plan for the distribution of assistance based on enrolment on 'lists of the poor' in each commune, in accordance with a classification that followed 'the degree of impairment of the capacity to work of the person to whom it is given'. The costs were to be financed from a national assistance fund through which resources would then be channelled to the departments, districts and cantons. This represented the linking of administrative centralism, which made assistance a right guaranteed by the nation, with the localization of the distribution of home assistance to the poor and the sick, under the control of the nearest local authority. This notion of *home assistance* meant that most medical and other forms of assistance could be administered in a way that avoided segregation. Thus there would be in each canton an assistance agency, with a doctor and a free dispensary for medicines. Only very specific categories (those with contagious or venereal diseases, beggars, the homeless poor, incorrigible vagrants, abandoned children and also – we shall come back to them – the insane) had to be uprooted from their living environment and set down in a closed institution.[35]

In order to put this policy into practice one of the first acts of the Constituent Assembly was, on 2 November 1789, to decree to be national property the hospitals and Church hospices, with the nation responsible for 'providing in a fitting manner for the expenses of worship, the upkeep of its clergy, and the succour of the poor'. The privileges and exemptions of the hospitals were abolished on 22 August 1791. The decree of 18 April 1792 abolished the religious orders.

The Convention wished to go even further. On 23 Messidor Year II, the Assembly decreed the sale of hospital property. At the same time Barère set out the Utopia of help without segregation: 'No more alms, no more hospitals. This is the goal towards which the Convention must unceasingly press, for these two words must be blotted out from the vocabularly of the Republic.'[36] Indeed, the decree of the Convention that instituted a Great Book of National Charity (22 Floréal, Year II) no longer made reference to the hospitals.[37] It is true that, two days before dissolving itself, the Convention, on 2 Brumaire, Year IV, suspended the application of its decree of 23 Messidor. It was finally abolished by the Directory on 16 Vendémiaire, Year V: hospital property already sold off as national property had to be replaced, the central government was relieved of all financial responsibility for the allocation of assistance, and management of hospital property was entrusted to administrative committees placed under the control of the municipalities. The Napoleonic state confirmed the tendency to return to the practices of the *Ancien Régime:* the donors of beds got back their rights, the foundation of new private institutions was authorized, the role of the religious orders was officially revived.[38] Thus the restoration of the hospitals after Thermidor followed roughly the main stages of the political restoration.

All had happened, however, as if at one moment history had wavered, as if there had been hesitation between two opposing models for assistance. The first was the totalitarian Utopia of the *Ancien Régime:* to wipe the slate clean of a host of deviants, as a first step, by neutralizing and isolating them. In a second step, they were disciplined by deploying, within a closed institution, a range of corrective techniques based upon manual activities, religious exercises and moral regulation. The second assistance strategy was already a Utopia that might be termed a capillary one. It aimed at stemming the risk of deviance at the point at which it appeared, in order to avoid an overspill dangerous to public order; it was intended to prevent a breach in the assistance given at home. This notion of home assistance had been very skilfully conceived as a middle way between a kind of nomadic state arising from the absolute freedom to move around and a state of being rigidly tied to the commune of one's birth, explicitly taking into account the necessities of the labour market.[39]

Hence two strategies for localization, which implied two opposing modes of implementing medical treatment. For the tendency to dehospitalization did not entail getting rid of medical treatment – quite the contrary. Most of the activities to which medicine laid siege at the end of the eighteenth century, and which gave it a new political dimension, occurred outside the arena of the hospital, in what today would be called the community. Hence the new assumption of responsibility for childhood: aware of the new evaluation of the population as a factor of wealth, medicine attacked the problems of infantile mortality by checking births more closely and supervising wet-nursing. The same was true for epidemics, hygiene in the towns, and morbidity in the countryside. It was represented above all by the creation of the Royal Society of Medicine in 1770, which consolidated this more ambitious conception of the doctor's role. From the royal power he received a mandate for observation, for data-gathering and surveillance of sections of the population within their natural environment. Through these practices the doctor assigned himself a new political function. The agent of the central authority – disinterested because he took on a public service that, according to certain revolutionary projects for reform, should be directly remunerated by the state – the doctor, in his assistance role, left behind him the special environment of the hospital and ranged over the whole area of society, offering his skill at the spot where misfortune and disorder emerged.[40]

This dual portent was full of promise: medicine as a *public* and homogeneous service implanted over the whole country, and *preventive* medicine, part of a general mechanism for detection and early intervention: 'It is undoubtedly a categorical duty for society to assist poverty, but to prevent it is no less sacred and necessary a duty.'[41] A policy of assistance given in detention is inevitable when the evil has been done, when the unfortunate or sick person is already isolated, swept along by a current that threatens to be irreversible. Yet, in so far as it would shore up structures that were in the process of change, medical intervention would also detach itself from the hospitals, where all is, in so many respects, too predetermined. Instead of breaking up natural ties, the policy of assistance would safeguard and reinforce them. It would save itself from taking the by-path of isolation by fitting itself into the spontaneous dialectic of the individual with his environment. It is within the framework of its criticism of hospitalization that the Committee on Begging thus spelt out the Utopia that served to underpin it: 'It is by caring for one another that the family spirit is preserved, the natural bonds are tightened, goodness is nurtured and morals perfected.'[42]

It is always preferable to give treatment on the spot rather than to isolate, to prevent rather than to attempt to 'reprogramme' after the event an individual who has become desocialized, to strengthen the ties that bind to the living environment rather than to mop up the individual wrecks that occur when they are broken. This programme fairly compehensively foreshadowed by 150 years the policy known as 'sectorial'. Hence the last 'progressive' project of the Convention concerning organized public assistance, on 22 Floréal, Year II, the listing of all those needing help in the Great Book of Public Charity. Instead of assistance given in hospital, a body of 1,500 to 2,000 doctors and auxiliary doctors paid by the state took over health problems.[43]

Thus if these two modes co-existed, why was the new medicine of mental health cast in the mould of the more archaic and the more discredited of the two? Why had it turned its back on the new formula that seemingly inevitably would prevail, so as to rework the old material of the totalitarian institution, cutting a piece out here and there, and indefatigably patching up – a task to which it had applied all its energies for more than a century?

A Reformist Compromise

If the burgeoning discipline of psychiatry bound its destiny to that of the totalitarian institution for so long, it was for neither purely technical nor purely political reasons, but through the conjunction of these two parallel phenomena, strictly regulated both in space and time. The asylum model was fashioned in the concentration-camp world of the *Ancien Régime* through a set of practices that can be reconstituted from Pinel's work. But this prosaic task at the same time epitomizes a political turning point for which Delecloy can be taken to be the spokesman.

From the political aspect, the complete 'de-institutionalist' day-dreaming of Barère merely represented one extreme tendency. It supposed the advent of a political organization capable, in the end, of doing away with misery, thus rendering useless institutions whose sole finality was the management of misfortune': 'Is there within them a portion of humanity that is suffering? . . . Then put above the door of these asylums inscriptions that announce their imminent demise. For if, once the Revolution is over, unfortunate creatures still exist among us, our Revolutionary labours will have been in vain.'[44]

This Utopia did not survive the defeat of the Montagne. The spokesman of the Thermidor reaction on public assistance was Delecloy. A member of the Convention, it was he who pleaded for the suspension of the implementing of the Law of 23 Messidor, Year II, which had ordered the selling off of hospital property. Having become a member, under the Directory, of the Council of Five Hundred, he returned to the matter and obtained the definitive repeal of the law. On this occasion he presented an overall plan for the reorganization of public assistance that contained the guidelines for the policy that would triumph.[45]

First, the liquidation of the revolutionary alternative: 'It is time to get out of the deep rut in which an exaggerated philanthropy has caused us to be bogged down since the Constituent Assembly. A mania for levelling out, for the generalization of the distribution of assistance seems again to have ended in causing the best of minds to be led astray.'[46] Nothing could be plainer:

> He who first said that the government alone owed the needy assistance of every kind and in all ages of life stated an absurdity, for the product of all the taxes imposed by the Republic would not suffice to cover this enormous and incalculable burden: it is perhaps much more truthful in politics to say that the government owes nothing to him who does not serve it. The poor person has a right only to general commiseration.[47]

The right to assistance was thus replaced by an appeal to the benevolence of the good-hearted. A return purely and simply to the former charity? No: indigence, misery and sickness were social problems. The state could wash its hands of them in so far as the existence of these misfortunes might jeopardize its stability. It must therefore show an example in benevolence, be 'the mainspring' of the impulsion that is to set in motion private initiative in giving assistance:

> Let us then lay down once more as a principle that the government cannot by itself take on the maintenance of the poor; but, by submitting the poor to the safeguard of the general commiseration *and to the guardianship of the wealthy*, it must set the example by a benevolence that is limited in its means; it must sacrifice funds, and thereby set the

seal of large-scale action upon all the mechanisms that can incite the universal sensibility.[48]

In Delecloy's eyes was it not plain, or did he not feign to believe that, 'when the government says sincerely to men that they should do good, then ineluctably they do so?'.[49]

Thus, so far as possible, assistance had to be decentralized, channelled directly to the local communities, where it could be revitalized by private initiative. Yet if denationalization, 'communalization' and privatization go hand in hand, one must nevertheless anticipate the assumption of responsibility in a certain number of extreme cases. A minimal structure of obligatory public assistance was therefore set up, upon the twin bases of an organization for home assistance and a hospital programme.

As regards the first, in each commune a very limited list of individuals that were completely unprovided for was drawn up: the totally indigent sick (their registration was only provisional), children that had been abandoned, the aged lacking absolutely all resources, for 'the government must take care of those generations that are setting out and those that are coming to an end, namely, those who are the promise of labour to come or who have given of their labour.'[50] So far as possible such assistance was to be given in the home. For – and it is significant – in this moderate context, criticism of the hospital was as virulent as ever: 'We shall not dissimulate from you that the more we have concerned ourselves with the poor, the more we have felt that the hospital was a vile institution; only administrators could have imagined, to suit their own convenience, the idea of huddling together men of every kind, in order to allow them to languish in opprobium and misery.'[51]

However, the hospital structure could not be completely abolished:

> I should have liked to be able to abolish this kind of assistance: but, among other considerations, I felt the need to offer the unmarried, individuals with no lodging, parents, or friends, a refuge in their distress or infirmity in a few communes. Thus the number of hospices has been considerably reduced, whilst increasing assistance at home and restricting, strictly speaking, to the one category alone, those with no parents or friends, the painful but indispensable resource of the hospices.[52]

In the countryside, the concrete ties that subsisted between men, which constituted a network of mutual assistance, dispensed with the need to provide for the public organization of assistance. Hospitalization was no longer more than the counterpart of urban *anomie*. Thus only small hospices were established, on the basis of some 50 places made available for towns of 10,000–20,000 inhabitants, etc. The gigantism of Paris justified the preservation of some ten hospitals (whereas there once existed about a hundred), but their capacity was considerably reduced. Thus the Hôtel-Dieu only had 400 beds available.

Hence the population that was dealt with formerly by detention was shrunk, like Balzac's 'skin of sadness' (*'peau de chagrin'*). Yet this very reduction revealed within it categories that belied even more radically the myth of total 'de-institutionalization'. These were the 'mad, the sufferers from venereal disease of both sexes, and all those who, by virtue of their having been sentenced, are detained for a fixed period'. For them, 'there will be established in every *département* a place of detention'.[53] Only in Paris did the size of the population allow two institutions specially for the insane to be envisaged, one for each sex.

This was the point where public assistance and repression began to become dissociated from each other because of the criticism of the hospital structure. The stress placed upon home assistance allows us to identify a primary ring of rejection, drawn around a limited number of isolates that could receive in their own living environment the aid that their condition necessitated. But this humanitarian argument allows the identification of a secondary ring, one of detention for all those who had to be separated from society because of the danger they presented to it. Thus, through criticism of the massive institutionalization of all deviants, and setting aside a limited number of the indigent who could benefit as of right from hospitalization, the insane alone, together with criminals and sufferers from venereal disease, remained legally liable to compulsory imprisonment. Thus, even before the form of prison and that of asylum were dissociated from each other, one can grasp the logic behind their constitution, which made their existence, paradoxically, a necessity within liberal societies.

Two mechanisms were brought simultaneously into play. On the one hand, a clarification of the finalities of detention: criticism of the totalitarian institution as an undifferentiated mode of assistance and repression that obliterated the differences between those who, from the indigent to the criminal, were dependent on that system. This criticism freed certain categories, responsibility for whom was formerly assumed through detention and, at the same time it revealed that others could benefit from such a liberation. The identification of criminality and madness as requiring a specific form of treatment thus emerged against a background of a 'liberal' regime: to the very extent that the contractual structure of society became generalized, it required the rejection of those who could not play its game. The liberal society and the totalitarian institution indeed functioned like a dialectic pair.

Moreover, 'liberalism' implies a maximum privatization of the administration of assistance. This trend became more marked and flourished under the Restoration. The minimum programme for a public service still contained within the Delecloy project would not even be applied. Assistance became more and more discretionary. Such a relaxation likewise pointed, *a contrario*, to criminality and madness as specific 'social problems': in a *laissez-faire* context dominated by a market economy, the criminal and the insane could most assuredly not be left to their own devices.

During the post-revolutionary period the totalitarian institution was therefore reduced to the bare bones. But this reduction did not lead to its disappearance; in certain respects the opposite occurred. Now dealing only with people who most definitely had no place in 'normal' society, its ends henceforth appeared to be rational. Its internal organization also had to rationalize and reform itself, so that technically it could manage the tasks for which it was irreplaceable.

This clarification began with Delecloy. The allocation of help was to the home; hospitals, hospices, and places of imprisonment were identified according to their different functions. Yet the process of division was not carried to its conclusion. The house of detention still lumped together criminals responsible for their actions and two heterogeneous categories of the sick: the sufferers from venereal disease, contagious and morally guilty; and the insane, dangerous but not responsible. It was the fact that such a classification was still too exclusively based on the fear aroused by such groups of reprobates that accounts for such a syncretic approach. The rationality of repression was to triumph by distinguishing more precisely between types of fear and by using specific techniques to exorcise them.[54]

It is not dogmatic to put forward such an interpretation based upon a single report by Delecloy, because here he was merely the spokesman in the field of public assistance for the class that conquered both the absolute power of the monarchy and the revolutionary alternative. Another 'specialist' in these matters, Cabanis, said much the same thing, but in terms that more directly served as an introduction to the technical and political problem that was to be solved by mental health medicine.

The same suspicion existed about the hospital:

> This lumping together of individuals bound together by no natural ties; whose lack of hope stirs to no activity; for whom a stupid sense of security lulls the future; who have only false and corrupting relationships with the objects that surround them and the persons on whom they depend: such an assemblage, I say, is it not capable of degrading to the utmost degree both intelligence and morality?[55]

'Every time that men are brought together, their health is changed, every time they are brought together in an enclosed environment their morals as well as their health are changed.'[56]

The same realism also existed: 'Hospitals are perhaps by their very nature defective institutions, but in the present state of societies they are absolutely necessary.'[57] But a solution began to emerge, outlined with reference, but in opposition, to the dream of Barère, who was interpreted without being named:

> The sudden destruction of institutions of assistance, and the rationalized slackening in individual charity, far from abolishing the numerous causes of misery, would assuredly aggravate several of them. Thus one must not take literally that profound saying of a man who, endued with the kind of mind whose property is always to press forward to great results, devoted itself very especially to the investigation and examination of the facts.[58]

What must not be taken 'literally' is the particularly political dimension of Barère's conception and of the radical members of the Convention. They aimed at *political* overthrow because they saw in the hospital a bastion of absolutism, a power mechanism founded upon the uprooting of the wretched from their living environment in order to place them, bereft of everything, in the grip of an absolute authority. The question was indeed therefore – even if the members of the Convention could not, or did not have the time, to define a programme for it – one of inventing a political alternative for types of relationships that were themselves couched in political terms. On the other hand, if the hospitals were merely 'through their bad organization a fresh cause of misery rather than truly beneficial, a principle for demoralization rather than the model or sustenance for benevolent virtues',[59] the problem then became only a *technical* one, with implications that were merely *moral*. This was a sociology of organizations before its time: to unblock structures, to do away with archaic practices, make up for past delays, rationalize procedures, make costing efficient, humanize relationships, etc. Realism, effectiveness, profitability, morality, good management: the hospital was capable of reform. Modernized, it could become the key in a new dispensation for a public assistance refurbished at the least political and financial cost. It was not a mechanism of power that crushed people and reproduced servitude. It was a badly run institution. It was no more than a matter of renovating this wing of the totalitarian institution, bringing it into line with the new moral environment of bourgeois society.

Cabanis even sketched out the application of these principles, technocratic before their time, in his 'Report addressed to the department of Paris by one of its members concerning the condition of the female insane detained in the Salpêtrière hospital' (6 December 1791[60]). First (at the beginning of the report), a concern for good management: 'The state of the female insane in the old quarters of the Salpêtrière is one of those disorders that no humane administration could endure.'[61] Cabanis therefore proposed a plan for new regulations that dealt both with admissions and the internal system. The female insane would be classified into four groups: 'women under treatment', 'violently and indecently insane without hope of cure', 'the scrofular and epileptic incurable', 'imbeciles and in general all those who have need only of special care'.[62] This classification was still deceptive, and one which could even appear to lag behind that proposed by Colombier and Doublet. Yet at the same time Cabanis recommended advanced techniques for the observation of the insane person: 'Observation will be made from every viewpoint: he will be observed by para-medical officers, and by those personnel who are the most clever and practised in observing madness in all its forms.'[63] He even went so far as to envisage keeping a day-book 'in which the record of each illness, the effects of the remedies, the dissection of corpses, will be countersigned with scrupulous exactness. All patients in the section will be listed in it by name, so that the administration can be kept informed of the condition of each one individually, week by week, or even day by day, if it deems it necessary.' Moreover, each service was placed under medical control: 'There shall be established for each section a para-medical officer, attached solely to those services dealing with the female insane, under the supervision of the head doctor.'[64] Madness was thus ripe for display to medical scrutiny. It would find in the asylum the specific arena in which its reduction to medical knowledge and the practical mastery of it could be developed side by side.[65]

However, Cabanis was still a planner of projects whose programmes embraced the whole of 'public assistance'. He was doubtless also a doctor – and this was no mere chance – but one who had spent more time translating Homer and frequenting the salon of Mme Helvétius or parliamentary assemblies than in practising his profession.[66] The policy he commended required practical operators. Efficient and humane managers were called for.

A Practical Operator

Cabanis and his friends found this new type of manager in Philippe Pinel. History does not record whether Pinel was explicitly given a mandate to carry out these views. In any case, he shared them, and belonged to the circles who spread them abroad. Pinel was appointed at the Bicêtre hospital in 1793 upon the recommendation of Cabanis and Thouret. Cabanis had already been the one who had introduced him to Mme Helvétius, the inspirer of that celebrated 'société d'Auteuil' where he met Lavoisier, Condorcet, Franklin, etc., and Thouret. With Cabanis and Thouret he belonged to the same masonic lodge of the Neuf-Soeurs, of which Pastouret, another doctor, was Grand Master.[67] Thouret, the last head of the former faculty of medicine during the *Ancien Régime*, was also the first director of the Medical School founded in Year III of the Republic. He appointed Pinel to the chair of physical medicine and hygiene there, and then to the chair of medical pathology. Thouret was a member of the Committee on Begging, then of the Tribunate, and finally of the legislative body. With Delecloy, Cabanis and Fourcroy he represented a movement of those reformers of public assistance, hygienists and philanthropists, who were often doctors and who survived all political upheavals, less through opportunism than because the divagations of the various regimes gradually effected that bourgeois synthesis of order and progress they recommended.

From what is known of the strictly political ideas of Pinel, he must be placed in this camp. Semelaigne, his biographer, wrote:

> He was imbued with a wise patriotism and a sincere love of progress, but he had a horror of blood and of those who caused it to be shed in the name of liberty and equality. His letters upon the death of Louis XVI, which he witnessed, and upon the hotheads who organized the Terror, do the greatest honour to his courageous common sense and the firmness of his convictions, which lacked fanaticism.[68]

Thus he too would be honoured by successive regimes. His hospital career having been made secure by the Convention, he was appointed consultant physician to the emperor in 1803. He received the Legion of Honour in 1804, and then, in 1818, the Croix de Saint-Michel at the hands of the Duc d'Angoulême. It was only after the reaction that followed the assassination of the Duc de Berry in 1821 that he was to be reproached for his moderate republicanism: he was dismissed upon the closure of the medical faculty in 1822. The radical Republic would preside over his legend much later.

Yet Pinel was neither an Ideologue, nor a politician, if by that is meant a member of assemblies (for a while a holder of municipal office under the Convention, he almost immediately abandoned all public activity of this kind). It was in, and through, his professional practice that he set up a system which divested the plans of reformers of public assistance of some of the weight of their historical past. Pinel was a practical operator in that reformist trend that proceeds from the Convention to the July Monarchy. Thanks to him – or rather, to the kind of practices that he was the first to implement in a systematic way – a programme of assistance that was somewhat vague became embodied in a hospital technology. On one point at least, the question of the insane, the philanthropic policy of the enlightened bourgeoisie was equipped with the means to carry it out.

To illustrate from the work of Pinel the principles of the technology of mental health is not to ascribe to a single man the merit of accomplishing a revolution (if revolution there were). It is true that the originality of Pinel and of his 'works' has been highlighted in the hagiography of psychiatry. Doctors in England such as Willis, Cullen (whom Pinel translated in 1785), and Haslam, in France, Colombier and Tenon, in Savoy Daquin, and in Italy Chiarrugi, etc., shared in the same background for 'reforms', and their initiatives in some fields even preceded those of Pinel (for example, Haslam and Daquin for moral treatment). But Pinel allows us clearly to see an evolution that particularly distinguishes mental health medicine. Before him, two lines of progress had developed in quasi-independent fashion. One may be termed theoretical: it consisted of a progressive refining of the classificatory framework of illnesses through the works of Boissier de Sauvage, Linneus, Sydenham, Tissot, etc.[69] The other was work on the totalitarian institution through practical initiatives such as those taken by Vincent-de-Paul, the Frères de Saint-Jean-de-Dieu, the administrators of the Hôpitaux Généraux or institutions for beggars, and reformers such as Colombier and Doublet etc. The treatments followed yet a third line of development, one moreover that was very slow. The medicinal techniques for madness were still scarcely specific: the administration of medical prescriptions and drugs such as opium deemed to have shown their worth in general medicine; bleeding, purging; more specifically, the use of various forms of hydrotherapy: enemas, baths, hot or cold showers . . . Doublet, in the annexe to the circular of 1785 whose innovating character has been noted, even recommended for stubborn cases, 'cauterizations, swabs, surface abscissions, inoculation with dermatitis', as well as a return to hellebore.[70]

Pinel joined together three apparently heterogeneous dimensions of mental health, the link between which constituted its synthesis: classification of the institutional area; nosographic categorization of mental illnesses; the imposition of a specific power relationship between doctor and patient (the 'moral treatment').[71]

First, classification of the hospital space:

(1) *A general order was established regarding the distribution of the sick:* the despatching of infants and young girls to orphanages; the removal of sexagenarians, husbands and wives, known as 'households', who should no longer be tolerated in a hospice devoted solely to females; the general division of the one hospice into several sections, according to age and type of infirmity or chronic illness, and in consequence the isolation of women of working age, septuagenarians, people obliged to rest after long years of work, the paralysed, epileptics, the mentally

deranged, and women stricken with cancer, known as 'incurables'. Each of these divisions will have its own dwelling-space and its separate courtyard; the workshops established for dressmaking, knitting, lacemaking and other crafts for physically fit females; finally, the refectory, for female employees. How many genuine proofs of a general and invariable order henceforth established in a place where once reigned countless abuses and extreme confusion![72]

It must not be forgotten that Bicêtre, where Pinel began his hospital career, then the Salpêtrière, where he carried it further, were the two largest institutions of the Hôpital Général of Paris, with its plurality of functions and diverse clientele. The Duc de Rochefoucault-Liancourt, three years before the arrival of Pinel, described this extraordinary scene of miracles as follows:

> The Bicêtre institution shuts away poor people, who are admitted free, other poor paying for their board (with four different classifi-cations of boarding), men and children who are epileptic, scrofular, paralysed, or insane, and men shut away by royal order, by decree of the Parlement – and these also with or without board; children arrested by order of the police, or convicted for theft or an offence, children without any vice or sickness who are admitted free; finally, men and women being treated for venereal disease. Thus this establishment is at one and the same time: hospice, Hôtel-Dieu, boarding establishment, prison and penitentiary.[73]

Pinel's initiative was not the removal of their chains from the insane, but this ordering of the hospital space. By 'relegation', 'iso-lation', 'removal' to separate buildings, the intermingling categories of those shut away were redeployed according to the various reasons for becoming an assisted person: poverty, old age, loneliness, aban-donment by relatives, and differing forms of illness. These clusters were joined together by the universality of misfortune. Detached from them, the category of madness then stood apart in its speci-ficity. And by virtue of this, it became an illness. From the moment when he was isolated, placed within his own living-space, the insane person doubtless appeared no less sequestrated than the others, but for different causes than theirs. Because of illness. What did this mean? What was mental illness?

It revealed its nature by replicating that same act of isolation. The illness was displayed through regrouping and discrimination between its symptoms, by carving out in the hospital space as many sub-divisions as it presented of broad behavioural syndromes. The 'methodical allocation' of the insane itself introduced a rationality into the illness.[74] The knowledge that went to make up mental health psychiatry could be discerned in the spatial arrangement of the hospital as well as in the pages of a book. A science was constituted as soon as the population of the insane was classified: those persons shut away were indeed sick people, for they presented symptoms that only needed to be observed:

> A hospice for the insane . . . is lacking in one fundamental purpose if, in its internal arrangement, it does not keep the various types of the insane in a kind of isolation, if it cannot seclude the most agitated or violent from those who remain calm, if mutual communication between them is not prevented, either to guard against relapses and render easier the carrying out of all the internal regulations, or to avoid unexpected anomalies in the succession of the complex of symptoms that the doctor has to observe and describe.[75]

But this text-book principle was also the immediate guide to practice. Ordered space calls for regulated behaviour. Knowledge and *praxis*, the recognition of the nature of mental illnesses and their treatment, are two aspects of the same hospital rationality that was achieved by classification. Let the hospital, provided that it is orderly, constitute the very instrument of treatment – this is to be taken absolutely literally. Pinel's text, cited above, continued as follows:

> A methodical allocation of the insane within the hospice to various departments allows one to grasp in a moment the measures to be taken respecting their diet, their cleanliness, their physical and moral routine. The needs of each one are then worked out and foreseen, the various defects in their understanding are perceived, according to their distinctive characteristics, the facts are observed, compared and brought together with other analogous facts, or rather, converted into solid results derived from experience; it is from the same source that the observing doctor can draw the basic rules for treatment, can learn to discern the kinds of madness that yield more or less expeditiously to time and to the regime followed, those that present the greatest obstacles to a cure, or that can be regarded as incurable, and finally those which require urgently the use of certain medicines.[76]

The flawed nature of the hospital did not therefore derive from the segregation of the society that it served, but to the propinquity that was the rule within it. This mixing together in the Hôpital Général of the various species of madness maintained a confusion whose effect was to nullify both the possibility of knowledge (no exact observation, no precise diagnosis), of treatment (no specific grasp of the illnesses because of the lack of differentiation between its kinds), as well as of moral regeneration (the 'demoralization' derived from the contagiousness of disturbing influences, the transmission of vices, like the illnesses, through propinquity). Conversely, it was the same action which, by bringing order from chaos, instituted a system of knowledge (nosographic classifications), an effective practice (moral treatment), and a reduction in the number of focuses of moral epidemics (moralization). There was no need to proceed to a radical critique of the hospital institution. There was even less reason to be sceptical, as were the proponents of home care, about its therapeutic virtues, seeing it as a lesser evil. On the contrary, it was an ideal observation post and a privileged centre for action. Hence the programme of mental health medicine was to make the hospital a docile instrument in the hands of the enlightened doctor, to deploy in it a technology that was not new, but drastically renovated through having at last discovered all those conditions capable of maximizing its effectiveness.

Pinel's Technology

'An administrative reform', Pinel himself declared of his work. But from this everything proceeded:

> I was led as a consequence of this spirit of order to determine the divisions of insanity within their distinct species, founded upon the numerous observations that were the most clearly perceived. This methodical division has also a very valuable advantage in establishing a consistent order within the hospice service and contributing to the curing of the insane.[77]

This reveals a rich ambiguity in the concept of order, of which the whole medicine of mental health was to be merely a lengthy commentary:

> This general organizing of the insane according to the nature of the place selected, the ways in which tastes and inclinations, the states of

calm or excitement coincide, first reveals on what bases rests the general order that reigns in the hospice and the ease with which one can eradicate all the sources of dissension and disturbance.[78]

It suffices to enumerate the principal operations through which this strategy of order proceeds, to realize that it laid the foundation for the whole of asylum practice.

1 *Isolation*

The first requirement of order was *to isolate from the outside world*, to break with that focus of uncontrolled influences upon which the illness may draw to sustain its own disorder. This was the justification for the celebrated 'therapeutic isolation'. It was also an astounding reversal of values.

Up to then the shutting away of the insane had been deemed in philanthropic circles to be an evil, doubtless necessary because of the dangers that the sick incurred, yet one that nevertheless constituted a harmful and extreme measure. Thus Mirabeau, in a violent attack that inveighed against both arbitrary acts of detention and upon the principle of secure institutions, decided to allow an exception to his liberalism: 'As for the insane that are to be found in some prisons, it is only too true that those who have lost the use of reason need to be shut away from society.'[79] The resigned 'need to' of Mirabeau became with Pinel a categorical 'must'. Moreover, Mirabeau continued as follows, denouncing before its time the defects of 'hospitalism': 'Yet I shall observe that most of the insane shut up in secure institutions and State prisons have become as they are, some by bad treatment, others by a horror of the solitude in which at every moment they encounter the manifestations of an imagination made more acute by pain.'[80] With Pinel, the viewpoint was exactly the opposite: shutting away the insane was the prime condition for any therapeutic treatment of madness.

Justifying in this way the necessity to use such isolation as a 'diversion from delirium', psychiatry would provide the scientific rationalization for sequestration required by administration and police (see chapter 5). On this principle the paradigm of internment was to dominate mental health medicine for a century and a half. The routes that lead to de-institutionalization, to home care, to confidence in the therapeutic value of family ties and non-professional relationships, etc., were cut off. Hospitalization became the sole needful response to the questions posed by madness:

> For the patient it is generally so pleasant to be within the bosom of his family, there to receive the care and consolation of a tender and sympathetic affection, that I find it painful to enunciate a sad truth, but one confirmed most repeatedly by experience, that of the absolute necessity of entrusting the insane to the hands of outsiders, and of isolating them from their relatives. The confused tumult of ideas that agitates them, which is caused by everything about them; their irascibility, which is constantly excited by imaginary objects; shouts, threats, scenes of disorder or extravagant actions; the judicious employment of energetic, repressive methods; rigorous supervision of the staff, whose coarseness and incapability are equally to be feared, require a set of measures adapted to the special nature of this illness that can only be effected in institutions devoted to the insane.[81]

2 *The asylum regime*

The second requirement of order was the constitution of the asylum regime, that rigorous combination of places, occupations, timetables, and hierarchies that wove around the daily life of the patient a web of immutable rules. The text above continues as follows:

> From this arise various precepts concerning local arrangements, the distribution of the insane, the internal services, the physical and moral regime, depending upon the character and the types of madness, its various periods of acuteness, decline and convalescence; this assumes thorough knowledge of the course it runs, and the most consummate experience.[82]

From the need to break with the outside world could therefore be deduced the complementary need to construct from nothing a new social laboratory in which the whole of human existence could be programmed. Segregation was thus something other than transplantation from one place to another, or even the impossibility, in an enclosed institution, of communicating with the outside world. It sought to be a change of environment that operated a reversal in values: the 'normal' world was henceforth the place where disorder was reproduced, whilst the great cemetery of the asylum became a site co-extensive with reason, in which the insane lived in the lucidity of the law and made it once more their own. Such a coercive act was indeed necessary so that the inordinate nature of madness might have the possibility of being subjugated through the reinforcement of every kind of constraint. Those who put forward the view that the normal world did not differ essentially from the world of the asylum doubtless did not think they had expressed matters so well: the asylum was no more than the three-dimensional model of society, the moral order reduced to its bare bones of laws, obligations and constraints. In the face of this model, it was the rules of everyday life that seemed pale and lax. Thus one can understand that the asylum could function as the paradigm of an ideal society in the sense of being ideally reduced to order. It was a phalanstery in whose midst no outside upheaval could any longer disturb the harmonious unfolding of the law. Yet all the same it represented a strange paradox, when we know that such a place enclosed that madness which we think of as an excess of subjectivity.

3 *The Power Relationship*

There was a third procedure for the imposition of order, the *relationship of authority* that bound the doctor and his ancillaries to the patient in the exercise of a power that lacked reciprocity and was constantly applied. For plainly madness signifies disorder, and only that. The return to reason can only be effected by the insane person's interiorization of a will to rationality that is at first foreign to him, because he himself is irrational. Hence all forms of treatment are a struggle, a relationship of forces between the poles of reason and unreason. When the alien will enters into him, gradually narrowing the area of agitation and delirium until it subjugates them completely, then the cure occurs:

> Maniacs are especially distinguished by constantly renewed wanderings of the mind, irascibility of the strongest kind, and a state of perplexity and agitation that seems destined to perpetuate itself or not to be quietened save by degrees. A single centre of authority must always be present in their imagination in order that they may learn to repress themselves and overcome their impetuous violence. Once this purpose has been attained, it is only a question of gaining their confidence and earning their esteem in order to restore them entirely to the uses of reason, through the abatement of their illness, and their convalescence.[83]

The doctor was the law of the asylum incarnate and the asylum was the world constructed in the image of rationality that he embodied. The arena of the hospital multiplied his powers and, conversely, the order of things came to life as a moral order of existence backed by the doctor's will. *Moral treatment* was the strategy whereby medical authority relied on all the institutional measures contrived to back him up. It would be naive to be astonished that this relationship often took on the appearance of a struggle. Such violence was legitimate: it was that of reason. The insane person was merely an 'invalid'[84] whose handicap, moreover, frequently fell into a mode of excess, of disproportion. He had to be made pliable, be dominated by means of a therapeutic relationship that took on the appearance of a contest between good and evil.

It is no accident that the burgeoning of psychiatry was encompassed within an institutional form that was a legacy of political absolutism. Its patient–doctor relationship, which represented the first paradigm of the therapeutic relationship in mental health medicine, was one of sovereignty. The insane person could only regain his humanity by an act of allegiance to a sovereign power embodied in a man. Bereft of everything, and above all of his reason, he had no access in his own right to the contractual order. If he could hope to aspire to it, it was by means of a guardianship relationship that had become outdated in the face of the new model thought to preside over all social relationships. In a contractual society, the medical relationship to the insane person was therefore established by reproducing an ancient relationship of allegiance. Not entirely, however. The new form of allegiance did not arise in relationship to the values of feudal society, but to those rational ones of the new contractual society. The power of the doctor was considered to be the result of knowledge and was cancelled out as a principle of domination when the insane person regained his rational autonomy. Hence an especially subtle interplay occurred between doing violence to reason and re-affording access to it, between subjugating and liberating, and this gave a structure to the whole history of the therapeutic relationship.

For the moment, however, this therapeutic relationship remained caught up in the institution where its elaboration began. Yet, just as the relationship between patient and doctor already resembled a sublimation of the relationship of sovereignty, the scene of the confrontation resembled a sublimation of the totalitarian institution. It was no longer the undifferentiated arena of heterogeneity and contagion, but a territory of order equipped with beacons that indicated the stages towards a cure.

The Special Institution: Legacy and Innovation

One could equally well say either that the therapeutic asylum represented a revolution, or that it took its place in the continuous development of disciplinary institutions. In fact, one needs to show how it saved these latter from discredit by a profound renewal of the complex of problems that gave such institutions meaning. It was a first *aggiornamento*, which operated at a threefold level: the 'recruitment' of the sectors of the population concerned; the application of disciplinary techniques; and the pursuit of political ends.

First, the mechanism of recruitment of the sectors of the population for which 'responsibility is assumed' had not changed. It was still a matter of tackling the mass of deviants and marginals, of uprooting them from their environment in order to transplant them into an enclosed arena, so as to maximize the effectiveness of the techniques to which they were to be subjected.

Secondly, these techniques were still of the same type: the teaching of regularity, obedience and work . . . Disciplinary techniques, therefore, which Michel Foucault has shown proliferate within the shadow of sovereign authority, above all within those closed environments that, since the time of the religious convents, functioned as laboratories in which they were tried out before being generalized. In the asylum (as in the prisons) these techniques revealed their systematic coherence.

Thirdly, the aims of these operations likewise remained the same. It was still a question of abolishing or reducing the distance maintained between certain modes of behaviour in relation to predominant norms: to correct the indisciplined, to force the indolent to work, to rehabilitate the sick, and also to break up focuses of disorder and disturbance. Places of detention have always been deemed to play a dual role, which the asylum also assumed: to reintegrate those detained into the course of normal life, if the techniques for inculcating discipline had been successful; at the very least, to neutralize them, and in the final analysis, if necessary, by segregation.

Thus there was a continuity with the policy of assistance of the *Ancien Régime*, at least in so far as it began to be systematized, while an authoritarian, centralized political power was gradually imposed. However, a decisive transformation had been effected. At each of three levels, the synthesis of mental health resolved an uncertain situation which confronted the old totalitarian institution.

I

First, under the former system, the arrest of those disturbing order was a police measure. It became a matter for medical intervention. The openly repressive character of the hunt for illegal acts had posed huge problems for the political authority under the monarchy. The arrest of beggars, vagrants, bad characters and even criminals often sparked off 'emotions', and even popular riots. The confrontation to which these arrests gave rise may indeed be termed political, since violence in the exercise of power was of an arbitrary character and aroused revolt among the victims. It was most certainly not for the good of offenders that the king's guards laid hold of them and cast them into these abhorrent institutions. But it was for the good of the sick persons that the specialist in mental health assumed responsibility for them. Detention almost then came to be seen as a natural measure, and in any case humane, because the necessity for isolation was based upon the nature of the illness.

The medical justification for detention therefore disarmed reactions to the intervention by the public authorities in certain ways of maintaining order. But it also ensured more accurate detection of the section of population concerned. If, under the *Ancien Régime*, detention had been sought as a political measure to control undesirables, its effectiveness had remained questionable. The multiplicity of royal decrees concerning the suppression of begging and vagrancy, often made at some years' interval, speaks volumes in this respect: since these directives had so frequently to be renewed, they must have been little, or badly, applied. Most of the host of deviants and marginals slipped through the over-large mesh of the net spread by different repressive authorities, whose actions were poorly coordinated. To identify medically a part of their number, to set up specialized mechanisms for the task of controlling them, meant first to be given more effective means of counting them, and then of rounding them up.

II

Secondly, the effectiveness of the disciplinary measures applied to those detained in prisons, general hospitals, institutions for beggars, etc., was even more dubious than that of the arrangements governing their arrest. Here the same contrast existed between the regulations of those institutions that spoke of work and obedience to moral and religious precepts, and the testimony and complaints about their functioning in reality, which unanimously denounced the predominance of roguery and vice. The venality and sadism of the warders was matched by the idleness, debauchery, quarrelling, and spirit of revolt among detainees. A prison is, in principle, an instrument of government of unsurpassable effectiveness. In an environment shielded from outside influences, administrators have discretionary powers over their subjects, who have no alternative but to obey. Not only did those in authority command an internal police force that dispensed at their behest sanctions and punishments, but in many institutions they also possessed wide discretion in determining the length of stay, depending upon the behaviour of the inmates.[85]

In reality, however, the administration of these institutions resembled those despotic governments that cause terror and laxity to alternate through an inability to impose a regulated regime of constraints. How can a power be absolute without stooping to arbitrary acts, how can it enforce its decisions, from which there is no appeal, by remaining 'moderate', i.e. effective and rational? Psychiatry proposed an original solution when faced with these contradictions, which had been an obstacle to the policy of detention and had in the end led to failure. It put forward an *instrumentalization of absolute power* that made its exercise effective and rational.

The order of the asylum was indeed the imposition of disciplinary techniques, but medical technology gave them a unity they lacked. The 'Charities'of the Frères de Saint-Jean-de-Dieu, for example, were stated by Fr Dunod to be at one and the same time religious houses, educational seminaries and factories.[86] These were three functions whose unity was both real (the same techniques were indeed imposed) and problematic (to pray, respect the internal rules and work – these related to three obligatory, heterogeneous basic principles). In the asylum the therapeutic justification for all activities was deduced from the same principle. The organization of daily life was treatment, submission to the orders of the staff was treatment, work was treatment. 'Moral treatment' was the deployment of an all-embracing technology held to unify internally the diversity of constraints (of an economic, administrative, or personal order, etc.) imposed upon the detainee. The slightest incident in daily life was subsumed into the overall plan of the institution and elevated to the dignity of a therapeutic adjunct.

This unity was reinforced by the unique character of the directorate under an absolute medical leadership. In the closed institutions of the *Ancien Régime* there existed competing focuses of power: director and administrators (religious or lay people), the accountant, the porter, the chaplain, supervisory staff (religious or lay), the doctor (when he was called in), etc. Pinel postulated the thesis of the supremacy of medical direction in the asylum from the outset. It opened up a long technical debate, to which we shall return, concerning the respective prerogatives of medicine. and the administration in hospital management. Nevertheless, the point had been conceded in principle that 'the doctor, through the nature of his studies, his breadth of knowledge, and the strong concern he had for successful treatment, had to be informed and become the natural judge of everything that occurred in an asylum for the insane.'[87] A miniature Plato's Republic, the asylum realized a synthesis of knowledge and power in the person of that modern figure of the philosopher-king, the doctor-in-charge.

III

Thirdly, it was in the asylum that the dual strategem of the totalitarian institution – of both neutralizing and re-educating – found its best justification. If, as Michel Foucault has shown, the control exercised over deviants can be implemented according to two opposing models – exclusion, and for disciplinary purposes, division[88] – neither strategy precludes the other. Everything occurred as if, from the leprosery to the asylum, through the Hôpital Général and the beggary, a mixed form was progressively being installed, in which segregation would represent the first stage to be abolished, thanks to the application, in an enclosed environment, of a programme of resocialization. Only the leprosery appears to have been an environment of total exclusion, if it be true that it was content to mark out a social no man's land in which rejected souls were merely dumped. Yet even before the leprosery had been instituted, the convent had realized another kind of enclosed space, one that was filled to saturation with rules and forms of discipline, in which isolation from the outside world was only a means of maximizing within it the effectiveness of disciplinary rules.

The ideal type of the convent illustrates the profound affinity existing between isolation, discipline and the transformation of the personality. It also reveals the set of conditions that realization of the totalitarian Utopia would demand: the harmonizing of a code that selects recruits (here the religious code of the vocation), of a rigorous institution technology (the Rule of St Benedict, for example), and the official goals of the institution ('to do away with the old man' so as to programme in a new man). In principle the postulant accepts –and even desires – the process of transformation of his personality that the organization of life in an enclosed institution aims to promote.[89]

The same does not hold good for the vagrant, the delinquent, the libertine, or even the merely indigent. *A priori* they have no reason to wish to be 'moralized'. In other words, there exists, arising from the interplay between the social and/or moral code that selects them, a programme of resocialization that cannot be made to measure. This is because of the heterogeneous nature of the elements of population it is supposed to treat, and the institutional goal of re-adaptation that is imposed upon them from the outside. Hence the almost inevitable failure of the totalitarian institution, in so far as the person detained was obliged to break with his culture and repudiate his group and class affinities, for the sake of a plan for his own regeneration in which he had had no part, because it merely expressed what his masters had decreed. Attendance within enclosed institutions gives rise to a trial of strength between governors and governed, the outcome of which is not decided in advance. There is a strength of the weak that is expressed in dissimulation and conspiracy, which twists and turns the rules of the institution, and which can block its functioning all the more effectively because those who in principle have at their disposal all kinds of powers lack a specific technology to instrumentalize them.[90]

In the asylum, the coincidence of the patient's interest with the official goal of the institution still remained to some extent fictitious. Yet it was more credible and, above all, there was the attempt to achieve it through a more elaborate technical apparatus. It was more credible also, because it supposed coincidence between the cure of the patient and the therapeutic nature of the institution. But the monopoly of power by the official representatives of the institution (the doctors) was here justified by reasons *intrinsic* to medical ideology: the 'misfortune' of the insane person being to have lost his reason, what was imposed upon him was not really done from the outside, but in the name of what he would do himself were he reasonable. Within the institutional framework of the asylum, and in a synthesis that was at least ideologically coherent, were harmonized the medical code, the technology of moral treatment, the status of the person detained – a non-adult whose condition required that an extraneous will should assume responsibility for him – and finally the position of absolute power occupied by the person officially responsible in the institution, the doctor who embodied that medical will.

There was only one objection: all patients did not get better – far from it. Yet, after all, God alone knows whether in the convents monks and nuns did not more often find the way to damnation rather than salvation. Nevertheless the fact remains that the convent was an admirable power machine, the most systematic institutional device for doing away with the personality and for reconstructing, on the basis of this extinction, a completely new definition of man –in short, the most technically developed of the laboratories experimenting on man. The effectiveness of institutions of detention lags far behind. At the end of the eighteenth century it had become clear that this version, cultivated in a vacuum, of a concerted, systematic counter-organization for human existence had failed to provide an overall solution to the problems of deviance. The asylum took up the question again *ab initio*. It started from a more carefully formulated definition of its population, a more rigorous ordering of its techniques and a more scientific justification of its aims.

This first metamorphosis was the birth certificate of mental health medicine. All mental health specialists waxed indignant at the scandal of shutting up the unfortunate patients in prisons. All emphasized the huge progress in philanthropy that the invention of the asylum represented. There is no reason to suspect their sincerity. Even more would it be an error to claim that they were entirely mistaken. They did operate a metamorphosis. They invented a 'different scenario', i.e. a very different arena of operation, but one which was also the same. However, absorbed in their practices, they did not recognize what remained of the old skeleton beneath the new construction. Doubtless they were unable to do so. May we, instead of condemning them, learn the lesson, from a perspective there is no great merit in assuming, since all this – at least let us hope so – is in the process of dying. But the phoenix can be reborn from its ashes. Is there not a mode of discourse concerning the liberation of the word that might be just as liberating and mystifying as that regarding the freeing of the alienated from their chains?

3

The First Social Medicine

From the bastion of the asylum, initially conquered by Pinel, there emerged in the first three decades of the nineteenth century a nebulous complex. Links were forged between practices apparently different in kind, both inside and outside the hospital, using reputedly new knowledge as reference point. Such practices defended the corporatist interests of a professional group, and claimed to prevail through purely technical competence, whereas they received legal sanction, etc. Yet all practices had one point in common: they were categorized as medical and prevailed because of the recognition of that medical label. Hence the preliminary question – before following, in the next chapter, their diffusion: specifically, how did such a medical linkage constitute this new field of phenomena? And, more precisely, what was the medical reference in question? What was the medicine, and of what kind were the doctors who were successful in processes that had apparently more in common with a problem of public order than with that patient exploration of the body through which, at the same period, clinical practice set modern medicine on new foundations?

'Special medicine', 'special doctors': it was as such that the actors dubbed themselves. What did they mean? In fact, this was a *social* medicine, of which mental health medicine sketched in the first outlines. In it a medical code that was already outdated and an ancient political dream found in their alliance a new youthfulness. The success historically of the medicine of insanity was due to the fact that it was able to tie together – or rather, not to unloose – a medical strand, the guarantee of scientific respectability, and a social strand, that of the philanthropists and reformers of the post-Revolutionary period, in the search for new techniques of public assistance.

Birth of a Specialism

Pinel represents a turning-point. In his person was realized the creative break-away of the first medical specialism. He was a 'general practitioner' – if the term can be employed before the appearance of 'specialisms' – who first gave us, in his *Nosographie philosophique*, the grand *summa* of medical knowledge in the eighteenth century. In middle life he was appointed, for reasons that relate above all to the political situation, to the Bicêtre and then the Salpêtrière hospitals, and began to devote the essential part of his theoretical and practical activity to the insane. Yet his principal renown is still that of being a great 'encyclopaedic' doctor. Moreover, after the creation of the School of Health of Paris, by the Convention's decree of 14 Frimaire, Year III, he held the chair of adjunct professor of physical medicine and hygiene, then that of professor of medical pathology (internal pathology), which he kept until his dismissal in 1822.[1]

Esquirol was the first 'specialist' in the sense that from him onwards there opened up a career that could be devoted entirely to mental health. He joined Pinel at the Salpêtrière from Year VIII onwards. In the following years he assembled round him all those who went on to become great names in the movement of mental health medicine: Falret, Pariset, Ferrus, Georget, Voisin, Leuret, and a little later, Trélat, Calmeil, Foville, Lassègue, Chambeyron, Evrat, etc.[2] This division from the common core of medicine was innovatory at the very time when the reorganization of the medical profession was tending rather towards reinforcing its unity. Thus it was that the basic reform of Fourcroy of Year XI, supplementing that of Year III, put an end to the separation that had occurred, at their very origins, of medicine and surgery, by imposing a common training on both disciplines.[3]

The group of mental health specialists effected in medicine an original division whose specificity was to be sustained right up to the reform of the statute for head doctors in psychiatric hospitals in 1968. The group achieved a unified homogeneous training, detached from the teaching in the medical faculties, and also the status of civil servant attached to a hospital institution. This situation was as different from the private practice of medicine as was the hospital career afforded by the Faculties. It was the crucible in which were forged the cadres of medical specialists in mental health (who became the medical heads of psychiatric hospitals in 1937) which have, right up to the present day, exerted the predominant influence in mental health medicine in France. Its distinctive characteristics – a training given outside the universities; the homogeneity and specificity of its recruitment; the weight of traditions linked to the conditions for practice within the closed environment of the asylum; and before long, a statute for a long while unique in the field of medicine, creating full-time civil servants appointed directly by the central authority – all these have their origin in this environment of the Salpêtrière. From it would go out the *missi dominici* of a new public service: 'From the promulgation of the law of 1838 onwards, young doctors, chosen mainly from among the pupils of the eminent teachers who taught the medicine of mental health in the hospices of Paris, were sent out to the departments to organize this new service. These missionaries had to create everything for themselves.'[4]

In fact the movement had begun long before 1838. By that date all the services in Paris were directed by protagonists of the School. Esquirol, who had the guiding hand in appointments, had already placed his pupils in Rouen, Nantes, Toulouse, Auxerre, Rennes, etc.

By 1830 an adversary, the lawyer Elias Regnault, inveighing against the claims by mental health specialists in the field of medico-legal expertise (see chapter 4), bore witness to this precocious autonomization of the specialism. The 'special doctors', on the basis of their common training in the asylums, were already presenting themselves as a body united against their colleagues:

> Some doctors, because they have been attached to a hospice for the insane, either as interns, or at a higher grade, discount entirely the voices of all others, and, entrenched in their own specialism, dispute the right of their colleagues from outside to know and to pronounce judgement . . . Thus on the one hand, are ranged the hospital doctors, with their special knowledge, taxing the rest with ignorance; on the other side stand the bulk of doctors who inveigh against these *privileged analysts of the human intellect*, maintaining that, if their own knowledge is uncertain, this uncertainty is general.[5]

Everything therefore began 'at the time, already distant, when the Salpêtrière School flourished'. Lasègue, 30 years later, evoked its warm atmosphere:

The lectures only took secondary place, but, besides the audience in the amphitheatre, there existed a more restricted coterie of the assiduous pupils. The service was open to all, without formality or imposed doctrines, each studying according to the inclination of his abilities, and reporting his personal observations, which were debated, discussed and disputed among ourselves, with the indulgent participation of our teacher. Thus we lived within an amicable activity of the mind, the memory of which not one of us has forgotten.[6]

There was a feeling of sailing with the wind, of opening up a boundless field of research, and at the same time of seeing its innovations generally welcomed favourably because they matched expectations so pressing that the quality of the response to them was not scrutinized too closely:

It was the time when mental health medicine basked in the favour granted to all medical innovation. There was little study of it, but it was not disputed, and the decisions handed down by the mental specialists were greeted with the deference granted to scientific statements that are of too recent a date to have undergone the test of contradiction.[7]

Hence beneath the enthusiasm a graver note emerged. Not only was this success a fragile one, but there might indeed be a contradiction in what was deemed to underpin it.

Esquirol had introduced into pathology a method to which his pupils remained devoutly attached. Whereas, with Broussais, physiology affirmed its preponderance in medicine, it was natural that psychology, that physiology of the intelligence, should claim the same rights. The normal state of the faculties of the mind had just been the subject of skilful, enthusiastic, almost passionate research. There was haste to utilize, to the benefit of pathology, discoveries as yet unexploited. Dr Falret had a maturely thought-out faith, both convincing and convinced, in the future of psychological medicine, and, like his contemporaries, he broke away, half wittingly, half unwittingly, from what the Germans have since termed 'somatic medicine'. This was the disappointing direction that was taken by a life that had been so amply filled.[8]

There is a paradox: side by side with the spectacular growth of the first medical specialism a gulf grew ever wider from what should have served as its basis, the parallel development of medicine in general. The 'too recent scientific statements' of mental health medicine were in fact founded upon a very old medical reference. This is a postulate that is worth lingering over. Either such a fixation was a mistake, and one would have to explain why this archaic phenomenon paid off in mental health medicine at the very time when modern medicine was laying its foundations in the same Parisian environment. Or indeed it was only by means of a very special medical model – and, unfortunately for the 'science', one that was already outdated – that mental health medicine could carry out its mandate, because that mandate was not essentially medical.

The 'selection' of this theoretical corpus of knowledge appeared to be determined less by its medically scientific nature than by its relevance in categorizing a social problem. Today certain people would say that the knowledge applied in this initial psychiatry was exhausted through its ideological orientation. Indeed, there was no 'epistemological break' here between the references to knowledge and the social demand that they primarily expressed. But such a disqualification would not make much sense. Positively, the strength of the synthesis accomplished by mental health medicine sprang, on the contrary, from its ability to instrumentalize the practical concerns of the hygienists and philanthropists. Hence the first question: in what way and why, was the body of mental health knowledge capable of providing an operational formula for the policy of these social reformers? The reply has been given in outline in the previous chapter, which showed how the rescue of a part of the totalitarian institution could be included in a strategy for the control of deviance. But it was the mental health system as a whole that reformulated 'scientifically' the demands of the new policy of assistance emerging at the same time.

A Very Special Knowledge

It was Pinel who produced the first overall formulation of the theoretical corpus of knowledge in the science of mental illness, just as he was the first to characterize the whole of his hospital practices. Yet, even more than Pinel's technique, his theoretical work must be read as a continuous part of eighteenth-century medicine. His *Nosographie philosophique* was the last of the great classificatory systems founded upon the methodical collection of the *external signs* of illness:

> A methodical and regular arrangement supposes in its purpose a permanent order subject to certain general laws. But do not illnesses that were wrongly regarded as diversions or deviations from nature possess this characteristic of stability, since their histories, as gathered together by ancient and modern writers, are so uniform, when the course of nature is in no way disturbed? Does not attentive observation, constantly repeated, allow them to be envisaged as temporary changes, lasting to a greater or lesser extent, in the vital functions, made manifest by external signs that are of a consistent uniformity in their main characteristics, but with countless variations in their ancillary ones? These external signs, . . . in their various combinations, provide isolated pictures, more or less distinct and very pronounced, depending on whether one's eye is more or less practised, or on whether profound or superficial observations have been made.[9]

The constitution of a science of mental illness was purely and simply a replication of that classificatory method of general medicine in the eighteenth century, itself inherited from the natural sciences:

> Why then should one not transfer to this part of medicine, as to its other parts, the method used in all branches of natural history? Are not the distinctive characteristics of mental illness, apart from some ancillary variations, the same in all the exact observations gathered at various times? And should not one therefore conclude from this that all the other facts that one is able to gather will fit naturally into the divisions that have been adopted? Moreover, this is what is confirmed daily by the insane of both sexes admitted to the hospices.[10]

Such indeed is the application of the general methodological principle on which Pinel summed up his work, and which included it in the medicine of species: 'For a given illness, determine its true character and the position that it should occupy within a nosological table.'[11] The scientific attitude is merely one of observing the natural course of morbid disturbances, having ensured that they have not been provoked by an outside interference. As in the case of fevers and bodily diseases, we shall also see mental illnesses that pattern into stable configurations based upon a mere description of their symptoms. The innovation that Pinel flattered himself at having introduced, as compared with his predecessors in the field of mental illness, consisted precisely of the following: to observe minutely the *signs* of the illness in the order of their appearance, in their spontaneous development and in their natural termination. This is why his method, according to him, is 'philosophical' in the sense of Locke and Condillac: the opposite of 'metaphysical', it rejected risky speculations about the obscure causes of phenomena. Pinel ranged himself within the philosophical tradition of the English school adopted in France by Condillac and the Ideologues, and specially applied to medicine by Cabanis: man is malleable through experience, since all his knowledge comes to him from outside himself; all ideas, all knowledge are a composite of the sensations and can be reduced through analysis to their simple components.[12] It is a metaphysical obscurantism to aim to go beyond the phenomena. Science is content to discover their rational arrangement by holding to what is manifested in experience. It distinguishes the essential from the ancillary, the unvarying from the accidental phenomenon, but bases itself upon what is apparent to attentive observation.

The practical consequence of this orientation in mental health medicine is to direct attention to the signs or *symptoms* of madness, at the expense of the search for its *seat* within the organism. The rationality that is gained in this way is merely classificatory. It consists in grouping in their natural order the manifestations of the illness that are apparent. Thus it is a purely phenomenological rationality, which is exhausted after the constitution of nosographies. This is paradoxical at a time when, by the 'opening up of corpses', a new model of scientific thinking began to prevail. The exploration of the organic substratum, which would become the 'scientific' attitude in medicine, was still assimilated by Pinel to the 'metaphysical' obscurantism of vague speculation concerning the hidden causes of phenomena:

> It would be a bad option to choose to take insanity as a special subject for one's research and then give oneself over to vague discussions about the seat of the understanding and the nature of its various lesions; for there is nothing that is more obscure and more impenetrable. Yet if one restricts oneself wisely, *if one keeps to the study of its distinctive characteristics as manifested by external signs*, and if one adopts as principles for treatment only the results of enlightened experience, one then falls into the line generally followed in all areas

of natural history; and, proceeding with caution in dubious cases, there is no longer any need to fear going astray.[13]

On this decisive point, Pinel was essentially followed by the Salpêtrière group, which thus ranged itself against the tide of contemporary developments in medical knowledge. Indeed this kind of descriptive phenomenology had nothing in common with that clinical gaze whose birth Michel Foucault has placed exactly at the same moment and in the same Parisian environment, a gaze that penetrated beyond the signs, broke up the superficial arrangement, and sought in tissues or organs the principle of an underlying intelligibility of illness.[14]

The rupture was too great not to be perceived by contemporaries. The polemics that opposed Pinel and Broussais, the prophet of 'physiology',[15] are well known. In more measured terms Bichat clearly expressed the incompatibility of the principles of the mental health school with those of 'scientific' medicine.

> Only a few years ago all those who were heads of hospices for the insane . . . held mental disorders to be ailments of the soul and mind in which the body had not the slightest part; their immediate seat was placed either in the chest or in the bowels of the lower stomach. Not only did this general belief distract attention from the real seat of these illnesses, but it also deprived asylum doctors of one of the most precious and fruitful means of discovering the relationship between changes in the basic faculties to change in the brain . . . I rejoice . . . at having effected the most felicitous revolution, not only for the study of mental illnesses but also for their treatment.[16]

Yet Bichat deluded himself on one point: he had not realized that 'felicitous revolution'. Bichat's influence was directed to the investigation of the organic infrastructure of mental illness, as was that of his contemporaries – for example, Bayle, the discoverer of general paralysis, or Rostan, the first theorist of organicism, and yet a friend of Pinel, although not a mental specialist. But his influence only prevailed later, precisely when the Pinel school had exhausted its credibility.

The contradiction was so real that it even appeared in the works of most of his disciples. At the beginning of his career Falret planned a treatise entitled, *Instructions à tirer des ouvertures de corps des aliénés pour le diagnostic, le pronostic et le traitement des maladies mentales.* He never wrote it, and increasingly repudiated its organicist temptations as he progressed along the path of mental health medicine, in the end formulating the doctrine of 'therapeutic eclecticism' to which we shall have to return.

The most typical case is that of Georget. He was undoubtedly the most perceptive mind of the School and the most medically oriented towards the new criteria. He saw clearly the dead end to which nosographic research led with regard to the exploration of brain lesions. By 1820 he therefore came out plainly against Pinel and Esquirol, postulating the need to grant priority to the search for the *seat* of the madness. He was the first to place delirium as a mere symptom of mental derangement that must not be confused with the 'nature' of the illness. He went one better: he would have liked to make the *treatment* of madness depend upon the building up of knowledge about the organism: 'Less imprecise knowledge about the seat of madness, about the nature, development, progress and termination of its various phenomena, assimilated to all the other pathological phenomena, puts us in a position to improve immensely the treatment of insanity and to base it entirely upon principles completely compatible with reason.'[17] Georget thus mapped out a new therapeutic programme that entailed a severe judgement of moral treatment:

> The empirical medicine of symptoms loses its credibility: *one knows that it is in no way the ramifications but the source of the illness that must be reached;* that one should in no way prescribe remedies without knowing how they act and without foreseeing the effect that they may have both on the diseased organ and also upon the rest of the body. . . . As for the empirical part, the so-called moral one, it is based upon opposing principles: to administer it has hardly any connexion with the assumed state of the brain; intellectual disturbances alone provide almost all the elements in it.[18]

Georget thus appears as the defender of a more scientific kind of medicine that would probe beyond the manifestation of symptoms and go beyond quelling the forms of delirium in order to return to organic causes. To this objective knowledge would correspond a differential treatment of mental illnesses that would give a large share to the administering 'of medical means that are both internal and external'.

Yet suddenly there was a reversal of the tenor of the argument: the treatments, 'always necessary, which we call direct, empirical or moral, produce almost invariable effects and are of much more proven utility than the others. By themselves they can cure many forms of insanity.'[19] These moral means, above all isolation and a medical pedagogy, are 'direct' because they act directly upon the delirium, namely, upon the symptom. Yet, at the expense of an astounding lack of consequentiality in a mind as subtle as Georget's, their superiority lies in the fact that they act also directly upon the *causes* of madness. For the main causes of madness are moral, whether it is a matter of 'diathetic causes' ('it is above all certain tendencies of the moral and intellectual condition that must be looked upon as apt to favour the development of madness') or as 'effectively direct or cerebral causes' ('out of 100 insane, 95 at least have become so through morbid states or moral disturbances'[20]). The principle of organicism is here denied to make room for psychogenesis.

Another example of the impossibility of including the movement of mental health medicine in the linear development of 'scientific' medicine was the discovery of general paralysis. As early as 1822 Bayle identified a succession of stages, marked by specific syndromes, that make general paralysis a special form of mental illness that takes its own course, and is not, as was commonly believed at the time, the final phase of degradation in dementia. This discovery appeared, after the event, to be an example favouring the organicist viewpoint, since it seemed to impose a necessary relationship between the presence of an organic agency ('treponema pallidum', the syphilis germ) and a precise set of psychic symptoms. Yet, if one looks more closely, things were far from clear at the beginning. Bayle was certainly conscious of the divergence of his method from that of most specialists in mental health: 'These learned authors [Pinel and Esquirol] have generally contented themselves with observing the phenomena without seeking to trace them to their source, with scrupulously describing the facts without seeking to link them to any generating cause.'[21] Yet he himself wavered between a physical and a moral aetiology (psychological and social) of general paralysis. For example, confirming that the ex-soldiers of the Napoleonic armies were more frequently prone to it, he linked this fact to the traumatic conditions of military life and, among other things, to the disappointment brought about by the fall of the

Empire. The role of syphilis was debated as one of the possible causes.[22] Likewise Esquirol, observing the large proportion of former prostitutes affected by general paralysis, attributed this as originating in their excesses and not in any syphilitic infection. Doubtless definitive proof of the organic origin of general paralysis would only be demonstrated very much later, when changes in the brain brought on by the pathogenic agent have been observed under the microscope.[23] But from the first half of the nineteenth century onwards, in those same circles of the Paris School, knowledge of the clinical forms of syphilis was perfectly up to date. In fact the 'scientific' question of the aetiology of general paralysis was considered in (and in our view obscured by) the great discussion at the time concerning the role of the development of *civilization* in the growth of mental disturbances. Lunier[24] and Baillarger[25] emphasized this connection, which led them to lay stress upon the social conditions relating to the appearance of general paralysis. Matters were so unclear that when in 1853 he summarized the position, J. Falret showed that the particularly 'organicist' line of thinking only represented one of the four predominant interpretations of the nature of the illness.[26]

Such hesitations were shared by all the mental health school, doubtless with the exception of Leuret, who produced from the outset a totally psychogenetic conception of insanity: 'Madness consists in an aberration of the faculties of the understanding; unlike ordinary illnesses, it is not characterized by physical symptoms, and the causes that bring it on, sometimes perceptible to the senses, most frequently belong to a range of phenomena completely foreign to the general laws of matter: these are, the passions and ideas.'[27] The complete divergence of mental health medicine from the mainstream of medicine was the logical consequence of this position. Other specialists in mental health did not wish to pay such a price. At the Salpêtrière, as in the new asylums that were built on its model, 'corpses are opened up', and signs of organic deficiency were sought in the shape of the brain, or even in an inherited malformation. Yet everything occurred as if, once this homage to the modern model of medical science had been paid, attention was turned to truly serious questions of a practical nature, to which anatomy did not provide an answer.

Reading the textbooks of the School, one can perceive that it wavered between two models of mental illness: an organicist schema that assumed there was a localized lesion accounting for the origin of the illness; and a moral and social nosography of the symptoms of the disorder that related to a psycho-pathology of the passions and to a pathogenic social background. Certain writings, among them the most 'theoretical', affirmed the supremacy of the first model. But always, in the last analysis, the mental health medicine school inclined towards the second.[28] As late as 1874 the report of the General Inspectors of Asylums still defended the great practical synthesis of mental health[29] according to the categories laid down by Pinel and Esquirol.

Such a consensus, maintained almost in the teeth of the countervailing force of medical evolution generally, must have related to some strong reason. It was because the stress placed almost exclusively upon symptomatology was the most appropriate for constructing a *reactive and psychogenic* conception of mental illness. This provided justification for the technique of moral treatment: 'The most prominent characteristic of madness being physical and moral disorder, since it is in this way that it manifests itself, the most uniform therapeutic tendency must be the re-establishment of order in the exercise of functions and faculties.'[30]

Thus subordination of a 'theoretical' conception of insanity to the practical demands of treatment is already made explicit in Pinel:

One of the most fatal prejudices for humanity, one which is perhaps the deplorable cause of the state of abandonment in which almost all the insane are left, is to look upon their sickness as incurable, and to relate it to an organic lesion within the brain or in some other part of the head. I can assure you that, in most of the facts that I have gathered concerning delirious mania that has become incurable or has ended in another fatal illness, all the results discovered by opening up the body, compared to the symptoms that have been manifested, demonstrate that this form of insanity has generally a purely nervous character, and that it is not the outcome of any organic defect in the substance of the brain, as I shall show in the fifth section.[31]

An apparently 'progressive' implication is that by becoming organicist, psychiatry at the end of the nineteenth century would more easily resign itself to the condition of incurability and abandon to their fate as beyond the pale those patients that the first school of mental health medicine attempted to treat. Yet we must also assess the cost of this therapeutic humanism. The School of the Salpêtrière constituted as 'true' knowledge what justified most immediately its practices, to the detriment of clinical research more open to the future, but whose implications within the framework of the asylum were not clear. For the arena of the asylum, dominated by the exigencies of moral treatment, is not the experimental field of the clinic, even if both are encompassed within the same environment, that of the hospital. Thus from the beginning there appeared a certain disjunction between asylum psychiatry and hospital medicine. This constituted the basic explanatory principle for an understanding of the evolution of mental health medicine. The conflict would flare up on several occasions between proponents of the asylum, intent on defending and improving the conditions in which to practise their 'special medicine', and the technological and modernist trend, relying upon the medical model, that had been built up in the ordinary hospitals and the clinics of the medical faculties, which have since become the CHUs (Cliniques Hospitalières Universitaires). We shall see that the decisive changes in the history of psychiatry (the creation of free services, the organization of mental hygiene, the separation of psychiatry from neurology, and even the present-day vicissitudes of the application of the concept of the 'sector') signify so many episodes in this conflict. The institutional struggles that lie in the future, the conflicts of authority between proponents of the asylum and those attached to the universities, will always present two opposing and incompatible medical patterns.

However, we must guard against seeing these as mere episodes in the conflict between ancients and moderns. The treatment of insanity represents something utterly different from a merely outmoded stage in the history of medicine. What will later 'resist' the impatient planning of technocatic administrators and technological doctors is an anthropology and a policy whose designation as progressive or backward is complex. Thus we shall see in the immediate aftermath of the Second World War a Marxist tendency that extols the return to a 'neo-Esquirolism',[32] as opposed to another model of social medicine whose search to establish norms relies on a modernist conception of medicine. There may be 'progressivism' in the belief – the legacy of the philosophy of the Enlightenment – that madness is no pre-ordained destiny, that man is the product of his works, his living environment, that he may be overwhelmed by his very conquests, broken by the changes and chances of history and restored once more by a rational, educative programme dispensed in a framework specially contrived to maximize the effects of medical intervention. There is also some 'conservatism' in encapsulating this programme for the transformation of man within the established order, borrowing from it at the same time both its derogatory conception of madness and its techniques for imposing discipline, in order to reduce it. Yet, independent of such value judgements, it is important to demonstrate how the elements of this power are articulated.

A Well-packaged System

1 *Symptomatology*

The first element of the system is symptomatology. The theoretical corpus of the medicine of mental health – the nosographic classifications – is merely the ordering of the signs that distinguish pathological behaviour from socially regulated modes of conduct. It is a purely negative perception of one aspect of order: the insane person is the one 'who has habitually no regard for any rule, law, or usage, or rather who fails to recognize them all; whose speech, bearing and actions are constantly at odds not only with the customs of the country in which he lives, but even with what is human and reasonable within himself'.[33] 'He is egotistical, lacking sociability; he is drawn outside the real world by his ideas and sickly feelings, and exerts only a weak control over his own ideas; having no self-control, he reacts only feebly against his sickly tendencies and dispositions, to which he allows free and unbridled rein, and which grow the more they are indulged.'[34]

Nosographies are content with coining a certain number of sub-species in this global perception, which is universally derogatory. Madness, that excess which is a deficiency: agitation, exaggeration, inordinate outbursts of rage, want of control, impulsiveness, unpredictability, dangerous behaviour – such characteristics signpost so many points of distance from, and contrast with, the enjoyment of a life that has assimilated all the disciplinary norms and made them second nature. Thus nosographic labelling only serves to formalize the immediate facts regarding the social consciousness of insanity.

2 *Social disorder*

A second element in the system, the area where mental illness breaks out most, is social disorder. Hence the countless texts of the mental health school concerning the relationship between insanity and civilization. This theme was treated from many different facets, whether these dealt with great political upheavals, the acceleration of progress, the degradation in morals, the abandonment of ancient beliefs, fluctuations in commerce and industry, or the misery and immorality of the lower classes.

> The movement of ideas and political institutions has rendered once immovable and stable occupations subject to change. Besides great benefits there have also resulted the excesses of boundless competition and indifference to what was good in theory and practice about the ancient institutions. Lacking any regulatory force, the present generation, which is in a veritable period of transition and organization, has launched itself upon the new course it has carved out and has encountered new causes of misfortune and destruction. Many minds, over-stimulated by a headlong and unlimited ambition, having worn themselves out, perverted in a struggle beyond their strength and ending up in madness, have found the cause of this mischance in indifference to virtue or insufficient education. Others, forced to grapple with need, deprived of the protective support of the ancient corporations, have felt themselves to be too feeble to resist, and discouragement and misery have led them to stray from the light of reason.[35]

It is social anomie that feeds a constant state of agitation and opens the way to the disorders of madness. A deep structural equivalence exists between manifestations of madness (its symptoms) and that sphere which is shaken by political events and social conflicts. Upon this general foundation are grafted countless analyses of the part played by a bad education, the relaxation of morals, the waywardness of women, misery, etc. in the genesis of psychological disturbances. 'Madness is the product of society and of moral and intellectual influences.'[36] Hence the great exploitation of the theme of madness and civilization, on which practically all specialists in mental health could be cited endlessly. Even in 1874 the Report on the mental health service harped at length on this refrain, which had been revived by the events of the Commune.[37]

Mental health medicine was indeed the first form of 'social psychiatry'. It is false to claim – save perhaps at the moment when organicism was triumphed – that mental health medicine reached a dead end concerning the historical and social conditions that are at work in the genesis of mental illness. On the contrary, these remained the object of its constant attention. Yet it interpreted them within the framework of a 'psychologicalizing' aetiology that concealed their objective dimensions. This is the ambiguity of all 'social medicine', to which we will return.

3 *The preponderance of moral causes*

A third element in the system is the preponderance of moral causes, which formed the link between the individual or anthropological level (symptomatology) and the social field (anomie) of a phenomenology of the disorder. Madness is most frequently a reaction to a situation of social disequilibrium, through the mediation of an aetiology of the feelings. The category 'moral causes' groups together all the traumatic happenings of existence. These traumas act upon the sensibility, which they weaken, sparking off the intellectual manifestations of delirium: 'Madness is most often brought on by the development of the passions, by strong moral emotions, by chagrin, etc. The struggles of conscience and remorse very often provoke it, particularly among women. Then come excesses of every kind, debauchery, misery, and the privations that they bring in their train.'[38]

On this point proof is particularly hazardous, and it would be a gamble to try to follow its elaboration. Instead of proofs we have outlandish statistics that are often contradictory, the playing down of facts that are nevertheless acknowledged, such as those relating to heredity, and an obscure casuistry concerning the relationships between the various types of causes (predisposing, secondary, or directly or indirectly effective, etc.). Nonetheless it is true that the mental health school stubbornly maintained against all the odds Falret's adage: 'It is an established fact that madness is more often engendered by moral than physical causes.'[39] It is difficult to see how such an assertion could assist the inclusion of mental health medicine in the physiological medicine of the time. On the contrary, it prevented it from assimilating the research being carried out on heredity or through autopsies. Yet without this theme of the paramountcy of moral causes the link would collapse that was believed to connect the syptoms of mental illness to the social sphere, which was held to be responsible for its manifestation. Above all, its psychogenesis afforded the surest practical power over madness: the moral causality of the sickness was eradicable through moral means of treatment.

4 Moral treatment

Thus the fourth element in the system is moral treatment. Just as the thesis of the preponderance of moral causes did not succeed in entirely covering the whole aetiological field, so moral treatment has never excluded the use of a whole range of physical means, from medicines to hydrotherapy. Yet if psychiatrists today can claim that what counts in the administration of a medicine is the relationship it allows to grow with the therapeutist, it is even easier to reinterpret in 'moral' terms the effectiveness of the 'physical' means of the times, such as shower baths. Falret termed this attitude 'therapeutic eclecticism',[40] which prides itself on using any and every means against the illness. The discourse of moral treatment benefited from such esteem, when it should at least have been toned down by the modest nature of the therapeutic successes achieved and by the knowledge that a host of other remedies were being used. This was because it had a direct connection with the moral perception of madness: the use of moral means was immediately mobilized to eliminate the moral disorder: 'The more the insane person is antipathetic to any regularity, the more it is necessary that a methodical orderliness hems him in on all sides and moulds him for a normal pattern of existence that sooner or later will become imperative for him.'[41]

This is why, with the most coherent theorists of moral treatment such as Leuret,[42] even the most physical remedies could never act save through being given a moral reinterpretation. Upon this conviction Leuret developed the first overall theory of psychotherapy. He stretched the attitude to the limit of coherence by deploying subtle tactics of disciplining strictly adapted to each individual case. His cures represented, before their time, veritable directive therapies. But most often the moral treatment was administered in a collective, impersonal way. A large body of patients was caught up anonymously within a network of general regulations. There was indeed an urgent necessity to deal with them, and this did only limited harm.[43] After all, madness is not original. The excessive sub-jectivity manifested is not worth exploring for its own sake. It comes down to a few types of transgression, of a monotonous nature, and always perceived negatively against a background of order. If the character of the delirium is less important than what it reveals to be lacking, the continued effects of general forms of discipline, fixed timetables, timed tasks, and regulated leisure can substitute without too much ill-effect for face-to-face therapy. Thus it is unsurprising that, in the whole of this psychiatric literature, there is very little question of madness 'in itself'. There is no concern to explore for its own sake its sickly subjective state, no questioning of the legitimacy of the monopoly that reason exercises over madness, nor the slightest scruple in imposing a unilateral power relationship upon the patient. Only the mechanism counts, for only the mechanism – and the doctor is solely the key factor in such a machine – has value as a rational, objective structure in doing away with a disorderliness that is merely a deficiency of existence:

> Order and regularity in all the actions of life, both in common and in private, the instant and unceasing repression of faults of every kind and of disorder in all its forms, the subjection to silence and rest at certain prescribed times, the imposition of work on all those individuals that are capable of doing it, meals taken in common, leisure breaks at a fixed time and of limited duration, the banning of those games that stir the emotions and encourage laziness, and above all the actions of the doctor in imposing submission, affection and respect through his unceasing intervention in everything that impinges upon the moral life of the insane: such are the means of treatment for madness, which give to treatment applied in these insti-tutions an indisputable superiority over that applied in the home.'[44]

5 *The asylum*

The fifth element in the system is, of course, the *asylum*. The asylum is existentially the locus for the exercise of psychiatry, because it is the most suitable substitute for the natural environment (namely, that of family and society). It is pathogenic because of its anomie, but a specially constructed environment which is therapeutic because it is systematically controlled. In the asylum, a pedagogy of orderliness can be deployed in all its rigour. In it the exercise of authority can be more energetic, supervision more continuous, the network of constraints more tightly drawn. A moral corset that well deserves the other, medical one:

> The asylum that is suitably organized constitutes for them [the patients] a truly medical environment; its unremitting effect is almost imperceptible, but this it breathes from every pore. It modifies the patients' behaviour in the long run much more drastically than one might be inclined to believe, at least to the extent that it is capable of alteration.[45]

However, it is appropriate to note that it is as the place ordained from on high where the strategy of psychiatric intervention can best be deployed that the asylum was the undoubted centrepiece for the mechanisms of early mental health medicine. Whatever its importance, it was thus only the means that maximized the effectiveness of a technology of power: 'Everything in a well-ordered asylum, the quarters, regulations and inmates, are as if imbued with that spirit of order and submission. It therefore contributes, unbeknown even to those who are its object or instrument, to the fulfilment of the general aim, which is the cure or at least the improvement in the state of the insane.'[46]

The fundamental aim of the mental health movement was to obliterate from the social landscape the focus of disorder that madness represents. An essential question for the future, because it governs the possibility of an *aggiornamento* of psychiatry in the community, the sector, etc., is whether such a policy is fated always to utilize the instrument of the enclosed space. Those who speak of 'revolutions' in mental health medicine in fact always refer back to institutional divisions. The break from the asylum link would most certainly be extremely important. Yet if one is as attentive to psychiatric strategies as to the places where they are practised, it is not certain that the breaking of institutional ties would be a meaningful factor in making a completely fresh start.

Such, therefore, has been the cohesive infrastructure for the system of mental health medicine. Its vigour did not spring from the strength of each one of its parts taken in isolation, but from their articulation within a practical synthesis. In all the psychiatric literature of the first half of the nineteenth century, there is a striking contrast between the certainty that an essential task has to be accomplished, and the hesitations, approximations, doubts, and even contradictions, *as regards knowledge*. It proves that this is not the viewpoint from which its strength is to be appreciated: 'Everywhere, today, the wish is to cure the insane, everywhere one seeks to modify, enlighten and reform criminals, and everywhere the scientific elements necessary to do so are lacking. Our knowledge is not equal to our feelings.'[47] Yet in a certain way the 'feelings' can supplement the 'knowledge'. It was the theoretical weakness of the system of mental health medicine that constituted its strength in practice. Or, to express it better, it was because it did not achieve autonomy as regards a specifically 'scientific' dimension that mental health medicine was able to become a reality in its practical objectives. Because the first specialists in mental health never instituted a breakaway from, or really even distanced themselves from, the 'ordinary' social conception of madness, because they reiterated in their nosographies the supremacy of order, just as they imposed in their treatment the authority of dominating power, they were from the outset in accord with political strategies that aimed at the perpetuation of such an order. A synthesis of theory and practice, the medicine of mental health laid down in its theory what it had as its purpose to struggle against in its practice: certain departures from that order.

The question of the 'scientific nature' of psychiatry is therefore a pseudo-problem. It wrought no changes in the field of medical knowledge. On the other hand, it was able to classify medically practices that relate more to traditional disciplinary techniques than to the operations of clinical exploration in modern medicine. In what way? By a twofold operation. By relying on a corpus of medical knowledge that was already archaic when psychiatry arose: first, that of the nosographic classifications of the eighteenth century. And then by enclosing them within the hospital ambit, which was in the course of being restructured through a new medical technology. Thus, it was a medical code, but one that was already outdated. It also represented a medical environment, but reinterpreted within the framework of an authoritarian pedagogy, with no relationship to clinical work. This dual redefinition itself proved sufficient to give a medical cachet to a synthesis which was not medical on the criteria of the 'live' medicine of the time. Yet, since the medical cloak was in this way so loosely cut, this allowed it to cover and legitimize practices that strictly speaking lay outside the sphere of its speciality.

At least as much as the constitution of a new branch of medicine, the birth of mental health medicine must be interpreted as being the hiving-off of a new group from among the *professionals working in public assistance*. 'At least as much' means neither more nor less. The medical link gave a certain degree of 'scientific' credibility to a political project, which in turn determined the choice of the kind of scientific character that developed. These are two facts of the same operation, through which the problem relating to public assistance advanced across a new threshold. However, to understand the importance of what was at stake, we need to make a detour.

The New Landscape of Public Assistance

The second half of the eighteenth century had been marked by a decisive discovery: that of the relationship which unites wealth and labour. 'For a long time we have been seeking the philosopher's stone: it has been found, and it is work'.[48] Wealth is no longer a gift, riches given away originally by the sovereign, passed on through natural affiliations, and freely redistributed by the giving of alms. It is the product of exchange and has its source in labour.[49] This recognition of work as value transformed the place that the indigent poor and other 'non-productives' occupied within the social structure. Instead of exiling them within an enclosed space in order to render them moral, they had to be diverted, without a break, into the circuit of production. This is a decisive implication for the policy of public assistance drawn by a contemporary: 'The question of public assistance is therefore not a *moral* question or one of pure charity, it is one that concerns policing and administration. To give succour to the sick poor is therefore in no way a *virtue:* it is a *duty* of government; it is even more, it is a *necessity* for the State.'[50]

This does not mean that the solution of detention had not already been a matter of policing, administration and government. Yet now the act of maintaining potentially productive segments of the population in a sealed-off environment and in idleness was revealed as a waste of resources. Coqueau also wrote: 'It is doubtless a necessity to forestall disorder and the mishaps that excessive misery may entail for the most numerous class in society. But it is a necessity also to look to the preservation of that immense and precious nursery of those destined to plough our fields, transport our foodstuffs, and man our factories and workshops.'[51] Royal authority, almost exclusively, had been sensitive to the prime 'need' for a policy on the indigent poor. It had effected their exclusion through an enclosed institution, where making them 'moral' by putting them to work, which was the presumption, had always failed. A more elaborate form of assistance might kill two birds with one stone: at the same time neutralizing the risk of disorder and exploiting that 'immense and precious nursery of people' by creating special conditions for access to work for all those who were not immediately employed.

This discovery of labour as the foundation of social wealth inspired the first policy of public assistance, devised by the partisans of a liberalism that might be termed naive, because it had not yet been made aware of its inner contradictions, and because the obstacles that it encountered appear as so many archaic phenomena bequeathed by a system that had had its day. 'Every healthy man must provide for his subsistence by work, because if he were fed without working for it, it would be at the expense of those who work. What the State owes to each one of its members is the destruction of those obstacles that might impede their industriousness, or disturb them in the enjoyment of the products that are its reward.'[52] Thus the rationalizing function of the state would be reduced to abolishing those measures of protection that are an obstacle to free access to work, at the very most supplementing it by a minimal task of organization, so that the most impoverished should find in public works at least a temporary means of escape from begging.

Hence Turgot worked out, in the financial district of the Limousin, a programme of land works on which the indigent might be employed. Having become General Comptroller of Finance, he wished to spread the plan more widely and at the same time to abolish the beggaries, which he held, as did most economists and reformers, to be outmoded.[53] With mitigated success: at the end of the *Ancien Régime* half such institutions remained and the royal administration in 1785 decided upon their reorganization. Although they functioned badly, the organization of public assistance workshops was almost as defective and their productivity almost as patchy.[54] However, when for political reasons the Paris workshops were closed down in 1791, they were keeping 31,000 people busy, which was three times as many as those in the Hôpital Général, and more than ten times the proportion of the 'fit poor' under detention.

If the system of assistance through work was far from technically perfect at the collapse of the *Ancien Régime*, two principles capable of reorganizing the whole policy of public assistance seem nevertheless to have prevailed: first, the recipe of detention was outmoded, at least for those in need that were fit; secondly, to organize labour freed from these archaic constraints could in essence wipe out the problems posed by vagrancy and begging.[55] 'Detention was a gross error and an economic mistake: it was thought that misery could be abolished by isolating and maintaining a *population of poor* by charity. In fact *poverty* was artificially concealed; and in reality a part of the population was eliminated as a potential source of wealth.'[56] Instead of the old formula of detention, assistance was entirely reorganized according to the differing possibilities of access to work: 'He therefore who is capable of work, and who does not lack it, should in no way obtain help; he who lacks bread and who asks for work should find both himself; he who refuses to work, although capable of doing so, not only does not deserve any public assistance, but should also be under the strict surveillance of the magistrates.'[57]

However, as freedom to work began to prevail (and we know that it became the charter of the new economic relationships with the Le Chapelier Law of 1791), that freedom produced more clearly all the social consequences that would contradict the optimism of the first 'liberals'. The principle of free access to work is in fact the legal framework for the exploitation of the worker, and not for the free admission of all to the means of subsistence. Wealth founded upon labour means in reality that the rich have need of the poor and must be able to dispose of them in order to ensure their own profit. Brissot had already expressed this in a forceful statement more than ten years before becoming the leader of the Girondin party:

> There will always be the rich, therefore there must also be the poor. In well-governed States, the latter work and live out their life; in others they assume the beggar's rags and imperceptibly undermine the State under a cloak of idleness. *Let us have the poor, and never beggars. This is the goal towards which good administration should strive.*[58]

The 'beggar' is the onetime poor person, he who had nothing and to whom alms were given, or who was shut away if he were too dangerous or too many in number. The new poor person is rich with a strength to be exploited. Undoubtedly he had to be set to work, but according to the laws of maximum profit. Now these had their own logic. It was not certain that the rational organization of the market would ensure the subsistence of all the poor. It even ceased to be evident that the bourgeois economy being set up required full employment. Hence work was no longer the universal solution to the problem of public assistance, even for the fit poor. The contrary in certain respects was true: the labour market, far from wiping out all misery, itself created indigence by a policy of low salaries, the constitution of a revolving cycle of unemployment, and the frequency of economic crises, etc. The spectre of pauperism would replace that of begging, and economic and political analysis would supplant moral condemnation.

These ambiguities in the notion of work burst forth with relative clarity in the heat of the Revolution. The Committee on Begging of the Constituent Assembly, it will be remembered, had, perhaps imprudently, forced the Assembly to concede 'that it places among the most sacred duties of the Nation assistance to the poor of every age and in every circumstance of life.' As the Revolutionary process developed, this conception of a right to assistance became more radical in the sense of becoming a right to work.

Before the Legislative Assembly, on 13 June 1792, Bernard d'Airy declared: 'Hence, gentlemen, this axiom which is lacking in the Declaration of the Rights of Man, an axiom which is worthy of being set at the beginning of the code for humanity that you will decree: every man has a right to his subsistence, by his labour if he is fit, by free assistance if he is unable to work.'[59]

Before the Convention J. B. Bô stated:

> Man, born to work, cannot be unhappy save when it is lacking or when, being excessive, it cannot provide him with the means of subsistence . . . Work is the sole aid that the State should employ to assuage indigence; for *man is not precisely poor because he possesses nothing, but because he does not work*. . . . You will eradicate, either by property or by industry, even the very notion of misery.[60]

The absolute right to work is a dangerous notion. If, instead of waiting for assistance or bowing to the laws of the market, the poor can exact their due, they intervene as full partners in the distribution of wealth, power, and, marginally, property. Undoubtedly the members of the Convention did not seize all the implications of this principle,[61] but Barère at least perceived them: 'The unfortunate are the power upon the earth; they have the right to speak as masters to those governments that neglect them.'[62] In the final analysis, the right to work might represent the equivalent in the social order of a right to insurrection in the political order: the recognition of a right turns its violation into arbitrary despotism. Popular violence would then be rendered legitimate, since it would do no more than re-establish the right.

The radical wing of the Revolution having been defeated, the obsession of the spokesmen for a policy of assistance appropriate to the new bourgeois society would be to fight this conception of a right to assistance, in whose name the poor might rise and demand their share of power. Such polemics were termed criticism of 'legal charity', that old-fashioned expression designating the incorporation into the law of a prerogative of the poor that does not derive from the reciprocity of contractual exchange. It was a criticism voiced both by those working for a return to the *Ancien Régime* and by spokesmen for the new business bourgeoisie in the field of public assistance. It assigned itself a dual target: clearly, the actions of the revolutionary assemblies, but also the organization of the allocation of assistance as in England, which was suspected of making life too easy for the indigent. One of the representatives of this tendency, Duchâtelet, who had more clearly seen the revolutionary potentialities of the right to work than had the members of the Convention themselves ('the principle of the right to work shakes the foundations of the social order'[63]), also drew radical consequences from his criticism: 'The workman gives of his labour, the master pays the wage agreed – to this boil down their reciprocal obligations . . . As soon as [the employer] has no longer need of his labour, he dismisses him, and it is up to the worker to make out as best he can.'[64]

This is to do no more than draw the logical consequences of the principles of absolute liberalism. The very concept of public assistance loses its meaning. The contractual rigour of mercantile exchange must govern not only economic transactions but also relationships between men. All forms of organized assistance would be threatening to the free function of the laws of the market, in the same way as did those obstacles to the circulation of wealth and men that the corporations represented under the *Ancien Régime*, and any coalition of workers would do now. Even institutions as 'humanitarian' as the hospitals for foundlings were not spared by the most consequential proponents of this morality of productivity.[65] The option of exercising private charity must suffice to rectify the most extreme manifestations, and thus those that most touch the heart, of social misery. This was all the more the case, because the distribution of the resources for such charity rested upon a tradi- tional infrastructure that was at the same time being reconstructed: the Restoration era was marked by the creation of a host of private charitable works under religious control, and by the return in strength of the religious orders, which regained roughly the same position as they had occupied under the *Ancien Régime*.[66]

However, despite the generally reactionary evolution of the policy of public assistance at the beginning of the nineteenth century,[67] this extremist option did not prevail as such. This was because, going beyond a return to the situation under the *Ancien Régime*, it denoted a regression regarding the problem of control. This the eighteenth century had begun to solve, having grasped the state's interest in intervening in matters of public assistance to safeguard the social order. Before the Revolution Coqueau had already clearly formulated what was at stake: 'The most extreme necessities are those that it [the government] is most interested in forestalling', and the disorders arising from this deprivation 'will form two hostile nations within the same empire'.[68]

Thus the protagonists of public charity ranged themselves against the defenders of purely private charity. This was not a reaction on the part of sensitive souls. They drew their conclusion from a political analysis that esteemed itself more realistic, although based on the same principles. The defence of private property and the search for profit were the foundations of the social order and could not be called into question. Thus the poor possessed no right that might contradict the laws of the market; there was no 'legal charity' in whose name the most destitute could lay claim to what could only be demanded as a counterpart of exchange. Yet, although the ine- quality in conditions was a just consequence of the growth of societies, its effects had to be controlled, so as not to arrive at a breaking point, from where those sacrificed would rush headlong towards extreme solutions, declaring a social war.

This position, more subtle and skilful than that of those cynics who hymned the praises of absolute liberalism, was the one adopted by that segment of the bourgeoisie that had specialized in problems of public assistance, and to which history has attached the label of philanthropists. There is no question of this being a marginal phenomenon. Philanthropy represented a laboratory for experimenting with ideas and practical initiatives. From it emerged the techniques for the subjugation of the masses that were indispensable for the domination of the bourgeois class.[69]

What was at stake will now appear as clear, and topical, even if to grasp it we have had to make this long detour. Between the order of contractual autonomy and the order of juridically decreed exclusions, there exist intermediate kinds of social status that have, in the strict sense, no legal existence, but represent dependent structures constituted by the policy of assistance itself. The poor person on the verge of indigence is maintained in a permanent state of need by the laws of the market: need for help in cases of illness, for the allocation of food in case of famine, for clothes if an unforeseen birth should occur, for lodging if the hovel he lives in becomes completely uninhabitable, etc. This misery is not an injustice, because it is a necessary consequence of the functioning of the social machine. However, it represents a misfortune and a danger. Thus the person living in misery should obtain at least minimum satisfaction of his needs, but in a form that is not one of satisfaction of a *right* that can be demanded (the only right is contractual). The means of survival are *granted* him in a personalized relationship of dependence, in which the economic relationship of wealth to poverty is changed into a human relationship between benefactor and beneficiary.

> *Poverty is to riches what childhood is to adulthood.* You rich, acknowledge the dignity with which you are invested. But mark this well, it is not to a vague and indefinite form of patronage that you are called . . . You have to exercise a patronage that is personal, individual, direct, immediate . . . *You are called upon to undertake a guardianship*, a free guardianship of your own choosing, but a real and active one.[70]

Economic relationships are impersonal: bourgeois society has reduced reason to calculation, and exchanges occur within the icy universe of contractual justice. But the inequality of position induces a flow of exchanges of another kind, generosity goes out to meet misery and encounters the gratitude of the person assisted. Charity is the bourgeois re-interpretation of Rousseau's pity. It is an increment of the soul that is also the adjunct to law and order, and which, naturally, works to serve them. The poor person is kept at the very extreme of survival through the iron laws of the economy. Yet in this way he comes close to welcoming his exploiter-cum-benefactor in a mirror-image relationship through which the joy of the donor that makes a gift without constraint enters reciprocally into the gratitude of the person assisted, who is saved from need through help to which he has no prescriptive right.[71]

In a social world given over to the pitiless rationality of economic exchanges there are thus reconstituted 'the enchanted relationships of the feudal world'. And they extend their ramifications further, re-establishing an organic link between men that runs counter to everything in their objective situation, insofar as the exercise of charity links the person assisted in a client relationship to his guardian. Thus the egoism of *homo economicus* is transcended, humanity is reconciled to both well-conceived self-interest and the outpourings of the heart, and, last but not least, the social order is saved:

> Instead of dividing society, through detestable epithets, through categories of 'owners' and 'proletariat', who are excited to hate, to attack, and mutually to despoil each other, let us, on the contrary, attempt to show those who are least happy how great are the abundant and sacred sources of sympathy and benefits that flood out in their favour from the hearts of the wealthy classes. Against every one of the misfortunes that may strike a working-class family, a generous charity sets up an institution that strives to forestall, or at least to assuage them.[72]

The new landscape of public assistance is now represented by this map, still for the most part blank, of concerted acts of subjugation. The enlightened exercise of charity is included in it as the best instrument for the surveillance and manipulation of the people. The guardianship relationship that it installs defuses any possibility of revolt, and reproduces and extends class domination. A simple solution, but one of genius: *whereas hardness of heart on the part of the rich stirs the unfortunate to revolt, generosity shown towards them is the political basis for their subjugation.*

The logic of the transformation in public assistance that we followed in the preceding chapter does not therefore cover the whole field – far from it. We reconstituted the moves made towards the separating-out of those segments of the population that were the concern of public assistance, which tended to redistribute them according to two opposing poles. The first polarity reduced the number of those liable to be taken into enclosed institutions and rationalized their treatment by a strict identification of them into limited, specific categories: criminality, mental derangement, incorrigible begging. Theoretically 'all the rest' remained outside such an organization for compulsory assistance. In other words, citizens as a whole should henceforth be governed by 'normal' social relationships, through contractual exchanges, codified rights and duties, administrative obligations and economic laws.

But such a bipolarization between absolute constraint and reasonable liberty corresponds to an abstract and idealist representation of the functioning of the capitalist machine. This social area 'freed' from arbitrary constraints is in fact an anomic territory, a prey to the ups and downs of economic crises, to revolts by those exploited, to the dramas of unemployment and misery. The paradox of liberalism is that freedom of circulation of goods and men is needed to secure a maximization of profits. Yet it is destructive of natural divisions in territory and organic social relationships, demanding for its own survival regulatory means that contradict its principles.

Hence a 'second line' for the reconstruction of the problems of assistance: to regiment, supervise and domesticate those segments of the population that have themselves been 'liberated', and foremost among them, that army of the poor swollen in number the very advance of progress. It is the opposite strategy to detention, since it means subjugating these groups where they are, without hiving them off from the movement of which they are the driving force. It is a problem that has also changed in scale, since instead of being content with mopping up the most dangerous of the social marginals, control has to be exerted over 'the most numerous class in society'. Yet it is a challenge that must be taken up with at least as much urgency, for the spectre of the 'socialist republic' is no phantasmagoria: 1848 and the Commune were looming upon the chronological horizon of a class becoming aware that the condition for its own survival resided in its capacity to colonize these hordes, which had become savage through the 'free' development of its rationality.

The Mental Health Specialist, the Hygienist and the Philanthropist

The experimental relationships that mental health medicine would entertain with these new strategies of domination were complex and ambiguous. We have established that the mental health movement forged its instruments by proceeding to the *aggiornamento* of one part of the totalitarian institution. It was therefore an occupation that placed it outside that search within the living environment for people to subjugate. Yet, although the philanthropic tendency indeed operates within a different social area and targets different segments of the population, at the outset it does not have an adequate technology to put its programme into operation.

Thus, in his *Le visiteur de pauvre*, De Gerando explained at length a technique of control that nevertheless remained somewhat rough and ready: to ensure a complete hold over some of the poor, their behaviour had to be minutely watched, their upward ascent guided. Such prescriptions did not break entirely with those of the charity of former times, and which in any case were not up to dealing with the new problems posed by pauperism. De Gerando indeed saw the necessity for proceeding to a 'general classification of the poor . . .' the foundation for the entire edifice that enlightened charity is called upon to construct'.[73] He sketched it out according to an assessment of needs, in three dimensions: the size of the needs (quantitative dimension); their nature (qualitative distribution: food, lodging, care, etc.); and their duration (certain needs are temporary, such as when an acute illness unexpectedly occurs, or those of dismissal from employment, and others are permanent, such as those of invalids). These three parameters combine to form a matrix of dependence. To intervene in 'enlightened' fashion for the needs of the poor, i.e. to satisfy them in measured fashion, watchful of the use that the beneficiary makes of the gifts he receives, is to arrogate to oneself the means of manipulating those assisted, to renew their dependent status, and institute permanent surveillance over families in need. Since the granting of help is meted out according to the docility of the poor, all forms of aid maintain and reproduce the process of subjugation.[74]

However, although such a programme may have been attractive, it demanded the availability of a set of resources that was not provided at the beginning. The Restoration era did indeed see the blossom of numerous associations of patronage, private institutions to help in various forms of distress, associations for savings, for insurance, for people's education – all inspired by these principles of concerted blackmail. Yet, however much their objectives may have converged, these initiatives occurred spadmodically and efforts remained disproportionate to the needs to be met.

114 *The First Social Medicine*

Everything happened as if this policy of control of public assistance had been clear at the outset about its purposes, whilst gradually becoming conscious of the weakness of the means for realizing them. Thus its problem was to institutionalize and professionalize a strategy of domination whose objectives were political, but for which resources remained rudimentary. It was all the more difficult a problem since to solve it by assuming official responsibility – for example, by the creation of a national body for the allocation of assistance – was impossible because of 'liberal' criticism of a recognized right to assistance.

This interpretation of the 'philanthropic' movement accounts for the type of relationships, both close and distant, that it developed with medicine generally, and with mental health medicine in particular. It is true that the segments of population in question were not the same and the techniques as such not transferable. Yet reference to the medical model represented a possibility of moving from amateurism to professionalism, from empiricism as to the choice of means to combining them through a scientific technology. Undoubtedly the appeal on the 'supply' side remained limited, but it met an old medical ambition.

It will be remembered that in the last decades of the *Ancien Régime* a new kind of medical Utopia developed, as evinced in the work of the Royal Society of Medicine. The doctor assumed the mantle of enlightened auxiliary to the political power in reducing misery and educating the people by contriving for it an hygienic and rational framework for existence.[75] To control the living environment, to counteract epidemics and illnesses, to rationalize procreation, to fight against obscurantism, to assuage misfortune, to distribute help – all these became less specialized modes of intervention but rather were complementary elements in a coherent strategy of intervention that required the organization of state medicine, invested with a real political mandate and endowed with wide powers.[76] Cabanis, who was, however, very measured in his assessment of the means that the medicine of his time had available to it, still defended this conception of the doctor as magistrate, 'the supervisor of morality as of public health'.[77]

Such a conception of a generalized medical order was a consequence of the optimism of the Enlightenment. The political mandate claimed by the doctor was, in his eyes, based upon the privileged knowledge of human life that he possessed. It was illuminating enough to be capable of dispelling prejudices, reducing arbitrariness and, in the last analysis, controlling by the use of reason the organization of daily life. The development of the real revolutionary struggles was, however, to belie these ambitious goals. As J. P. Peters remarks, groups other than the doctors were better placed to impose their hegemony. Interests other than those of reason were to occupy the foreground of history. Thwarted in his overall political plans, the doctor would have to resign himself to being a specialist, *but a specialist in questions of general interest.*

The hygienist movement thus transferred to what were apparently more modest programmes this will to dominate social contingencies and to promote a more rational form of existence. This *political* investment, which sought for itself an arena for *technical* intervention, constituted the originality and brought about the progress of the French hygienist school during the post-revolutionary period. In it the ideology of the Enlightenment and the sensualism of the English school, made topical through the theory of the influence of the moral upon the physical, as set out by Cabanis, gave rise to a practical reformism that was medically inspired: by controlling the influences *of the environment* through knowledge, man would succeed in mapping out for himself a more sensible existence.[73] Although the doctor is a specialist, his speciality relates to what is most fundamentally at stake in social life: 'There is then formed a kind of intermediate science between Legislation and Medicine . . . This science, which I call political medicine, is properly speaking the result of the links that can exist between social institutions and human nature.'[79]

In 1867 Bouchardat gave a tardy self-criticism of this orientation:

If at the beginning of this century an effort was made to understand everything about hygiene, today a host of details must be left in the shadows, either because they are useless or because they cannot be proved . . . Before hygiene's new phase, the authors sought to enlarge its scope. The attempt was made to draw up a general inventory of human knowledge; the programme was boundless.[74]

The circles in which such preoccupations developed were both the group to which the first mental health specialists belonged, as well as being their reference group. The same men were to be met with in the same places, particularly on the 'Conseil de Salubrité de la Seine', set up in 1802 according to the plans of Vicq d'Azyr, the one-time inspirer of the Royal Society of Medicine. There one met Parent-Duchâtel, Marc, Pariset, Villermé etc., and Esquirol, who was to become its president in 1822. In 1829, at the instigation of Marc and Esquirol, they founded the *Annales d'hygiène publique et de médecine légale* whose secretary was Leuret. Seven out of the twelve members of the editorial board of the review belonged to the Conseil de Salubrité. In the prospectus presenting the review was set down the scientific and political consensus of the group:

> Medicine's purpose is not merely to study and cure illnesses; it has close links with the social organization; sometimes it assists the legislator in harmonizing laws, often it enlightens the judge as to their application, and always, with the administration, it watches over the maintenance of public health. Applied in this way to the needs of society, this part of our knowledge makes up *public hygiene* and *legal medicine*.[75]

Thus there are two main points of application of medicine, 'in its relationship to the social organization': 'public hygiene, which is the art of preserving the health of people gathered together in society, and which is destined to be very greatly developed and to provide numerous applications for the improvement of our institutions'; and legal medicine for which 'the deeper study of insanity has allowed the satisfactory solution of several questions relating to moral liberty, to the civil status of a large number of individuals, and to the criminality of certain actions'.[82]

Yet such specialities were not narrowly circumscribed, nor did they rule out wider interventions that touch upon the overall problem of misery, deviance and the social order. Finally, the hygienist movement sought to promote the idea of *prevention*, whose rich ambiguity characterizes even today the dilemmas of social medicine. In attempting to elucidate this concept American authors have recently demonstrated its insurmountable ambiguity. If 'tertiary' prevention deals with the living conditions that are oppressive for a given individual, 'secondary' prevention already implies the assumption of responsibility for vulnerable groups, and neither the one nor the other can formally be divorced from a 'primary' prevention that would require the control of all the factors conditioning existence within a community.[83] Without such a theory having been explicitly spelt out, it was indeed this claim to reduce the sum of pathogenic conditions in the living environment that underpinned the ambitions of social reformers in the nineteenth century. From the physical insalubrity of the environment to its misery, immorality or vice, one is dealing with a continuum of degrading conditions that cried out for remedy.

Timely and specialized action thus led to a generalized policy of interventionism:

> The finest and most sublime duty of the doctor to society is to be diligent, through his philanthropic art, in all times and in all places, not only to preserve public health and restore it when it has been lost, but also to seek to base morality on firm foundations, to point out to authority how the idle can be brought to work, to lead the corrupted man back to virtue, the indigent to easeful living and happiness.[84]

'The philanthropic art' is the combination of a special skill, dependent upon medical knowledge, and a strong desire to treat all 'social problems'.

Mental health specialists have also shared in this vast ambition. For example, Fodéré, whose *Essai médico-legal sur les diverses espèces de folie* (1832) is one of the first treatises on mental health medicine, published between 1822 and 1824 his *Leçons sur les épidémies et l'hygiène publique* and an *Essai historique et moral sur la pauvreté des nations* in 1825. 'Faults in distribution in all parts of the social system having always been one of the principal causes of the sicknesses that beset the physical and moral nature of man, I thought it necessary to follow my *Leçons sur les épidémies et l'hygiène publique* by the publication of this present work.'[85] In it he discussed all the 'social problems' of his time – pauperism, begging, hospitals, foundlings – and demanded 'a sound public economic policy from which will benefit not only the few, but all members without distinction in the different human societies, each according to the rank that he occupies'.[86]

Another example was Leuret, who was not only directly the pupil of Esquirol, the head doctor of one of the services at Bicêtre, and the theorist of moral treatment. He was also principal editor of the *Annales d'hygiène publique et de médecine légale*, and occasionally set out the position regarding the allocation of public assistance and recommended reform of the system.[87] Is this soaring ambition a psychiatric imperialism before its time? Expansionism assumes possession of a clearly delimited territory from which are deployed the techniques for annexation. But here it is more a question of a primal source that is still relatively undifferentiated, shared by different sub-groupings that will gradually define their identity in relation to one another, without ever succeeding in becoming completely autonomous.

From the revolutionary assemblies onwards, privileged relationships were struck up between doctors and those politicians specially interested in 'social questions'. Thus doctors were in the majority among the 36 members of the Committee of Public Assistance presided over by Tenon, which under the Legislative Assembly succeeded the Committee on Begging of the Constituent Assembly (the Legislative Assembly, however, only included 28 doctors). Thus from the outset doctors and philanthropists constituted an almost indissoluble group. As soon as it came into existence, mental health medicine would 'naturally' be included in this grouping. Without any break in continuity there was a transition from the 'special art' of the doctors to the collective programmes of the hygienists and the political projects of the philanthropists. 'Without any doubt, the question of the insane is one of the most important branches of that political and social medicine whose activities seem destined to loom ever larger in the existence of modern societies.'[88] Prophetic words.

Such solidarity nevertheless did not imply complete interchangeability of roles. Along the continuum mental health medicine occupied a special place, both in relation to hygienism and to philanthropy.

First, let us consider hygienism. If the hygienist trend at the beginning of the nineteenth century had brought with it great hopes, it wrought – until the era of Pasteur – somewhat limited accomplishments in practice: emptying of drains, denunciation of the toxic nature of certain industrial products, prevention of certain occupational illnesses, even assessment of the dangers of prostitution[89] – such modest outcomes fall far short of the statements of intent concerning the necessary contribution of hygiene 'to the improvement of our institutions'. This was because the medical linkage through which hygiene sought to authenticate itself scientifically was too generalized to ensure it had effective instruments at its command. Even Cabanis – who, among his manifold activities, was also professor of hygiene at the Ecoles Centrales from Year III onwards – had clearly perceived the problem of a medicine caught between its political projects and the weakness of its means to intervene technically. On the one hand, he declared: 'In certain respects, the profession of medicine is a sort of priesthood; in other ways, it is a veritable magistracy.'[90] On the other, he was perfectly aware of the 'degree of certainty' – and just as much, of uncertainty – of a medicine whose technology was precarious and which was overseen by diabolically risky speculations. For him the crux of the matter, through which ran as much the political programme as that of the technical development of medicine, consisted in 'simplifying above all the art that is the most important and most difficult, that of applying these rules to practice'.[91]

One can indeed deem the knowledge and techniques of the mental health specialists to have been disappointing. However, it was they who were best placed, within the context of the times, to put forward a coherent operational scheme for intervention in the hospital arena (or – and this amounts almost to the same thing – in it they worked out a formula that has yet to be demonstrated to be ineffective). If clinical medicine already enjoyed greater scientific prestige, it still remained hemmed in within an individual, somatic framework. Mental health medicine treated a *social* problem and developed a *collective* set of practices. Thus it could represent itself as figuring in the vanguard of the hygienist movement by putting forward its treatment scheme as being the most credible scientifically and the most effective technologically.

The same argument, with certain reservations, was valid for 'philanthropy'. *Social philosophy* was common to both tendencies. Let us merely juxtapose two selected texts, among the dozens that spring from the same inspiration:

We now understand better the influence of civilization, which counts its dead and wounded after celebrating its victories. Trends in commerce and industry, the development of the arts, and intellectual activity, – these, which constitute the glory of the nation, must not cause us to forget the unfortunate who have fallen before arriving at the goal. Society must break off a few morsels of its prosperity in order to extend a helping hand to those defeated by social progress. Among the defeated, the insane certainly most deserve our sympathy

in their misfortune, for the needs of public security accord perfectly
with humanitarian prescriptions.

If civilization, in the course of its progress, causes inequality between
conditions to increase, and makes it more perceptible; if, in this way,
it therefore partly occasions misfortune; if, calling man to ever
higher, ever more powerful destinies, it leaves behind in distress those
whose enfeebled or paralysed faculties cannot respond to its call; if,
on its upward march, it encounters some obstacles, occasions some
injury and increases the chances of misfortune, as well as the
prospects of success, would it not be fair that it should be troubled by
those victims that have been sacrificed through the very task that
leads it to its goal, and should indemnify those that are stricken down
in its path?

The first quotation is a passage from the *Commentaires médico-
administratifs* of Renaudin, which constituted the bible of the mental
health school.[92] The second is from De Gerando, the leader of the
philanthropic movement.[93] The dialogue between mental health
specialist and social reformer could be continued. If 'the insane
person is almost always one who has been hurt by civilization, and
the asylum is his ambulance',[94] he shares with the very sick, the
destitute and aged, the incurable and indigent, the blind, the deaf
and dumb, and abandoned children, in an order of deficiencies
which, although ineluctable as regards their specific causes, are
nevertheless related to a general and common social aetiology.
'Progress', says De Gerando also, 'links the increase in common
wealth to the inequalities in condition between individuals, as two
connected phenomena',[95] and 'inequality is the inevitable consequence of the freedom to work, which is the source of all
prosperity.'[96] Yet 'it matters little if some persons are better
endowed, if by this means those who are less so secure greater
ease.'[97] And Renaudin again echoes him: 'If every day is marked by
a new conquest why, after having confirmed the results of victory,
should one not concede to the vanquished and the wounded the
benefit of the ambulance or of the home for the unfit?'[98] The madman thus appears as the marginal figure, the last to be excluded in a
process of rejection that wears men down. The necessity for such
acts of exclusion is not questioned, for they are the counterweight to
the march of civilization, which is identified with the development of
bourgeois society. The goal of public assistance, whether for the

mentally ill or other segments of the population abandoned on the path of 'progress', is always to preserve the social or ideological order by dispensing to the most unfortunate that help which is to maintain or restore their dependence on that order.

The *means* employed will therefore also be of the same type. It is still a matter of deploying strategies for subjugation. It is the same armoury of disciplinary techniques that is capable both of effecting the recovery of the reason (i.e. a return to the predominant form of normality) and also of subduing the people (i.e. causing them to internalize the rules that ensure the reproduction of the bourgeois order). From this viewpoint, moral treatment functions as the ideal model. Since it deals with a strictly limited problem in a special enclosed environment, it represents the paradigm of every authoritarian pedagogy. It is therefore understandable that the philanthropists, groping after techniques applicable to more diverse segments of the population in mixed environments, were fascinated by this model. There was need to be. Nineteenth century philanthropy was spared neither 1848 nor the Commune. Mental health medicine brought a real and complete solution to the problem of madness, at least in the sense that for over a century it stifled its challenge. Mental health medicine, in the wake of, and doubtless more effectively than, religion (love of which could also take on an inquisitorial form, for the greater good of heretics), demonstrates one of the early successes of relatively mild techniques whose generalization would dispense with resorting to open violence in order to solve the social question.

The sameness of the situation, however, did not rule out a fundamental heterogeneity in *the places where they operated*, a fact which would maintain the separation between the two activities, at least so long as mental health medicine remained rooted in the asylum. Significantly, it was almost exclusively when dealing with the problems arising from another enclosed site, the prison, that all these reformers came together in practice.

We know that at the beginning of the nineteenth century the problem of criminals and prisons constituted the focal point for all the obsessions of reformers: to exercise surveillance, punish, intimidate, re-educate, forestall, and cure . . .[99] In this grand concert the mental health specialists played their part. Thus Ferrus, the first Inspector-General of Asylums from 1836 onwards, was also Inspector of Health for penitentiaries from 1842. His work, *Des prisonniers et de l'emprisonnement*,[100] carried as much authority in the prison world as did *Des Aliénés*[101] in the mental health world. Both worlds were in a condition of osmosis to each other. Moreau-Christophe, Inspector-General for Prisons of the kingdom, based his policy on the reports of commissions on which sat numerous mental health specialists such as Esquirol, Pariset and Ferrus. In the great dispute of the day between the proponents of complete incarceration in cells and the upholders of a more flexible regime, it was their authority that led the former policy (called the 'Philadelphia system') to be adopted at first: 'Pariset and Esquirol, having had to express their opinion on this question, did not shrink from maintaining that isolating those convicted would be employed to a certain degree of severity and with great persistence, with no resultant harm to their mental condition.'[102] The same Moreau-Christophe, moreover, felt himself sufficiently versed in mental health ideas to present to the Academy of Medicine a memoir entitled: 'De la mortalité et de la folie dans le régime pénitentiaire' (1839), which would be endorsed by the doctors upon the recommendation of Esquirol, their rapporteur.

The linkage here could be made particularly close because, both in prisons and in asylums, isolation imposed a complete break from the outside world, through which a whole programme of resocialization could – at least in theory – be implemented in an environment free from any disturbing influences. In comparison with other spheres of possible application, the model position occupied by the mental health movement was doubly paradoxical.

First, it was paradoxical because of its inclusion in a movement for social reforms through the mediation of a technology essentially relating to the hospital. Whereas the realization of the hygienist and philanthropist programmes would have required control of the social environment, mental health medicine in practice only dominated one section in the hospital. Whereas in the one case emerged a will to achieve a general form of prevention, in the other the most effective interventions by the 'special doctors' took place after the event, upon segments of the population that had already been segregated.

Secondly, it was from the fact that the mental health movement seems best linked to medicine that it drew most of its prestige. Yet, as we have seen, this relationship was based upon a body of theory and techniques already lagging behind what represented for the times the spearhead in medicine (clinical medicine). The progress of mental health medicine thus ran the risk of paying dearly when there burst forth into the full light of day this fission between its own 'scientific' authentification and the criteria of a medical science that had become more demanding. Not only would the movement be in danger of becoming discredited, but another form of social medicine would attempt to latch on to a different medical pattern, more technically oriented. The centres of innovation in mental health medicine would then move from the asylums to ordinary hospitals, and especially to the clinics of the medical Faculties.

Mental health medicine was really to enter a decisive phase of crisis when these two movements coordinated their actions. A thorough questioning of the preponderant use of asylums was to go hand in hand with the supremacy of a new medical pattern, which was to contemplate breaking definitively with the almost spontaneous social (or moral) perception of madness, so as to establish it as a 'true illness'. Then the 'struggle against social scourges', inspired by the tuberculosis model, was to have a different medical technology as its referent, and at the same time the setting up of systematic prophylactic programmes was to outmode the idea that the hospital could constitute a privileged institutional mechanism in leading this struggle.

This is a story to follow, but to understand it depends upon the genealogy attempted here. In fact, all was to become very confused, and not a few good minds and men of good will led astray. However, in future attempts there would always be the two strands, the medical and the social, now separated, now intertwined in different fashion. The success of mental health medicine in its golden age arises from the fact that it seized possession of both strands at their origin, at the moment when they co-existed still in their pre-critical unity, and before the process of their division had become objectified in rival forms of practice based upon different forms of knowledge. Later, Durkheim, for example, would seek to rescue a social and homogeneous field from contamination by psychological and pathological phenomena.[103] The doctors would effect an opposite and complementary withdrawal, by attempting to limit strictly their concern, basing it upon the organic (or the unconscious). It would then become necessary to discover more sophisticated ways in order to reconcile 'theory' and 'practice', the 'social' and the 'psychological'.

Benefiting from a certain naivety as compared with later research, the first mental health medicine never broke with the predominant

conception of madness: it was *from the outset* social. It did not even
have to pose the problem of its 'applications' to recover the place it
had never left within the dominant social order. Its propagators had
never any difficulty in serving that order, because the theoretical
code of mental medicine contented itself with classifying its shortcomings through its nosographies of symptoms, whilst its forms of
treatment strained every nerve to re-establish the order by strategies
of subjugation.

Thus let us round off this attempt to assign psychiatry to its real
affiliations, which relate to public assistance and are political as
much as medical, by reflecting upon a passage of the great philanthropist, the Baron de Gerando:

> It is not only a matter, as is assumed, of procuring work for the
> indigent poor person: it is a matter often of educating him for work at
> any age; that is to say, of giving him a taste for it, to cause him to
> acquire the ability and habit of work. It is not only a matter, as is
> assumed, of attaining an economic goal . . . it is above all a matter of
> attaining a moral goal . . . There is little to be hoped for from specu-
> lation regarding the product of such industriousness; but there is
> much to be expected from its effect upon the morals of the poor, even
> when speculation would be unrewarding.[104]

Replace 'indigent' by one of the many terms applied today to the
diverse varieties of those 'excluded' from a system of exploitation
and normalization. You will then have the general formula for a
policy of public assistance in a class society, with a place also for all
kinds of social and mental health medicine, past, present and future.
And also the key to the relationship of classical psychiatry to the
problem of labour. It is in no way – unless by way of a bonus – the
recovery of a form of surplus value. It is rather the restoration of an
order in which the extraction of surplus value can be the economic
law, because subjugation to various disciplines constitutes its moral
law.

4

Providential Experts

Expertise: technical competence surpassing itself. On the basis of his knowledge and know-how, the specialist is called upon to decide between options that involve the fundamental values of existence. Delegation of power is part of the very definition of expertise. Through a process of technical or scientific reasoning, a decision is taken concerning a third person, which henceforth will seal his fate. The development of this function of expertise is one of the characteristics of Western-style civilization, and the essential agent in the process of rationalization, in the sense meant by Max Weber. It is a mandate imparted to competent specialists granting them the monopoly of making significant assessments, with, as their consequence, bureaucratization, disenchantment with the world, and the deprivation of the common man of all autonomy of decision.

Doctors in general, and psychiatrists in particular, have occupied a strategic position in the development of this process. It is perhaps a function, in part inherited, of the traditional role of the doctor. Even in societies where those areas of intervention that have been conquered through rational thought are limited in extent, he arbitrates in the name of his art, with the priest (which he often is also), a contingency that has arisen in the body social through accident, famine, epidemic, injury or death. Yet this prerogative will shift elsewhere and become generalized with the linking of medical arts to rational knowledge. Eliot Freidson has described under the heading of 'professional autonomy' the objective basis for such interventions, showing at the same time why doctors possess it to such a high degree.[1] By manifesting the external signs of science and cultivating an esoteric technique, doctors distance themselves from commonplace know-how. Thus they impose their legitimacy not only on the technical treatment of those questions deemed to fall within their competence, but also on the form of such questions: 'Their mandate consists in defining whether a problem does or does not exist, what is "truly" its nature, and how it should be tackled.'[2] Thus experts define reality for society as a whole, and in particular for those who live out its contradictions in the flesh. The psychiatrist effects this operation in exemplary fashion: from the moment when his diagnosis wholly defines the status of the mentally ill patient, he can, as Thomas Szasz declares, 'transform his judgement into a social reality'.[3]

Criticisms of this kind generally insist upon the pseudo-scientific character of the operations deemed to justify these acts of force (mental illness is a 'myth', etc.). Apart from the fact that we then have difficulty in understanding what imparts such power to the psychiatrist, this is undoubtedly not the essence of the matter. An expert is not, and does not have to be, a theorist. What determines him as one is less the force of what is true than the need to settle certain given elements of conflict in a concrete situation. That his assessments will have a more or less approximate character is conceded, in as much as he occupies a strategic position in the decision-making process.

It is true that the doctor is not alone in exercising this role. The town-planner, confronted with the need for a highway to serve a large conurbation, and the wish to preserve green open spaces, and with the demands of the promotor as well as the wishes of the inhabitants, voices an opinion structured similarly. However, there are two essential differences. The competence of the doctor sanctioned by law in fact makes him more than a person consulted, and he becomes the true 'decision-maker', as the term goes today.[4] This decision arbitrates between essential values, those of security and liberty, to retain the language of the time. The originality and grave nature of what will become the ' "psy" function' is that it elevates expertise to the level of a veritable magistracy.

Hence there is perhaps something missing in analyses of the type made by Freidson and Szasz, and by A. T. Scull, who made on this basis a remarkable study of the conquest by English psychiatrists of a monopoly in the treatment of madness at the beginning of the nineteenth century.[5] What is missing is that they fail to make us understand why the trap functions. Why does such an act of dispossession always work? Why has the psychiatrist received the somewhat inordinate mandate to transform utterly the definition of madness, and wholly condition the anthropological status of the insane? It is because his own power springs from other power systems. The process of negotiation, which decides the social destiny of the patient, does not take place between the expert and those who 'pose the problem', but between the expert and other experts or those persons responsible who have a mandate (and the power) 'to resolve the problem'. It is always a matter of equilibrium, of exchange, of competition between the representatives of various mechanisms: justice, administration, the police . . . If anyone exists who has never been asked for his opinion regarding his 'treatment' it is certainly the insane person himself.

Thus it is perhaps worthwhile to follow in some detail these strategies of 'responsible' specialists through those means that mental health specialists have exercised in the process of 'taking power'. In fact, it is a threefold strategy of conquest, one carried on unevenly towards its goal. Whereas the mental health movement ensured without much difficulty not only medical, but administrative, domination of a part of the hospital structure, it started to impose its paramountcy at a pivotal point, where the asylum and the outside world meet over the problem of admissions. It also, using medico-legal expertise, attempted with greater difficulty to break through into that outside world, one that is also more promising for future developments.

The New Managers

The first line of expansion of the mental health movement consisted in annexing the administrative functions within the hospital.

During the post-revolutionary period the situation of the hospitals and the hospices was catastrophic. As we have seen, the initiatives of the Legislative Assembly and the Convention had disorganized the former complex of hospitals without there having been time to set up new structures. The abolition of the religious orders, the selling off of an important part of the hospital patrimony as the property of the nation – these acts brought an acute crisis that was prolonged for a long while after such measures had been revoked. Under the Directory most institutions were short of staff. Famine was often rife, many refused admissions and in certain cases even tried to put their inmates out on the street.

By giving up a national programme of assistance (see chapter 2), the post-Thermidor regimes unloaded on local administrations the task of dealing with this situation. From Year V onwards, it was therefore administrative commissions under municipal control in the provinces, and then, in Paris, from Year IX, the General Council for the Administration of Hospices which assumed the task of restoring order.[6] In such a muddle a new formula, capable of ending the confusion even in a limited area, had every chance of being adopted. This is what could be observed, first of all in the Paris region, in the case of the insane.

The Directory (27 Prairial, Year V) abolished admission of the insane to the Hôtel-Dieu and closed the 'minor institutions', which, together with Bicêtre and the Salpêtrière, had taken in the incurable. At the same time Charenton (which had been closed under the Convention) was re-opened and raised to the status of a national institution for the treatment of the curable insane. But almost immediately it was swamped by patients paying board and lodging either personally or through the city of Paris. About 1800, therefore, there still did not exist in Paris any general admissions structure for the assistance of the insane.

As soon as it began to function, the Council of Hospices, motivated by the ideas of Pinel, wished to acquire two former convents in the Faubourg Saint-Antoine so as to devote them especially to the treatment of the insane. Negotiations having failed, the Council then undertook the transformation of Bicêtre and the Salpêtrière. From 1806 these two institutions were enlarged, modernized and equipped with treatment beds (180 at Bicêtre from 1806 onwards), and the squalid rooms were done away with. Five distinct areas were marked off based on the classificatory requirements of Pinel. The latter, according to the eulogy delivered by Hallé before the Academy of Medicine in Year XI, ruled over 800 of the female insane at the Salpêtrière, providing them with all the help science could give.[7]

Thus before the 1820s the Paris institutions met roughly the criteria laid down by the mental health specialists. Between 1801 and 1821, Desportes, the administrator, who was a member of the Council of Hospices, reckoned a total of 5,075 discharges as compared with 12,900 admissions, figures that were fairly impressive (as was also the number who died – 4,968). The average stay of the insane released in 1821 was 80 days for men, 149 for

women. In short, rates are comparable to those of an era very close
to our own. In this highly 'medicalized' environment they were not
content to administer: experiments and innovations occurred. For
example, young epileptics were forced to live alongside cows for a
long while – a therapeutic experiment, but farcical and based on
scientific criteria not easily discernible.[8]

In the provinces the situation was much less satisfactory because
of the distance of mental health medicine from the centre of values.
In his celebrated report to the Ministry of the Interior in 1818,
Esquirol reckoned that for the whole of France there were only eight
'special institutions'. Those who submitted to 'medical direction'
were even fewer. Elsewhere the insane were mixed up together, as
they were under the *Ancien Régime*, in hospice quarters, beggaries
and prisons. Esquirol contrasted the condition of the insane in most
provincial institutions with the medical norms approximately
respected at Charenton, Bicêtre and the Salpêtrière:

> I have seen them covered in rags, having only straw to protect them
> from the cold humidity of the flagstones on which they lie, I have seen
> them roughly fed, deprived of air to breathe, of water to slake their
> thirst, and of the things most necessary for living. I have seen them in
> wretched holes that are cramped, dirty, filthy, lacking air and light,
> chained up in dens in which one would fear to chain the wild animals
> that the government's extravagance maintains at great expense in the
> capital. This is what I have seen almost everywhere in France, this is
> how the insane are treated almost everywhere in Europe.[9]

However, from the 1820s onwards, the situation began to change,
precisely as the mental health movement developed. Esquirol, who
joined up with Pinel at the Salpêtrière in 1802, in 1817 opened a
clinical course there for mental illnesses. Although the first doctors
trained in this way strengthened the services for the insane in the
capital, they soon proliferated in the provinces, becoming the *missi
dominici* of the new learning. They gradually replaced the old-style
doctors, for whom service to the insane represented a sinecure. The
task of the newcomers was at least as much administrative as
medical. They altered the material organization of the institution,
discussed the budget and put forward plans for the construction of
new asylums. They did not get their way without disputes.[10] But, as
in Paris, they often succeeded in gaining the ear of the local and
departmental authorities who, although they may have scrimped

upon the financial resources asked for, generally agreed to delegate to these new specialists the management of an especially thorny problem. Thus, by the time of the preparatory work for the 1838 law, the situation had been redressed. Since Esquirol's report the number of 'assisted insane' had doubled (10,250 in 1835 as compared with 5,153 in 1818). There were now 41 institutions in which the insane were placed in categories that were treated separately.[11] In 1835 Ferrus was appointed Inspector-General of lunatic asylums; he gave a fresh impulse to the movement. But then he was invested with an official mandate. He had available the results of the enquiry on the position of the insane that the Ministry of the Interior had requested from the prefects in 1834. He was charged with putting forward detailed proposals, which were intended to arrive at a law.[12]

A threshold had been crossed. A unified movement had grown out of local situations, through the diffusion of the Pinel model. The central authority, by proposing a law, was only, for its part, taking note of a continuous development that has proceeded for over thirty years.

Thus, the mental health specialists progressively laid siege to a section of the hospital space; there was a consolidation and geographical extension of their hold. But the movement did not merely connote progress in the 'medicalization' of madness. Such medical practices were also indissoluble from administrative and managerial ones. The administration was to recognize this by explicitly delegating some of its own power to the doctor. The developing hold of psychiatry in the first half of the nineteenth century, running parallel, as it did, to the expansion of medical practices, signified the progressive recognition of the function of the *medical director*.

This was an impressive conquest if we take into account the fact that, from an historical viewpoint, the hospitals and hospices had been only recently, and then imperfectly, laid siege to by the doctors. This should have been all the more true in the case of the 'special institutions', which inherited their functions of guardianship and discipline from the Hôpital Général and the beggaries. Yet this appropriation of administrative authority within the hospital was a direct consequence of the new technology of the asylum:

[The doctor] must be in some way the living principle in a hospital for the insane. It is through him that everything must be set in train. He directs every action, called upon as he is to regulate every thought. It is to him, as the central actor, that must be surrendered everything that concerns the inmates of the institution, not only as regards medicine, but also everything relating to hygiene. The actions of the administration, which controls the material means of the institution, the supervision that this same administration must exercise over all the staff, must be covert; never will the director question a decision made by the doctor, never will he intervene between him and the patients or personnel. The doctor must be invested with an authority from which none can be exempt.[13]

At the end Esquirol's text opened up a debate that has only been definitively settled, and then to the detriment of the psychiatrists, by the 1968 reform of the statute of public-service psychiatrists, which abolished the functions of medical director. In the mental health era, the position of Esquirol was one of the most moderate, since he still referred to a duality of administrative and medical functions, whilst subordinating the former to the latter. The other direct disciple of Pinel, J. P. Falret, was more categorical: 'I seek in vain the part played by the director, I only encounter there that of the doctor.'[14]

Indeed, on what basis could be founded any autonomy of an administrative authority, when the moral treatment orchestrated by the doctor constituted the only real law in the asylum? If it were true, as Pinel's son himself, Scipion, said at the time,

> that one cannot instill too much into the insane the persuasive force of the power of him who alone holds their fate in his hands, who punishes, pardons and delivers [and that] such should be the unlimited power of the head doctor; then his influence enhances even more the esteem in which he is held, and allows him to regulate all elements of the service, by the impetus he gives to them through a firm will, one persevering in doing good.[15]

Only an absolute medical leadership would be able to carry out such a programme of governance.

Here we touch upon an essential and constant phenomenon in mental health medicine, one which institutional psychotherapy, whether analytical or not, would do no more than rekindle (the paradox is that institutional analytical psychotherapy represented the ultimate expression of the will of medical imperialism in relation to the administration, precisely at the moment when the functions of medical director were about to be abolished). Already Renaudin, in one of the great summaries of the medicine of mental health published under the title of *Commentaires médico-administratifs*, systematically formalized this idea by completely reinterpreting all administrative actions according to a psychiatric matrix:

> When one examines superficially the most important managerial actions of the administration, one discerns in them a form and correlatives which at first sight seem to possess nothing medical about them and not to differ from what occurs in any body. Yet if one studies more closely the elements of the problem that each individual has to solve, one sees that their character is essentially modified.[16]

Thus Renaudin concluded in another text: 'The direction of a mental asylum has become a medical science that is interesting in more than one respect. *By becoming administrators we have become, if I may so express myself, more 'doctor-like'.*[17] And he explained:

> This organization, which we have every reason to consider to be the only normal one, will one day doubtless be applied to all institutions; for the material and moral directions, far from being capable of separation, must be submitted to a unity of view for which the essential condition is the unity of authority . . . Moreover, the doctor is at the heart of the asylum, it is upon him that the moral responsibility rests, and he alone is competent to resolve or study the most important questions; his initiatives give life to the dead letter of the regulations. He is therefore the natural administrator of such an important hospital institution.[18]

This somewhat extravagant claim met with resistance, but in its essentials was to be endorsed. The 1838 law and its applicatory ordinance of 18 December 1839 left the doctor, save respecting a few minimum requirements (the existence of distinct quarters, the separation of adults and children of both sexes), with absolute power over the organization of the internal working of the asylum. At one stroke the problems of authority and hierarchy were in principle resolved, for a long period, by the removal of any authority from those 'collaborators' of the doctor who do not derive the source of their power from him. Hence this first depiction of the solidarity between the members of the 'team', insofar as they are content to embody medical thinking:

Such are the instruments the doctor has available to prescribe the physical and moral regime of the insane and to exercise over the patients his personal and medical supervision. The supervisor receives his instructions in this respect directly from the doctor; he passes on the details of how these are to be applied to the nursing staff and custodians, whose activity is thus coordinated and unified in a way that promotes the service. The doctor does not look after patients directly, he does not act himself; he states the way in which care should be given and in which one should act; he supervises the way in which care should be given and in which one acts. The supervisor is the immediate repository of the doctor's thinking, as it is to be applied to the care of the insane; he cannot alter it, put a different gloss upon it, or assign it an opposing goal; he can only detail it, develop it, and translate it into reality.[19]

Is this a myth of the mental health school? In one sense the technology of moral treatment functioned as a system of rational- izations. Any empirical study of hospital practices shows that the real behaviour of those detained, just as that of subordinate staff, can be organized in accordance with principles – what Goffman calls secondary adaptations[20] – that are diametrically opposed to the explicit finalities of the 'caring' institution. What, however, is important, is that this flattering representation of therapeutic effec- tiveness was able to gain official recognition. It is an indication, to which we shall return, that, at least for the representatives of administrative and political power, what was most important was not what mental health medicine effected in reality on the level of practice, but what it was thought to do by rationalizing away the contradictions of the managers.

Thus the minister progressively appointed an increasing number of medical directors. The movement reached its peak at the end of the great period of the asylum. One statistic in 1863 shows that, out of 45 'special institutions' and hospice quarters (Paris excepted), only 13 were not directed by doctors.[2] As for Paris, a lengthy discus- sion on this question of medical direction was launched by the Conseil Général of the Seine department, in order to settle the question of the siting and organization of future asylums in the Paris area. An administrator as 'serious-minded' as the celebrated Baron Haussmann declared in the course of the debate: 'It is to medical thinking that everything must be subordinated in establishments of this kind.' And Dr Linas summed up the discussions as follows: 'It is

clear that the doctor is the absolute master and the director only the
administrator of his wishes, the executant of his orders.'[22]

Unifying in order to Rule

The spread of Pinel's asylum techniques in the first half of the nineteenth century had another consequence essential for the history of
mental health medicine: the unification of care mechanisms and the
refusal of the mental health movement – right up to and including
the protagonists of this branch of medicine at the end of the Second
World War – to treat the different categories of the asylum population, and above all acute and chronic cases, in separate institutions.

Nor were these things inevitable from the beginning. It will be
recalled that the 'English model' that inspired the reformers at the
end of the eighteenth century proposed institutions for intensive
care, treating 'new' patients for one year at the maximum, at the
end of which, if therapy had failed, they were to be transferred to
hospices for the incurable. Thus when Tenon planned the setting up
of the first French institution devoted especially to the insane, he
naturally reproduced this distinction between curable and incurable,
one that bid fair to become institutionalized in the very name of
modernism.[23] It was also this conception that inspired the first concrete achievements of the Directory. It made Charenton an institution for the curable, which got rid of its failures by sending them
off to Bicêtre and then the Salpêtrière, armed with a certificate of
incurability. Again, Esquirol, in his first project for the overall
reform of the asylum system in 1818, envisaged a special institution
for intensive care in every appeal court town.

Pinel's practice seemed likewise to be hesitant on this point. His
'gesture' in freeing the insane related to those detained at the
Hôpital Général, at Bicêtre, and finally at the Salpêtrière, i.e. to
groups considered incurable or as not worth treating. His
therapeutic optimism, which led him to reject definitive diagnoses of
organic causes, will also be recalled. However, he insisted upon the
need for early treatment; the largest proportion of the insane could
be cured in the year that followed the onset of their illness, and the
prognosis becomes more and more gloomy as time passes. Above all,
there were categories of the insane that Pinel considered not
amenable to any treatment, for reasons that were more moral than

properly medical: they were those whose rebelliousness or 'perverse inclinations' hampered any collaboration with the doctor in the task of cure. In the examples that Pinel took, such incorrigibles were women, and it is abnormal sexual usages, debauchery, masturbation or homosexuality that made them irredeemable:

> All modest shame is then dead; vice shows itself openly. One sees these unfortunate victims of debauchery indulge in the most disgusting talk, and make a mockery of all the means of repression that one can apply: thus there is no help for it but to confine them in isolated rooms, and let them plunge into all the filth that their brutish imagination may suggest, without infecting others by their example.[24]

But whether 'incurability' proper, or irreversible perversion – why not, as the 'modernists' will suggest later, frankly consign such irredeemable cases to less expensive institutions and make the asylum a place for intensive care?

It was the logic of the asylum technique itself that in fact would resolve the question. The referent of moral treatment – even if it functioned in part as a rationalization – would progressively unify the hospital sector and make it a 'therapeutic environment' that was as homogeneous as possible, taking into account the existence in it of different categories of the insane. For, if there were several kinds of madness, the doctor's power itself, as displayed in moral treatment, could neither be shared nor limited. Even when he did not cure, he still treated: 'Whatever the circumstances of admission, placement in an asylum has only one aim, that of treatment of the affliction whose existence is attested to on the medical certificate. It would therefore be wrong to believe that one should restrict efforts directed to this goal only to those cases capable of being cured. The doctor's task could not be limited, for he must never forget that, particularly *vis-à-vis* the insane, his mission consisted sometimes in curing, often in assuaging, and always in comforting. *Every insane person is therefore a sick person who must be treated*; and consequently must be subjected to attentive observation.'[25]

Parchappe, finding that from 1851 onwards the choice between one single institution and separate institutions had been in reality decided, gave ultimate expression to the 'unitary' attitudes of the mental health specialists:

The curable and incurable insane can be assembled and brought
together in one institution without the presence of the incurable being
an obstacle to the effectiveness of the treatment of the curable insane.
Their presence, on condition that suitable divisions can be arranged,
is even, in the hands of a prudent doctor, a powerful adjunct in
assuming and preserving a supremacy over the curable insane and in
imposing upon them the habits of discipline that make up an essential
part of the moral treatment.[26]

There has been an open struggle throughout the history of mental
health medicine between a selective medical and technical approach
– and thus one that *rejected*, one which wishes to choose its patients so
as to treat them intensively – and a globalizing trend, which ill
distinguished therapy from public assistance, or acute from chronic
cases. The latter trend discarded the notion of incurableness –
doubtless for humane reasons, but also because it marks the extreme
limit of its power. The mental health specialists threw all their
weight into causing this latter attitude to prevail. On the whole they
have succeeded – the 'sector' is even, as we shall see, devised in part
in order to make this choice a viable one – because the conjunction
of technology and the mechanisms that they set in motion imposed
this option. For them, to make madness a medical matter did not
consist in treating its acute attacks (that had been attempted before
and was to be again after the crisis in the asylum system). The
founding act of the first mental health medicine was to cause from
the polymorphous masses of the former detainees one single
category to emerge (mental derangement is singular, even if it consists of species; it was later that there would be mental *illnesses*). This
category was included in a single institutional framework (even if it
was essential to classify, as regards their location, the various groups
of patients) under a single medical direction. If one can reproach the
mental health movement with having had a somewhat narrow conception of mental illness, at least that conception was coherent. But
this was because it obeyed a logic that was as much administrative as
mental. The two should go hand in hand, and it is at this price that
the progressive assault upon the hospital could be systematically
undertaken. The imposition of the 'special institution' as the sole
mechanism for care, the refusal to recognize absolute differences
between the different species of mental illness, and the appropriation
of the administrative prerogatives of the director – these were
different elements in a single strategy that had been related to 'moral

treatment' as its reason or rationalization. The deployment of this same power was manifested in controlling the very inmost being of the patients, the staff and the venture of the asylum itself.

Thus the persona of the mental health specialist, who completely dominated a part of the hospital complex, was already something more than that of a mere technician or strict specialist. He assumed those tasks of administrative organization and social disciplining that flowed both from his professional skill (or from that which he pretended to, or others attributed to him), and also went beyond these. This increment of skill, spreading out from the focus of the practices in the asylum, would ensure outside it his recognition in the new role of expert. Yet, whereas the accretion of power occurred within the asylum at the expense of administrative authority, it would then prevail to the detriment of legal authority, with the support first of local, and then central, administration.

The Certificate of Non-conformity

The problem of admissions appears to be a limited, technical one. Yet, situated at the pivotal point between the world inside and the outside, commanding access to patient status, even in the eyes of contemporaries it brings out the ambiguities in the function of expert:

> 'The fortune, the life, the honour of these sick people, their relatives and the persons who surround them, and public order itself, would be compromised if the insane were not prevented from doing harm by assuming physical charge of them . . . The suspension of the right possessed by each individual to dispose at will of his person and property is so grave a dispensation from common law in the social order that one is at first surprised that doctors, and above all jurists, have not indicated positively those cases where an insane person can and should be deprived of his liberty. It is astonishing that the law in all countries has not established any rules at all to indicate the cases requiring the suspension of an insane person's liberty and to fix the procedure to be followed when this suspension, if judged necessary, is implemented.[27]

Yet the question was even more complicated than as stated here by Esquirol. It was not only a question of there being a gap in the law, or the absence of a law, but of the real impossibility (see chapter 1) of bringing forward a measure that was a direct extension of the bourgeois reform of the law. Esquirol tried to narrow down the problem as closely as possible by making it a question of *periods of time*, postulating 'a law to regulate the measures of isolation and legalize the series of acts that intervene between the onset of madness and interdiction'.[28] In fact, it was interdiction itself that would be suspended so as to be replaced by a legitimacy of a quite different type, based more on medicine than the law.

The answer was first provided in the practices that were followed. Concrete procedures were set up, and it was when these had progressively displaced the initial contradiction that the law had no alternative but to sanction them.

Here also Paris played a pioneering role. The population density of the conurbation meant that very soon a critical threshold was crossed concerning the admissions problem. An initial solution was found by playing on the difference between 'acute' and 'chronic' cases, the institutional implications of which have already been seen. A discretion was instituted for conditions of crisis: the administrative authority could take custody of an individual in a case of emergency and place him in a hospital. But this was conditional on it being a *provisional* measure. It could not be extended without the court having to pronounce through the procedure of interdiction. Chaptal, the minister of the Interior, on 18 Vendémiaire, Year X, issued regulations for admission into hospices that contained in Article 7 some 'special rules for the admission of the insane'.[29] As for those 'acute' cases who might later turn out to be incurable, their case was carefully provided for in a supplementary measure promulgated on 8 Brumaire in the same year:

> When insane admitted into hospitals for the sick are judged incurable by the para-medical officers to whom their treatment is entrusted, the commission shall cause them to be admitted for settlement into institutions designed to serve as refuges for incurable cases. This admission, which is essentially provisional, will only be made definitive when their condition has been pronounced upon through an authenticated judgement, to effect which the commission, if there is no request from the relatives, shall be bound to instigate through the ministry.[30]

This solution did not carry the day for two reasons. First, the cumbersome nature of the judicial apparatus made it incapable of assuming that part of the task imposed upon it, namely, the legalization, by interdiction, of the segregation of the incurable. This does not mean that at first it did not attempt to apply this process. But from the beginning, the slowness and costliness of the procedure made it impossible to follow. A letter from the prefect of the Seine department of October 17, 1806, leaves no doubts on this score:

> The court, through one of its members, proceeded to the visits and interrogations as prescribed. But the numerous forms that the laws presently existing on this matter prescribe to be followed, and the considerable expense arising from each interdiction, to date have not allowed a single one of them to be completed. The court was even forced to suspend its operations because the resources of the insane were often insufficient to pay the expenses.[31]

Thus in 1821 Bicêtre housed only 18 under interdiction as compared with 651 insane deemed incurable.[32]

Secondly, the institutional dichotomy between establishments for treatment and establishments for the incurable on which this procedure was based, was at the same time undermined by the practices of the mental health specialists, as we have seen. This same year of 1806 saw the opening of treatment sections at Bicêtre and the Salpêtrière. Mental health science, whilst insisting on the desirability of early intervention, refused to fix a time limit for treatment. Another fact made the situation worse: only the institutions of Paris had much repute for the medical treatment of the insane, who flocked to Paris from all over France.

The Conseil Supérieur des Hospices of Paris, whose reforming role has already been seen, was thus impelled to take the situation in hand. It progressively installed a parallel procedure giving doctors the preponderant role. From 1802 onwards emerged the distinct role of the medical certificate, which represented not only a technical diagnosis, but the attestation of an expert who officially decided an individual's future: 'The central bureau can only admit those individuals whose state of insanity is evident, or those provided with a certificate attesting to this and signed by two doctors and two witnesses of acts of madness.'[33]

Even those insane committed by order of the prefect of police had to pass through the central bureau of the hospices, which in this way controlled the admission of emergency cases (this was the origin of the 'special infirmary' of the institution for incurables). In 1806, when treatment services were set up at Bicêtre and the Salpêtrière, the admissions procedure was based upon the medical certificate. There was no longer any substantial difference between admission to a centre serving the insane and to an ordinary hospital.

The major part played by medical control prevailed in another important aspect of the way responsibility was assumed for the insane. In the confused state of institutions and legislation existing at the beginning of the nineteenth century the number of private hospitals had grown considerably. At the end of the 1820s there were more than 200 that could admit the insane, and many of their directors were suspected of being lured by profit and of falling in with the wishes of families seeking to get rid of one of their members.[34] In 1823, to regularize this *de facto* situation, De Belleyme, the Prefect of Police, issued an ordinance important because it would be one of the bases of discussion for the law of 1838. The opening of a (private) hospital was made subject to the authorization of the prefect of police, who also had to audit the admissions registers. The prefecture doctors had to verify the validity of the grounds for admission. The hospitals had to be directed by a doctor, who was obliged to reside in the institution. The royal prosecutor was to be advised of every admission and a commission formed from members of the Conseil de Salubrité would visit all such hospitals regularly.

Thus preliminary steps were taken towards that collaboration of administrative, judiciary and medical authorities that would characterize the law of 1838. Yet, although these were called upon mutually to support one another, they did not all enjoy equal ranking. The medical authority enjoyed a *de factor* privilege, for it possessed the function of expertise: the certificate that validated or invalidated the condition of the illness in fact decided whether detention was justified or not. Moreover, only the doctor was continuously present in the institution, whereas the intervention of the other responsible authorities was intermittent and, in practice, would become optional.

The result was that practically, both in public institutions and private hospitals, in Paris at least, the essential part of the admissions procedures progressively passed under medical control. In the provinces the situation was very mixed, but here it was on the whole characterized by a time-lag for such a medical take-over. In numerous regions, as for instance at Dijon, the local administrative authorities were only too happy to require respect for strict legality, under a judgment of interdiction which was so difficult to obtain, so as to avoid assuming the burden of too many of the insane.[36] But these practices appeared outmoded. They were not capable of meeting the new requirements. *A contrario*, therefore they highlighted the prestigious role played by Paris, which appeared as the innovator both from a medical and administrative standpoint.

During the discussions preparatory to the law of 1838, the mental health specialists consulted would refer in glowing terms to this Parisian model, which gave so much the lion's share to the doctor. Thus Scipion Pinel declared: 'Unless we are mistaken, in Paris the detention of the insane now requires formalities that seem to us to afford every surety.'[37] Esquirol said:

[The law] has only to generalise throughout the kingdom the measures for isolation that are already employed in several departments, and particularly in Paris. Over thirty years of applying these measures proves their effectiveness. Thus no individual affected with a mental illness can be isolated and shut away save on a certificate signed by two doctors, who must confirm the necessity for detention.[38]

These procedures relating to admission had their counterpart in those for discharge. This was much less discussed, inasmuch as the problem of an indefinite stay in a medical institution only exceptionally gained the light of day. Yet on this score also the doctor exercised effective sovereignty. In reality, it was the whole status of the detained person, from his admission to his hypothetical discharge, with all the implications for deprivation of human and civil rights during his detention, that depended upon medical authority.

In this concert of praise from the mental health specialists for the success of their own strategy, there was only one discordant voice, that of Ferrus:

This exclusive authority of the doctor has always seemed exorbitant to me, and I am strengthened in this view by the major difficulties I find in exercising it . . . All such questions are so knotty, so bristling with difficulties and subject to dispute, that it seems prudent to me not to limit their resolution to one single man, no matter what surety his knowledge may afford, and however incapable one may suppose him to be of abusing the prerogatives attached to his functions as a mental health doctor. . . . Finally, and let it be said for the last time, the present state of affairs is too imperfect, it may give rise too easily to arbitrariness, or merely to error and carelessness, it chimes too little with our other social guarantees for it to be put up with any longer, for my conscience. [39]

Ferrus concluded with a proposal for a new law that would give the dominant role to the judiciary. He would not be followed in this matter either by his colleagues, which is understandable, or by the government or parliament as a whole. The practices now set up gained such coherence that by 1838 they seemed to provide a solution to the contradiction pointed out by Esquirol. [40] Yet by sanctioning them the legalism of the law itself was to be stretched: its authority covered an element of decision that was not included in interdiction, and which was not of a juridical but a medical kind. The authority of the expert was thus to be legitimized by the law.

Monomaniacs and the Insane

Although recognition of the competence of doctors over admissions was still located on the boundary where 'normal' society meets the enclosed institution, the first clear sortie that the mental health specialist made outside the asylum consisted in setting himself up as an indispensable part in the functioning of the judicial apparatus.

The problem apparently, whether looked upon from a medical viewpoint or from that of justice, was neither novel nor central. It was not new because (see chapter 2) some kind of role for the doctor as the ancillary of justice had arisen very early on through witchcraft cases. It did not appear to be central either, because at the beginning of the nineteenth century a clear division seemed established between what fell within the purview of medicine and that of justice. Thus Article 64 of the penal code, which moreover revived ancient judicial practices, recognized that there 'is neither crime nor offence when the accused was in a state of dementia at the time of his action, or when he has been constrained by a force which he cannot resist'.

It is therefore in connection with a problem that is at first sight marginal, introduced by the significant equivalence established in Article 64 between madness and external constraint, that the question would crop up again. Madness and external constraint were absolved from the realm of punishment, because they *exonerated from responsibility*. But the problem arose precisely because of the difficulty in furnishing proof of lack of responsibility in a certain number of situations where the evidence of delirium does not necessarily characterize an act as pathological, and in which, nevertheless, justice cannot intervene because it cannot be assured of the culpability of the accused. The casuistry of psychiatry and justice, so important in the future evolution of both institutions, would develop within this margin, narrow at first sight, but which would progressively be enlarged through all the forms of criminal behaviour in which the responsibility of the person concerned was uncertain. Thus there is a casuistry of responsibility and irresponsibility, or of the voluntary and the involuntary. This is why, faced with this problem, mental health medicine was embarrassed. Let us say generally that it felt comfortable when it was a matter of diagnosing disturbances of the understanding, i.e. a pathology characterized by delirium. Then the case had already been rehearsed and medical authority acknowledged: the diagnosis of the mental health specialist entailed the direct application of Article 64 of the penal code. Yet, faced with involuntary actions in which there was no delirium, mental health medicine would have to furnish proof of its ability to make this new aspect of behaviour a pathological matter.

Now, there was nothing in its tradition that had prepared it to take on this problem. Almost all the cases described by the first mental health specialists concerned disturbances of the understanding. The most innovatory mind of the School, undoubtedly Georget, could still write in 1820: 'There is no madness without delirium.'[41] The few encroachments made by experience on this system had not been granted any theoretical status. It was Pinel who had first been troubled when in his practice he met with 'examples of raving mania, but without delirium or any incoherence in ideas'. These examples 'show how very distinct the lesions of the will can be from those of the understanding, although often they are also combined together.'[42] Yet for Pinel these discoveries constituted a 'surprise'[43] that he could not integrate into his conceptual system, because they constituted 'a sort of enigma, according to the notions that Locke and Condillac have given us about the insane'.[44]

This question therefore came to psychiatry from the outside, from justice. In Chapter 1 we sketched out the complete restructuring the latter had undergone round the notion of contract. As Michel Foucault has shown in *Surveiller et punir*, from the second half of the eighteenth century onwards (cf. Beccaria), it was no longer the purpose of punishment to wipe out the crime or offence by crushing the criminal under the excessive power of the sovereign; it set out to correct an imbalance whereby an individual had incurred guilt through preferring his individual interest to that of the general interest. This was a fundamental change, since it supposed a calculating rationality at the origin of all criminal acts. No responsibility without rationality of the act, and thus no sanction, nor even an offence, without responsibility.

Justice was thus confronted with a problem parallel to that encountered by medicine. Just as the classificatory categories of insanity ceased to be operational in the domain of the will, the impossibility of applying to certain forms of behaviour the new categorization in terms of responsibility and rationality posed a question of principle for justice.

These forms of behaviour, according to Hoffbauer, are 'states that cannot at all be termed madness, but in which it is impossible to overcome the impulsion to this or that action'.[45] Faced with these 'unaccustomed impulsions to a determinate action', Hoffbauer's position was particularly equivocal and betrayed clearly the embarrassment of justice. He could not make such impulsions a pathological matter, since he could not discern in them the classic signs of madness. He could not condemn them either, since the subject was not in command of the impulsion. He thus resorted to an expedient: these 'unaccustomed impulsions' would be considered, despite everything, as being devoid of responsibility. Yet this was to contradict the spirit of the new legal codes, which recognized only two conditions of irresponsibility (cf. Article 64): madness and *external* constraint.

The definition of mental health medicine had therefore to be extended to include a new type of *internal* constraint. Significantly, it was to the end of this embarrassed passage of Hoffbauer that Esquirol tacked on his celebrated note on 'monomania'. The notion of monomania assumed in the psychiatric literature of the times the place of this question. It was the first reply of the mental health school to an uncertainty that was less its own than that of justice. The notion operated, with difficulty, to designate a new area of modes of behaviour that eluded the classic description of madness as delirium. Thus it opened up room for an extension of what was pathological, but at first was ill defined.

Initially it occupied a very modest place. The inventor of the notion, Esquirol himself, at first included it in the traditional intellectualist conception of mental illness. His first definition essentially ruled out mania understood as generalized delirium. Monomania is that 'micro-mania' that is manifested when delirium focused on a special object, moreover leaving intact the reasoning faculty, instead of subverting it completely, as in mania proper: 'The character of mania is a general delirium whose principle lies in the disorder of the understanding, a disorder which entails also that of the moral feelings . . . For partial delirium we keep the term "monomania".'[46] At the very most Esquirol outlined another distinguishing principle by making monomania depend on 'passions that excite, are expansive and gay'. and by adding that, whereas with mania the phenomenon proceeds from a disorder of the understanding to one of the passions, in monomania 'delirium derives its source from disorder of the moral sentiments, which react upon the understanding'. But he said much the same for melancholia, and he continued to characterize monomania by terming it 'fixity and concentration *of ideas*'.[47]

'Criminal monomania' began its career before the courts in this ambiguous form. This is doubtless one of the reasons why it received a limited welcome. Adopted by the defence, which was only too pleased to have available a novel argument in desperate cases, it was denounced in the courts by a large number of magistrates, who saw it merely as a skilful manoeuvre or a tautology, consisting simply in dubbing as homicidal monomania the criminal act itself, with the sole aim of rendering it guilt-free. A lawyer, Elias Regnault, would win for himself a certain degree of success with a pamphlet entitled *Du degré de compétence des médecins dans les questions judiciaires relatives aux aliénations mentales*, in which he refused mental health specialists the slightest right of audience in matters of justice: 'Let us repulse these courtiers of humanity who claim to do honour to it by making out a crime to be an illness, and a murderer a madman.'[48] One magistrate declared that if monomania existed it should be cured on the Place de Grève (the square for executions) and another counselled: if an accused person has a monomania to kill, have the monomania to condemn him.

The concept was apparently too fragile, at least in this form, to sustain the manoeuvre that was aimed at: to win a share in the traditional prerogatives of justice. Hence the mental health specialists reformulated it. Georget, who in 1820 asserted that there was no madness without delirium, distinguished clearly in 1829, and in fact within the framework of a discussion concerning expert competence, between 'lesions of the will' and 'lesions of the understanding, or delirium'. These are, respectively, 'firstly, a state of perversion of the inclinations, affections, passions and natural feelings', and 'secondly, a state of aberration of ideas, of disturbance in the combinations of the intellect'.[49]

Esquirol, starting from his confused note of 1819, returned to the question in 1827 and, like Georget, did so within a framework of thought concerning penal responsibility: 'Since that time I have observed forms of madness without delirium, and have had to submit to the authority of the facts.' These new facts are principally revealed in the activities of expertise itself. They

> show that if the insane, deceived by delirium, hallucinations, illusions, etc., kill, that if the insane, a prey to a *reasoning monomania*, kill, after having premeditated the homicide and reasoned about what they are about to commit, there are other monomaniacs who kill because of an instinctive drive. These latter act without conscience, without passion, without delirium, without motive; *they kill in a blind exultation, instantaneous and independent of their will*; it is in an outburst of monomania devoid of delirium.[50]

In 1840 Marc gave ultimate shape to this doctrine of monomania:

> Since the facts demand it, we must therefore admit two kinds of monomania, the one instinctive, the other reasoning. The first impels the monomaniac, through an original feebleness of the will, to commit instinctive and automatic actions that are preceded by no process of reasoning; the second determines actions that are the consequence of an association of ideas.[51]

This is a somewhat muddled distinction, and the notion of a pathology of the will or instinct which supports it cannot be accepted without misgivings.

Yet it was not so much the notion of monomania that was in itself important as what, through it, was sought as its theoretical elaboration, and as the delineation of a field for practical intervention. The fate of the notion itself was fragile and fleeting. From 1854 onwards Falret meted out sound criticism of it, declaring that one would not be able 'to have a complete idea of the motives that impel the insane to commit some of their acts save when one has rid oneself of the error of monomania'.[52] The question gave rise to two important discussions at the Society for Medicine and Psychology in 1853–4, when it was violently attacked, particularly by Morel, and in 1866, when it appeared completely outmoded.[53] What was important was that a strategy existed, relying upon approximate knowledge, which it elaborated and transformed for the most part for the needs of its cause: namely, so as to carve out for itself an area of intervention in those peripheral regions where the judicial apparatus functioned. Falret, with a fine display of frankness, admitted it:

> Administratively and legally we are not dealing with absolute certainties, but with mere possibilities and strong presumptions. Now, it is on this new ground that doctors must agree to take their stand. We can no longer dodge this urgent question and brush it aside by refusing to accept it. If we refuse to study it, others will decide it without us, in spite of us, and against us.[54]

Such an undertaking naturally stirred up resistance and unleashed polemics, such as that inspired by Elias Regnault, to which Leuret replied at length in the *Annales d'hygiène publique et de médecine légale*. In several circumstances mental health specialists intervened as a veritable pressure group, in order to win a decision by proving their 'special competence'.[53] Yet this rivalry between the representatives of the two factions did not rule out a certain complicity between them, provided that exaggeration between opposing systems could be avoided, a request voiced in the introductory passage to the section given over to medico-legal questions in the first number (1843) of the *Annales médico-psychologiques*. Now, on the whole the mental health movement had carefully guarded against such 'excesses' by upholding a double requirement: to make it impossible for an insane person to be convicted, but also for a criminal to be declared innocent by being wrongly imputed to be mad. 'May it please God', cried Esquirol,

> that we advocates of materialism and fatalism should not wish to create and defend theories subversive of morality, society and religion. We do not claim to set ourselves up as the defenders of

crime, nor to transform great acts of criminality into outbursts of madness; but we believe that the doctrine of monomania is something other than crime excused by crime.[56]

Georget, who had adopted a fairly liberal stance, was disavowed by Marc in these terms: 'To see monomaniacs everywhere is to come to the point where one does not see them anywhere. In spite of the great merit of his work, the late Georget seems to me to have been wrong, and in wishing to spread the doctrine of monomania he has perhaps brought it into disfavour in the minds of criminologists.'[57] Yet Georget himself had strongly emphasized the fact that in trying to establish the dividing line between criminality and insanity by relieving the mentally ill of responsibility the aim was not to excuse all crimes: 'He who would uphold such a doctrine in theory or in practice would himself have lost his reason . . . The view that equates the effects of the passions to those of madness appears to us to be both erroneous and dangerous; it tends to confuse two different states and place on a par immorality and innocence, the assassins and the insane.'[58]

Thus there was no syncretism, and, in principle, no will to annex the prerogatives of justice. Such an expertise sought to be strictly specialist. It claimed to mark out spheres of competence, eliminate areas of uncertainty, and separate out floating categories of the insane. In short, it was a matter of giving everyone his due, – the insane to the psychiatrists, and criminals to the judges. Thus Lelut, after having deplored the fact that, between these two types of specialist, both equally honourable, there existed 'a spirit of antagonism and, as it were, mutual suspicion which, amid the pomp of criminal justice, has more than once given very sorry results', summed up the explicit intentions of the mental health specialists as follows:

> I am far from wishing to enlarge the ambit of madness so as to remove in this way from the effect of the laws, and the sword of justice, errors, offences and crimes that must strike fear into society and that it has the right to punish. I share Aristotle's opinion: before the individual comes the family, before the family the body politic, before the body politic the State. Therefore let us restrict to its narrowest confines the circle of unreason, that unreason which belies or destroys free will and causes guilt to vanish away. Yet once this circle has been drawn, let those unfortunates who have been placed

within it by virtue of their condition, and who step outside it in order to carry out a dangerous act, see opening up before them, not the gates of the prison or penitentiary, but the doors of the charitable institution.[59]

This is why mental health medicine first gained a sphere for intervention through cases that, in short, were offered to it by the judiciary, because they posed for the latter an insoluble riddle. We have in mind those hugely monstrous and motiveless crimes that filled the chronicles of the time at the beginning of the nineteenth century: Léger, Papavoine, Lecouffe, Henriette Cormier, Pierre Rivière.[60] These exceptions, which were literally staggering, question fundamentally the right to punish. They were acts that were so outrageous that they cannot be categorized in accordance with any motives. They put to flight any rational justification for punishment, because they cannot be measured against any yard-stick. Therefore, let the mechanisms for the management of madness take over. One should certainly take into account profes-sional sensitivity, esprit de corps, the defence of areas that have been delimited by tradition – all these increase the lack of understanding and the number of quarrels. Yet fundamentally the mental health operation that marked out new sectors of behaviour as pathological was complementary to the judicial operation, which sought to refur-bish the right to punish by placing it on an entirely rational basis.

A Conquest that Burns its Boats

However, although such exceptions are not liable to condemn judges to unemployment, they are not destined either to remain pictur-esque dummies in a chamber of horrors. As Michel Foucault states, these huge, rare monsters in the annals of crime will engender a host of petty perverts, psychopaths, abnormals and other degenerates – right down to 'the delinquent child'. The discomfiture of the judge shows itself less in the spectacle of great, bloodthirsty crimes than in the daily task of sorting out family and social influences with regard to minor offences, or in envisaging the effectiveness of a punishment in some case or another. Rational and responsible judgment shifts from the criminal act to the individual person, who is assessed according to his deep motivations, the vicissitudes of his life, family and social relationships. To take into consideration these dimensions becomes essential both in weighing up the sentence and in assessing the possibility of rehabilitation. The 'service' that the mental health specialist rendered the judge at the beginning of the nineteenth century could therefore be continued on a different scale; namely, it was shifted qualitatively whilst being increased quantitatively. Through monomania psychiatrists achieved fairly satisfactorily the difficult task of giving an answer to the reason for what, socially, they did: to spell out the degree of subjectivity, in order to classify those forms of behaviour that remain problematic in other classifications, and which cannot therefore be managed by the other mechanisms. For to classify is to manage, by virtue of a social mandate. The diagnosis determines the institutional fate. First, the asylum or prison, depending on whether or not the accused is acknowledged to be a monomaniac. But later, and more subtly, the gamut of possibilities is enlarged through deploying a range of institutions whose degree of diversification goes hand in hand with a refinement of the matrices for the interpretation and diversification of those groups in the population for whom 'responsibility is assumed'. The activity of expertise then ceases to function as an 'either . . . or' dichotomy: either insane, or criminal. It places the person in question on a scale of responsibility or performance. It becomes a sorting activity, one of detection, orientation and classification. At the same time it is led to embrace a growing number of people. One example of this shift: today 'toxicomaniacs' pose a problem that is equivalent to that of the 'monomaniacs' of about 1820. The same difficulty arises of suppressing these forms of behaviour through the traditional pattern of punishments; the same tendency exists to unload the problem on to the psychiatric service (the law of 1954 concerning 'dangerous alcoholics', the law of 1970 concerning the fight against the forms of toxicomania). And also, with some, the same temptation to refine the psychiatric (or psychoanalytical) classifications in order to respond to this new 'demand'. Whether one is dealing with monomaniacs, toxicomaniacs, or other 'abnormals', there are still experts who think as did Falret: if it is not us who deal with them, it will be others, and it is preferable for it to be us, for we are the most knowledgeable and the most humane (and thus we shall become the most powerful). These claims are perhaps not always pernicious, but their consequence is always to transfer the 'assumption of responsibility' for the subjects concerned to a mandated group of competent specialists.

This 'small' matter of monomania was therefore pregnant with a whole future, which is now our present. But at the time it had already brought about an important shift, on the threefold level of the perception of the insane person, confidence in the validity of treatment, and credibility of the asylum as the privileged 'therapeutic' environment.

Because it was situated on the boundary between the medical and the judicial spheres, the question of monomania focused the attention of mental health specialists on a field of behaviour that was · not a priority for them. We have indeed noted that mental health medicine was built on a differentiating perception (and an institutional cleavage) between the mentally ill, criminals and other deviants. But this operation created a gulf between pathology and criminality, and placed the stress on the guiltlessness of the insane as compared with the other categories with which they had been unjustly lumped, through the relative lack of differentiation effected by the 'Great confinement'. Hence that general benevolence on the part of the first mental health specialists which, although translated into a paternalism that was sometimes tough, was none the less sincere. He who loveth greatly chastiseth greatly. Significantly, the harshness of a Pinel, for example, in the case of certain 'perverts', found, properly speaking, no justification either in his theoretical work or in his practice. He shut them away in rooms and did not speak of them much, as if he wished to forget them. And forgotten they were.

The need to handle more subtly the distinction between the mentally ill and the criminal (for it is still a matter of distinguishing between them) led to a more detailed assessment of the traits they possess in common. At the top of the list, comes the *dangerous* character of the mentally sick. Not that it is a question of discovery here either: from the beginning the dangerous character of the madman colours the way he is perceived. Yet a dual transformation will be effected. On the one hand, irresponsible dangerousness was associated, as we have just stated, with the compassion engendered by the fact that reason, that supreme possession of man, has been lost. Now the danger that the madman presents will be associated with the evil nature of the 'instinctive monomaniac', given over to his wicked inclinations, to indulging his automatic reactions, and to the weaknesses and failures of the will. On the other hand, dangerousness was traditionally associated with great agitation. One had early warning of the outbursts of the 'violently insane', which allowed one to guard against them in advance. The dangerousness of the monomaniac, and soon, particularly, of more tortuous categories of the sick and psychopathic, was unforeseeable, for it is rooted in drives that are undetectable and which can develop slowly in the shadows. Paradoxically, the sick person that one exonerates from responsibility is at the same time half suspected of acting with premeditation: 'Improvement is often only apparent; often there is no manifestation of a return to delirious ideas; the explosion is almost always swift; the individual ponders his projects in silence, and strikes amid the most perfect tranquillity.'[61]

This is as much as to say: if you already hold one of these dangerous 'impulsives', it is better not to release him, even if he apparently manifests signs of being cured. For the mode of discourse has changed: it is no longer a question of a 'return to reason' that redresses the pathological interlude, but of a permanently perverse nature that can simulate the external signs of normality. The practical implication is this:

> The legal doctor fulfils a great duty to humanity by preserving the monomaniac from infamy, by saving him from the hands of the executioner, but the mental health specialist would fail to recognize the sacred rights of humanity by exposing it to new attacks through the patient's untimely discharge. *Every insane homicidal person, I state it for the last time, must be shut away for ever in an institution for the insane.*[62]

Amid the outcry Aubanel demanded new legal requirements and the setting up of secure quarters for the dangerously insane.

The same attitude is valid *before* the commission of the criminal act, opening up possibilities of a new means of tracking down the insane that can be called, if one likes, *prevention*. It ends in intervention that is founded upon the *potential* threat that the sick person presents, without any objective reason for representing it as his real behaviour. Lunier commented as follows on reading one of those small items of news that feature outbursts of violence by the mentally ill, items that were already particularly favoured by nineteenth century journalists: 'If, in order to shut away an insane person, one did not have to wait until he had committed some crime or offence of a certain gravity, one would not have daily to regret such occurrences.'[63]

By abandoning reference to real behaviour in favour of surmises concerning future behaviour, psychiatry began to arrogate to itself a margin of interpretation (and thus of intervention) whose bounds were no longer discernible. This is all the more so because, as J. Falret noted a little later: 'upon reflection, one quickly comes to recognize that Society must protect not only the life, but also the property and honour of individuals, as well as public order. Hence the number of the insane that can, on various counts, be prejudicial to public safety is singularly increased'.[64] We must add that since, by virtue of the official mandate entrusted to him, he can be held responsible in case of 'imprudence', the psychiatrist will tend to stress the danger (even without taking into account professional prejudice).

Let us give one example. An insane person named Griffith had escaped in circumstances that had required great ingenuity. Arrested at an inn, not for having displayed any signs of pathological disturbance, but for not having paid his bill through lack of money, he preferred to let himself be sentenced to seven years in prison rather than admit that he had escaped from an asylum (which tells us a great deal about the living conditions in such a 'therapeutic environment'). He was freed from prison before the end of his sentence for good conduct, found work, and lived perfectly 'normally' until he was accidentally unmasked as a former insane person. This is the commentary by Moreau de Tours when he learnt of the story as told in a newspaper:

> The behaviour of an insane person can in many circumstances resemble that of a reasonable man. The facts given above are one example out of a thousand. Confronted with such facts, one thought comes to the mind of the legal doctor: how many sick people like Griffith cannot but be dangerous when thoughts of murder prevail in them! How greatly can appearances take over and deceive regarding the real mental state of an accused person![65]

This attitude has three implications. First, madness becomes a stigma that adheres to the flesh throughout one's life. If a cure risks being only 'apparent', the only good insane are those in the asylum. The generalized lack of differentiation between the new types of dangerousness justifies, on the doctor's part, prudence regarding its far-reaching effects, since an impression that is for the most part unverifiable may well entail lifelong sequestration. At the same time it is proof of the largely fictitious character of the psychiatric diagnosis, from the viewpoint of knowledge, but a diagnosis essential from the angle of social control: it is through a prognosis of dangerousness, for which even the most scientifically minded psychiatrists have never succeeded in providing indisputable positive criteria, that the balance is weighted heavily against a person, even conditioning completely his social destiny.

Secondly, there begins an era of generalized suspicion. Rationalizing itself, the psychiatric attitude is no longer merely one of help to suffering (public assistance), but is a suspicious gaze cast over every type of social behaviour. Here again the beginnings of the transformation are modest. Thus, from their publication in 1843, the *Annales médico-psychologiques* ran a regular feature that brought together all the small news items that concern those insane implicated in murders, arson, moral offences, thefts, etc., and even trivial incidents. The commentaries were stereotyped. It was always a question of warning against a widespread threat, of affirming the exclusive ability of the new specialist to detect that threat and neutralize it. The dichotomic nature of the antinomy, normal-pathological, still determined this attitude, in the search for the 'truly mad', those whom their simple-minded companions cannot detect. Yet this check was fragile, insofar as the attitude itself destroyed any objectivist perception of insanity: it searched out the hidden signs of disorder behind the appearances of reasonable behaviour. This initiated a reverse procedure whose consequences we have not yet ceased to undergo: it is normality that is suspected of being an 'appearance', and which must be proved before a tribunal of specialists in pathology. Nor should we see in this relativization of the conceptions of the normal and the pathological a dawning revenge on the part of insanity, for so long oppressed by the reason, which would begin to emancipate itself from the latter's protection, so as to put an end to its own ordeal. It is the same normalizing characteristics borrowed from the dominant values in society that continue to provide the criteria on which new judges invalidate non-conforming behaviour.

Thirdly, the asylum no longer bids fair to be the best institutional arrangement to deal with all the problems relating to insanity. It is a significant paradox that, within the framework of an attempt at modernization of the psychiatric set-up at the beginning of the twentieth century, 'progressive' psychiatrists would, medically speaking, turn back nostalgically to the 'pre-psychiatric' system of the eighteenth century. On degeneration, in line with the thinking of Morel who systematized a certain number of facts that first made their appearance in connection with monomania (see chapter 6), they discovered that classic mental health medicine provided too narrow a definition of those groups for whom responsibility was to be assumed. The 'abnormal' category was to be distinguished from that of the 'mentally ill'. If the latter could be looked after in a therapeutic environment, a reception institution was lacking for those who are 'too lucid for the institutions of the insane, but insufficiently responsible for the prison'.

Finally, there was in the Bastille a numerous category of prisoners recruited from among those miscreant degenerate, those *constitutionally abnormal* whose congenital brain deficiencies did not allow their adaptation to the social environment. Even today these kind of abnormals are a scourge against which Society remains almost unarmed. Most of them, with whom psychiatry, legal medicine and comtemporary justice are equally inadequate to deal, are not delayed in being released from prisons and asylums, however patent their dangerous state may be. *And yet, if they are too lucid for institutions for the insane, insufficiently responsible for prison, are they not, above all, too miscreant to be left at liberty?*[66]

The parallel development of hospital practices and those outside the hospital thus gave concrete expression to the basic contradiction discovered in the previous chapter, and in which mental health medicine was caught up in the first half of the nineteenth century. The conquest of the hospital by psychiatry was the most assured and the most regular gain, because the hospital structure offered a set-up in which the technology of mental health could be deployed as in its natural environment. For outside interventions the mental health movement had not as yet any specific technology available. However, this implied more than technical backwardness or a historical time-lag. The export to the world outside of a model constructed in the asylum had a boomerang effect, undermining the base from which it started. For example, when Esquirol stated of the homocidal monomaniac that he 'does not display any appreciable change in the intelligence or the affections: he is impelled by something indefinable that incites him to kill',[67] he doubtless did not realize clearly that such a proposition could not be integrated into the synthesis of the asylum, but ran the risk of shattering it. For how could such an impulsion be reconcilable with the reactive conception of madness that the mental health school had built up, or with the role of the environment and of culture in the genesis of mental disturbances, and the preponderance of moral causes over organic aetiology? And how could such a drive, represented as irresistible, indefinable and mysterious, yield to the technology of moral treatment, which postulated that madness is malleable when faced with the deployment of an armoury of rational means? The place of the incurable may well be in the asylum because, as Parchappe said, by his passive docility he contributes to the reign of order in it. But what of the pervert who is ineducable? Even more so: if the asylum runs the risk of not being the essential place for the cure or detention of such an 'abnormal' case, it is even more inadequate in ensuring *prevention* of those new manifestations that lay on the frontier between pathology and immorality.

Thus, whether what was at stake was to discipline the seething mass of instincts and drives that bubble beneath the lid of monomania, or to intervene in time so as to neutralize them, the asylum began to be outmoded at the very moment when it prevailed as the initial solution.

5

Psychiatry as Political Science

However numerous and progressive they may have been, at the beginning of the 1830s the achievements of the mental health specialists were very sporadic. Moreover, they remained improvised answers to localized problems. Most frequently they had been arrived at by negotiation; in the provinces, with the local authorities, administrative commissions and departmental Conseils Généraux; in Paris, with the Conseil Général des Hospices. Thus progress was made uncertainly, marked by successes obtained one by one. If the positions acquired in this way began to benefit from the authority of custom, they also ran the danger of being called into question so long as they were not recognized by the law. The ultimate stage, that of integration within the apparatus of the state, remained to be achieved. This end-result was itself prepared by a series of steps, and its genesis in this way sheds light upon relationships between state authority and local centres of power. It was not a matter of a centralized machine imposing its will from on high. 'Mini-powers'[1], at first uncoordinated, were progressively organized into networks that became ever more tightly meshed. The final integration merely marked the attainment of a threshold in the development of that process.

Here we shall follow the principal vicissitudes in this alternation of exchanges and reciprocal acts of equilibrium between the practitioners, the mental health specialists, and the political actors charged with the central management of social antinomies. It is the story of an alliance of conflict through which the political authority proper merely arbitrates between pre-existing practices, and which poses for us such questions as: Why did the mental health specialists find in centralized integration of their practices the best means of realizing their objectives? Why did the political power – and indeed, *what type* of political power? – recognize in mental health strategies a means of implementing its own options?

Towards Integration into the State Apparatus

The Napoleonic regime – and one will not be astonished at this – represents the first, manifestation of this generalized will to intervention by the central authority in psychiatric problems. The implanting of an administrative apparatus to cover the whole of the national territory with a tight network of surveillance was also – and perhaps this was its principal aim – to try to pin down 'marginal' groups in the population. On 5 July 1808 the Imperial decree concerning the suppression of begging, whose main features have been analyzed already (chapter 1) was published: the resettlement of the floating masses, their assignment to work as well as to a place of residence. The beggaries were to eliminate the uncontrolled movement of social 'marginals'. The same tactics were adopted for criminals: by a decree of 1813, a network of 23 state prisons was established, one at the seat of each court of appeal.

On 25 March in the same year (1813), another Imperial decree required the prefects to undertake a census of the insane and an assessment of their situation: who provides for their expenses, what treatment is given them, what rules are followed for their sequestration, what abuses require reform, what improvements can be proposed, what proportion of the insane is publicly assisted as compared with those who remain a charge upon their families, etc. Regretting the disadvantages arising from the absence of a common system for the insane, the decree made its intentions clear: 'This state of affairs results in disadvantages from the viewpoint of accountability, uncertainties regarding the sums that need to be allocated in budgets, and continual obstacles to the admission and stay in public institutions of the insane, whom it is nevertheless important to keep shut away from society.'[2]

Political circumstances meant that this enquiry was not followed up systematically. However, the Napoleonic administration kept to its plan sufficiently to decide, even in such difficult circumstances as the month of December 1814, to convert the asylum at Mareville, near Nancy, into a central hospital for admitting the insane of the

Moselle and neighbouring departments. Even on 5 March 1815 the Minister of the Interior took the trouble to send a despatch to the prefect of the Moselle confirming the decision.[3] In fact, it came down to adopting for the insane the solution decided upon for criminals: to set up a score of large regional institutions that would cover the whole territory and thus settle permanently, after the turn of the vagrants and criminals, the last uncontrolled nomads.

An unsigned note in the archives of the ministry of the Interior dated 9 September 1813, confirms this intention, but at the same time evinces some significant hesitation:

> Up to the present there has been no uniform mode of procedure for the treatment and maintenance of the insane. There is a fairly large number of hospices that take in these unfortunate persons. Many others are placed in prisons and beggaries. It is thought that there would be many advantages in putting a stop to such confusion and *in setting up for the insane, following the example of the prisons, a certain number of central institutions* in which quarters would be assigned to those insane that are amenable to treatment and other quarters to the incurable. It is difficult to determine whether institutions for the insane should be considered as hospitals or as places of detention. On the one hand, for the incurable insane, it is a matter of shutting away individuals who could do harm to society, and on the other hand, for the curable insane, to secure means to effect a cure for sick patients and, for the indigent poor who fall into either of these classes, it is a matter of ensuring the existence of individuals who have no means of providing for their needs. It appears that the institutions for the insane are *mixed institutions*, which can neither be classed as hospices, nor as prisons.[4]

If, from 1813 onwards, the need was felt for a public service for the insane, indecision remained regarding the nature of the institutions: merely prisons, or hospitals, or rather 'mixed institutions', the composition of which was not yet fixed? This was because the essentially medical character of the 'special institution' had not yet carried the day at this political level. The 'mixed' institution was a hybrid that placed side by side in one single area two institutions whose official purposes were contradictory: the hospital and the prison.

Six years later, the situation had changed. A circular of Count Decaze, the Interior Minister of Louis XVIII, appeared on 16 July 1819:

The commission I appointed has not yet finished its work, but it has unanimously recognized that the position of the insane cannot benefit from the improvements that are desirable until they are placed in institutions that are designed exclusively for them . . . Living quarters that are healthy and well ventilated, numerous divisions and sub-divisions, complete isolation, constant and assiduous care – these are the conditions that the treatment of the insane demands, these are conditions that it will be almost impossible to give them in other institutions which take in different classes of individuals, and which they will find only in special hospices.[5]

Thus the entire programme of the mental health specialists was endorsed by the Minister of the Interior. What had happened? There had been some very significant exchanges between the representatives of medicine and those of the central administration.

On 27 November 1817, Edouard Lafont de Ladebat, head of the Office for Public Assistance and Hospitals, sent to his minister a note whose content already differed from that in the note of 1813.[6] For the first time the concept of the 'special institution', as it had been set up by mental health specialists in Paris and in some provincial cities, was taken as the general model for an administrative reform. The note also referred to the conditions of 'physical and mental treatment' that required the insane to be classified according to the nature and seriousness of their illness.

On 9 October 1818, there was a second note from Lafont de Ladebat, in which the medical reference was even clearer, and alluded by name to practical collaboration with Esquirol:

At the moment when I was settling down to prepare a report on a subject that merits so much interest, I was informed that M. Esquirol, a general doctor at the Salpêtrière, was busy with an extensive work upon the state of institutions for the insane in France and the changes he would demand. M. Esquirol, the pupil and worthy emulator of M. Pinel, has for several years devoted all his attention to the treatment of mental derangement. He has caused considerable improvements to be introduced at the Salpêtrière, from which he has obtained the most favourable results. He has travelled over almost the whole of France . . . I thought that there was nobody who could be consulted with more profit upon such a subject than this doctor. At my request he has kindly handed me a memoir that is to some extent the résumé of the work he is proposing to publish, and I shall present an analysis of it to Your Excellency in this report.[7]

In fact, there followed a faithful résumé of the Esquirol report. In conclusion, Lafont de Ladebat suggested purely and simply the adoption of the programme of the mental health specialists: the establishment of a score of regional asylums, rigorous classification of the patients, and the preponderance of medical direction.

These two notes remained unanswered until Guizot was appointed in January 1819 as director-general of Departmental and Communal Administration. As early as 19 February, he in turn wrote to Decaze, merely endorsing the note of Lafont de Ladebat:

> The possibility of establishing in large institutions the divisions and sub-divisions that are so useful to the wellbeing of the patients, the option of having available dormitories and exercise yards in common, of bringing together in them all the conditions tending to contribute to the cure of the insane, the possibility of placing at the head of such institutions skilled doctors who, observing and assembling a great body of facts and observations, will be able to draw conclusions that are invaluable for the advancement of science and the alleviation of one of the illnesses most deserving of concern; such are the main advantages that this plan appears to present.[8]

In order to implement this plan Guizot proposed to his ministry the setting up of a commission wielding extensive powers and able to call upon the cooperation of the prefects. Presided over by a doctor who was a member of the Conseil d'Etat, Baron d'Oissel, it was made up of the three head doctors from the three 'special institutions' in Paris (Esquirol for the Salpêtrière, Pariset for Bicêtre, Royer-Collard for Charenton), Desportes, a member of the administrative Commission for the Paris hospices who had rallied to the mental health cause, an architect, and Lafont de Ladebat. Even better, Pinel wrote to the minister a few days later, setting out 'his long services and the classic works he has had published on this subject', and was appointed to the commission in March. The mental health specialists had virtually *carte blanche* for what constituted a real delegation of power on the part of the administration.

The commission immediately undertook the modernization of Bicêtre, the Salpêtrière, and a few other services in the provinces. It sent a questionnaire to the prefects in order to prepare for a general reorganization of assistance to the insane. Esquirol was later to say that these efforts 'marked a new drive towards help for the insane'.[9] More than a new drive, it seemed that all the elements were present for rapid success in defining an overall policy. However, the process was abruptly blocked and halted for 15 years. The mental health movement continued its progress surreptitiously, but the gap was patent between the strengthening of practices and the vacuum that existed at the centre. Between 1820 and 1833, there was no circular at all upon the question of the insane. On the other hand, in the archives are to be found descriptions of the catastrophic situation, such as this note from the hospices division, which is dated 26 November 1822.

> The position of the insane in France demands the most urgent attention of the government. On all sides complaints are arising. Humanity is groaning, public peace is threatened; the evil constantly grows worse, and the authorities lack any means to deal with it. Disorders that cannot be suppressed – a scandal that cannot be prevented – occurring every day, are being caused by the insane, who go free because of the lack of asylums.

The note recalls once more the proposals of 1818–19 and even goes as far as to estimate the cost of building 15 regional asylums for the 9,000 insane that are in need of help.[10]

However, nothing happened. We have to wait until 1833 before the question is taken up once more at central level. On 14 September 1833, the Comte d'Argout, the Minister of the Interior, sent a circular to the prefects that recalled the Napoleonic circular of 1813 and requested a report on the present situation. The Conseil Général des Hospices commissioned Ferrus and one of its members to visit asylums in England and to investigate the ways in which the two Bills of 1827 and 1828 had been applied which, after the uncovering of scandals in British asylums and the appointment of a Parliamentary Committee, announced intentions for reform.[11] Ferrus's report concluded with detailed proposals that were an adaptation of those recommended by Esquirol in 1818.[12] On 25 June 1835 a fresh circular to the prefects was sent out by the Minister of the Interior. The necessity for new legislation was clearly acknowledged:

> Public safety is often compromised by the insane at liberty, murders are committed and fires started by them. The Justice Minister requests the cooperation of the administrative authorities; it is indispensable for the administration to concern itself seriously with devising means to regulate this important branch of the public

service. Since the difficulties of the administration arise from one single cause – the lack of guaranteed adequate resources – these difficulties can only be resolved through legislation.[13]

In 1836 the Special Inspectorate of Services for the Insane was set up and entrusted to Ferrus. The prefects were advised in another circular of his pending visit. They were to collaborate with him in drawing up a precise report on the situation regarding the insane. The finance law of 18 July 1836 provisionally lumped together, until the promulgation of definitive legislation, the costs incurred for the indigent insane with the miscellaneous expenses of each department. In the same year the Conseil d'Etat prepared a Bill that was introduced into the Chamber of Deputies by the Comte de Gasperin, the Minister of the Interior, on 6 January 1837. The process that integrated psychiatry into the mechanisms of the state was now ripe for completion.

Yet why had there been this long peregrination and these failures? It is not sufficient to talk of administrative hold-ups. Over this period of some 30 years the practical operators and political actors had several times drawn close to one another and then distanced themselves again. Why? The question must be considered in relation to each of the partners in turn. First, in the system of practices and doctrines that psychiatry sets out to perfect, what lends itself to being adopted by the political power? Then, what is the type of policy that is discernible from these practices, which integrates them into its workings, and officially mandates them to carry out a part of its functions?

What Can Become a Medical and What an Administrative Matter

A first element in the answer is that if psychiatric developments are taken up by the administration, it is because they are capable of being administered. This is little wonder, because they are constructed to comply with the demands of management.

Thus, for example, Esquirol's celebrated report in 1819, 'Concerning institutions devoted to the insane and the means of improving them'. This had a decisive influence in coordinating the practices applied by mental health specialists with decisions promulgated at governmental level to define what today would be termed an overall policy on mental health. There is no certain proof to enable us to decide whether Esquirol, in his conception of regional asylums, was inspired by the model of the central prisons of the Napoleonic administration, or whether he merely generalized the model of the special institution constructed by Pinel and himself (see chapter 2), neither option being in contradiction with the other. But his exposition, written at the request of Lafont de Ladebat, was constructed as a real expert's report: a summary of the situation, analysis of the causes of the present disorder, discussion of the different means of remedying it, and concrete proposals for reform. On the one hand, the whole argument is given a medical reference, its explicit goal being the improved treatment of the insane. Yet at the same time it is structured around administration: there is a calculation of costs, a comparison of the relative effectiveness of the different options, and discussion of the possibility of generalizing what were 'pilot experiments' before their time, in the event, the experiment at the Salpêtrière.

The 'White Books' of mental health medicine are not of recent date, and they are always addressed to the same audience. In them medical competence divides itself in half and looks at itself in the mirror of administrative requirements, in order to adjust to them. Conversely, the latter are to be found in them, and discover in them a solution to their own difficulties. Hence this exchange between Esquirol and Lafont de Ladebat, and Esquirol and the Minister of the Interior. In other words, there exists: the progressive installation of new practices – administrative demands – a realistic medical transposition of these – reinterpretation of them by the bureaucracy – fresh negotiations between experts – the seal of approval by the mechanism of the state. The logic is identically the same, whether it leads to the law of 1838 or the circular of March 1960 on 'sectorization' (or, if one prefers an American example, the Community Mental Health Act of 1963). Professionals and administrators functionally constitute a pair, because they negotiate on the basis of common options that define what is termed a 'policy of mental health'. It is an affair, as the saying goes, between 'responsibility holders': high officials of the state entrusted with the control of marginal groups, and specialists whose competence is in the field of deviance, essentially the doctors. Since more recent times (cf. the US) a third 'rogue', the specialist in the social sciences, is sometimes called upon to make his contribution, on condition that he endorses the objectives of the 'demanders' and helps the administrator and the professional to negotiate the optimum compromises. Thus both scientific objectivity and the reproduction of a power relationship that is inherent in the social structure are mixed up together. A policy of 'assistance-control-and-guardianship' expresses the view of those who have officially received a mandate to manage the problems of mental illness, whilst ruling out from the outset the viewpoint of those to whom the policy is 'applied'.

In our next book we shall analyse the reciprocal benefits that each of the parties to the compromise has drawn from the 'policy of sectorization'. Yet the way in which this exchange functioned in the nineteenth century already allows us to exemplify the political logic behind any attempt at 'medicalization'.

In the first place, the medical notion of 'special institution' allows one to escape from the administrative ambiguity of the hybrid 'mixed institution', and the insoluble problems of management and efficiency that it poses: under what budgetary head should it be classed, to what ministerial department should it be attached, etc. Yet, through this technical solution to a management problem, a political solution to a question of principle is found.

The contradiction existing between the need for the sequestration of the insane and the respect for juridical rules that should accompany any measure that deprives a person of liberty (see chapter 1) is recalled at the level of principle. On the one hand, it is a matter of safeguarding public security; on the other, that of the liberty of the person. Concretely, it is a question of accepting or rejecting a new type of *administrative internment*, the modern form, but more subtle, of the *lettre de cachet*; the administration draws upon its technical prerogatives for support in order to adopt measures of a political order. For example, quarantine in the case of an epidemic is undoubtedly technically justified. The administration allegedly aims to promote a solution of the same kind for the insane, i.e. to assess, *on its own responsibility*, the opportuneness of a measure that can deprive a person of his liberty. As the Minister of the Interior stated in the preamble to the 1838 law, 'it is a matter of forestalling events such as those included by a watchful administration in its solicitude, for which very events it has been constituted, such as floods, fires, scourges of every kind, the dangers that threaten the public well-being or even the peace of its citizens', and he immediately added this self-justification for the legitimacy of administrative intervention, based upon internal criteria: 'Gentlemen, the time is past when administrative authority was held permanently in suspicion, in whose actions was seen only the danger of arbitrariness. Today its responsibility is real, its procedures legal, its interventions protective. It is recognized that, like all legitimate powers, it provides guarantees.'[14]

This is precisely what the affair is all about. The memory of *lettres de cachet* was still vivid among the class of politicians that had carried the day against royal 'despotism'. The Napoleonic State, moreover, had revived the use of administrative internment against its opponents, and had even begun to employ to this end the burgeoning institution of psychiatry: Vivien, the rapporteur of the 1838 law for the Chamber of Deputies, mentioned detention in asylums for political reasons.[15] Finally, the Restoration police themselves continued practices that were at odds with the constitutional charter. It was not by chance that the most eloquent defender of legal principles was Isambert, the deputy who had been condemned under the Restoration for a press campaign against the practices of the 'scoundrelous police'. Even today Isambert's argument is irreproachable:[16]

> I believe I have demonstrated that what is at stake in this law is a huge shift in power; shifting the magistracy of family law to the administrative authority; putting the judicial authority into conflict with that of the prefects and the Minister of the Interior, in conditions that do not in any way involve governmental policy, but rather place that judicial authority in a state of subjugation, subordinating it to that of the police, downgrading the one and compromising the moral authority of the other. It is another law of disjunction. It is a law that overturns the Civil Code and, in the most serious cases, abolishes the necessary control of the process of interdiction. What the laws of 1790 and 1791 had not dared to grant, save indirectly and timidly, to the municipal authorities, this the government arrogates to itself, and exaggerates. Gentlemen, what is in question is the re-establishing of an ancient confusion of powers, the very principle of *lettres de cachet*, if not the thing itself. The first of all our liberties is at stake, that liberty of the individual guaranteed in Article 4 of the Charter, since one is destroying the judicial guarantees that serve as its basis.[17]

On the level of principle, the contradiction was insurmountable. Mental health medicine would *shift* that contradiction. Isambert, moreover, erred on one point. *Before becoming a medical matter* (and when he intervened, it was in response to the Minister of the Interior, who proposed in his preamble a version of the law that had only a slight medical flavour), when administrative and juridical logic confronted each other without any mediating agency, then properly speaking there was no 'power shift'. Either a gag might be put upon the contradiction, or there might be purely and simply an annexation by one party of the other's prerogatives. *Through making it a medical matter* there was truly a 'shift', i.e. the transforming of the initial situation by the transfer of certain attributes of opposing authorities to a *third power*. This shift constituted the operation by mental health medicine itself, whereby it became part of the political problem.

First, mental health medicine could 'displace' the contradiction because it set itself on the ground occupied by one of the parties and endorsed completely its demands; it insisted upon what the administrative power also demanded absolutely, the *sequestration* of the insane. But it changed the meaning of this by using its own justifications. The notion of 'therapeutic isolation' was the magic agent in the act of alchemy. As has been said, therapeutic isolation was, according to Pinel, Esquirol and the whole mental health tradition, the medical activity that 'effects a diversion from delirium' by 'modifying the evil course of the intelligence and sentiments of the insane'.[18] In an emergency it was the first measure to be taken (it must therefore short-circuit the long drawn-out judicial mechanisms), for it constituted a necessary condition for a cure. Therapeutic isolation was therefore not a *sequestration*, the arbitrary act of a usurping authority: it was a *placement* required by the special condition of the insane person. It was without any doubt a measure as imperative, rigorous and sure as the harshest police custodial action. Yet through it the place of detention became the best therapeutic environment and, reciprocally, the 'special institution' ensured an isolation as effective as that of the best prisons. 'Mental health medicine makes it the first condition for treatment; the family . . . triumphs over its fear of committing an arbitrary act and, using the inalienable rights of reason over delirium, subscribes to the teachings of science in order to obtain the benefit of a cure for the insane.'[19]

The sequence of administrative and police action was: safeguard of public order – arrest – sequestration. It had thus become a medical and humanist sequence: welfare of the sick person – isolation – placing in a special institution – treatment – possible cure. If the wicked-minded still stubbornly insisted on speaking of repression (for plainly it was a matter of the authoritarian exercise of a painful constraint), at least it was fully justified for the most scientific reasons, and carried out by the most competent and most respectable specialists, the doctors. 'A happy coincidence,' as it was admirably termed by the rapporteur of the law in the Chamber of Peers, the Marquis de Barthelémey.

> This legislation must ensure that the woes of a suffering and unfortunate human being are mitigated, and his cure obtained if possible, and at the same time must take measures to remove from a person dangerous to others or to himself the means of doing harm. To attain this double goal it must prescribe the isolating of the insane, for this isolation, as well as shielding the public from their ramblings and excesses, in the eyes of science presents the most powerful means of effecting a cure. *It is a happy coincidence that, through the application of rigorous measures, causes the wellbeing of the sick person to accord with the welfare of all.*[20]

Indeed, it is a marvellously pre-established harmony, which gives the key to the political role of mental health medicine (and doubtless to all forms of psychiatry, for, as we shall see, if modern mechanisms are more subtle, they give expression to the same logic). The shifting of the contradiction that has been operated here must be exactly understood: the contradiction is neither repeated nor resolved.

It is not pure *repetition*, for one has passed from a relatively disappointing mechanism of detention to a more elaborate one of placement, which supposes that a new institutional space has been contrived, a new set of rationalizations constituted, and a new body of specialists etc., appear. It would be a more delicate matter to say who gained and who lost by this. The mental health specialists gained without a shadow of doubt, because it was a question of winning their place in the sun. The patients very probably also, in comparison with their previous situation, but this is already a value judgement. In any case a real metamorphosis of the system had taken place.

Yet it was not here a matter of finding a *solution* to the contradiction, because there had been no complete transformation of the situation. To turn a problem into a medical matter is more to change its ground than to resolve it, because it is to render autonomous one of its dimensions, working on that dimension technically, and thereby so glossing its overall socio-political meaning that it becomes a 'purely' technical question, falling within the competence of a 'neutral' specialist. This is an operation whose effects are felt at two levels. On the 'ideological' plane, it means to resolve or verbally to defuse the contradiction by a new synthesis that at the very least guarantees that the formula worked out was the best possible: 'It is not with a heartfelt joy that one contemplates the isolation of an insane person: necessity is a law unto itself. The calamity resides in the insanity, and not in the measure itself. To cure wherever possible, to prevent dangerous attacks – this is one's duty according to the laws of humanity and social preservation.'[21] The act of force is no longer arbitrary and scandalous, but a solution carefully thought through, which takes into account the interests of all concerned. It reduces prescription to what is immediately manipulable in a technical and scientific framework, blotting out all that is irrelevant in so technical a 'treatment' (psychological or organic).

This logic of subjectivization (or individualization) constituted the specific mode of intervention of mental health medicine and gave it its particular political significance. Thus, in the rationalization and effective practice of 'therapeutic isolation', it was clear that the antinomy between public order and individual liberty was not eliminated. But the second term of the antinomy as a legal position was invalidated and became a 'case' for which to 'assume responsibility'. Henceforth the sole problem would be to know whether the case had been dealt with effectively or badly, according to autonomous scientific criteria. Thus a problem of power first posed elsewhere and couched differently was displaced into an entirely medical problem. Henceforth, with the best will in the world, the doctor, in his medical capacity, would never be able to operate save within this technical framework, in order to refine his armoury of specialized intervention techniques. Medical neutrality had assumed outwardly what it always possessed internally. Necessarily appearing *as if* the set of problems with which it was presented were relevant to its competence alone, it henceforth reproduced, through each concrete intervention, the political choice that determined the social status of the insane person. Thus mental health medicine reproduced social exclusion. But it imparted to it its most 'humane' form by justifying the reasons for it medically, and by treating its effects medically. At least some of the nineteenth century specialists in mental health medicine had the merit of being aware of this. From this humanism, this devotion to the patient, this technical competence, they derived so many professional qualities that were certainly indispensable, but which took their meaning from accept- ance of a social mandate that made their profession subordinate to a political requirement: 'If the individual has rights, society also has rights . . . To disturb public order, to compromise the safety of the person – these are the dangers with which the madman threatens society. That he should therefore lose his individual liberty when it places these social benefits at risk is entirely fair.'[22]

Such clarity of thought will be destroyed for two reasons. The perfecting of new technical processes that increase the scope for intervention by mental health medicine will reinforce its feeling of independence. The professionals will tend to confuse a relative autonomy of a technical kind, which they win by perfecting their instrumentation, with political autonomy or neutrality. At the same time, as these instruments are perfected, they better conceal their objective. In contrast to what can be fairly clearly seen through the brutality of 'therapeutic isolation', the more sophisticated technologies will be both more 'gentle' and better equipped to hide the relationships of force under relationships of meaning. An analysis such as the present one will then run the risk of being termed reductionist, even paleolithic. It is true that minds as subtle as the techniques they employ jib at seeing their practices objectivized.

However, without claiming to reduce a situation to a simplified model, we can begin to understand that it was never gratuitously, nor merely for its own sake, that the apparatus of mental medicine gained power. It was recognized as a legitimate partner insofar as it resolved a difficulty peculiar to the authority or authorities that acknowledged it as partner. Its expansion thus procured for the administrative or political authorities an 'ultra-power' that they in turn used to encompass their own ends.

Two implications follow. First, the equation – which forms part of psychiatric holy writ – of the administrative authority with the evil genius that sabotages or betrays specifically medical initiatives is for the most part a rationalization. Conflict can indeed exist on the level of the technical allocation of tasks and rivalry between the represen- tives of the two set-ups (for example, between the doctor and the director within the hospital). But these vicissitudes occur against the backcloth of a competitive reciprocity between two parties that share the same mandate to manage. Secondly, what is at once perceived as a triumph by the representatives of the psychiatric Establishment – for example, the passing of the law of 1838, or the 1960 circular upon 'sectorization' – can bring a disenchanted awakening. This is all the more painful when, whether naive and/or generous, the medical protagonists, out of professional ethnocentricity, distance themselves less from the most nobly disinterested rationalization of their initiatives. For, in a mental health policy, the specifically mental dimension is, in relation to the whole set-up, only the emergent (and, consequently, the only visible) part of the iceberg. For the alert administrator, the medical dimension is, at best, the means of carrying out his own managerial tasks. It may happen also that it is taken as a mere cover for an operation whose objectives may be at odds with the intentions of the medical protagonists. In the event of conflict, the latter rarely carry weight (cf. the present application of the 'policy of sectorization').

Thus there is a whole problem (which has to be taken up later) regarding the stance of the professionals in relationship to their mandate, and their level of awareness of it. This is one indisputable difference between the situation in the nineteenth century and that today. The mental health specialists stuck to their mandate. They knew what they were doing and wished to do it. Later, in the process of the downgrading of the synthesis of the asylum, attitudes hitherto unknown began to surface: bad faith (not to know, or not to want to know what one is doing), bad conscience (not to wish to do what one is doing), the distortion of the mandate (to wish to use what one is believed to be doing in order to do something else), and nihilism (to do nothing). If we can speak of psychiatry in the first half of the nineteenth century as being a golden age, it is especially because of that happiness, born of good conscience, in having a duty to perform, and encountering only technical problems in carrying it out.[23]

The Political Operators

However, the administrative and political apparatus can realize certain of its objectives through techniques whose respectability is borrowed from medicine. There can be less sophisticated means of disciplining the marginal elements in society and reducing the sources of deviance. One can, for example, imagine that a fascist state would have no truck with the 'problem of the mentally ill', unless it were to contrive for it a kind of 'final solution' as German Nazism attempted to do. Thus it is not enough for doctors to put forward schemes capable of being administered. This technical organization must be at the same time symbiotic with the political options, so that acceptance of the technical proposition appears as a means of realizing the political option. Historically the problem presented itself approximately in this way. Even before 1820 the mental health specialists had worked out a technical arrangement that was capable of resolving certain acute problems concerning the control of marginals in the population. How and why did this technical potentiality become at a given moment a political decision?

'How', asked Esquirol, 'can one restore to these unfortunate people the modicum of care that is due to them from public charity? How satisfy the claims of local administrations who complain about the state of abandonment in which the insane are suffering, and who are seeking means of improving their lot? How can one respond to the wishes of the government?'[24]

Above all, we shall ask ourselves why these 'wishes of the government' were to be carried out through a *medical* synthesis. De Gasperin, the Minister of the Interior, as if he were replying to Esquirol's question in this curious exchange, answers:

> Several different reasons can, as has already been remarked, require the person affected by a mental derangement to be placed in an institution designed for this end: the concern for public safety, compromised by the danger of violence, fires, etc.; concern for the safety of a third party, of relatives and others near and dear, whose lives can be threatened because of monomania; concern for the very existence of the sick person, threatened by attempts at suicide, to which one third of the insane are inclined; concern for public morals, which can be offended at the sight of the insane and idiots wandering abroad in public places; finally, the ever-sacred concern for the treatment of the insane person himself, the success of which, in order to lead to a cure, requires the precautions in question, the principle of isolation have been declared by science to be the foundation for all treatment of the insane.[25]

If we have seen how these different and very divergent 'concerns' can be brought together by mental health medicine on the basis of acceptance of its social mandate, as we have previously analysed it, there remains to be delineated the type of political power that finds its own interest served in confiding to it such a mandate.

Four or five successive periods can be distinguished in the political jurisdiction that separates the Revolution from the passing of the law of 1838. During the first period the practices of mental health medicine were installed in the midst of political upheavals, under the inspiration of social reformers of the stamp of Cabanis. These are enlightened intellects struggling against royal absolutism, but who, once the latter had been overcome, became the convinced defenders of the new bourgeois order. We have seen that Pinel had been reinforced by this group. However, in the first stage, acknowledgement of the merits of 'special medicine' remained restricted to a comparatively narrow circle. The second period consisted of the attempt by Napoleon to generalize and centralize the system. It proved abortive, but one cannot definitely decide whether the failure was at first ascribable to the premature collapse of the regime, or to the weakness of the positions held by mental health specialists at that time. Yet it is likely that, if the Napoleonic administration had had time to set up its system of regional institutions for the insane, it would not have been one that, at least at the beginning, was very much a medical concern. The third episode is when, with the convulsions of the Restoration hardly over, there was a new attempt to set up a service of assistance for the insane in which doctors, under Esquirol's leadership, played the main part. This attempt appeared to be on the verge of success, when it is followed for 15 years by a long eclipse. The fourth episode is from 1833 onwards, when the process is restarted, i.e. immediately after the danger of the July Monarchy being overthrown and sliding into a social republic has been counteracted.

Without claiming to write a political history of that time, we can discern in these vicissitudes some indications of a deep-seated complicity between psychiatry and a certain policy. Moreover, such a perception can be valid beyond this period. A situation of the same kind recurred at least once more, about 1960, at the time of that other great turning-point in the development of psychiatry, as represented by the adoption of the 'sectorial policy'. If certain psychiatrists marvel that even today they have met men like Lafont de Ladebat in the private office of ministers, it is perhaps worthwhile to ask oneself what that 'coincidence' conceals.

Guizot can be taken as a marker. In January 1819 he was appointed Director-General of Departmental and Communal Administration in a ministry that attempted to bring about a liberalization of the Restoration by strict application of the Charter, in spite of the out-and-out opposition of the Ultras. Guizot's functions were apparently technical, but he immediately undertook an ambitious reform both of the administration and of public assistance. Confining ourselves to this latter field, there is not a single sector in which he did not intervene, in the course of one year, by means of numerous circulars. Not only did these concern the insane, as we have seen, but also prisons (three circulars), penal reform (one circular), foundlings (two circulars), the position of hospices and charity offices (four circulars). In that same year of 1819 Guizot was one of the founder members of the Royal Society for the Improvement of Prisons, and his hygienist preoccupations led him to preside over the Central Committee for Vaccines.[26]

It should merely be recalled that under the Restoration Guizot was one of the most dynamic representatives of the political trend that made bourgeois France. From the enlightened minds at the end of the *Ancien Régime* to the present advocates of 'reforms', through the Radical politicians of the Third Republic, a line runs which, before triumphing, underwent a diversity of fortunes and was covered by many kinds of label, but which remained firm on a certain number of principles. In the first half of the nineteenth century the fight was waged on two fronts. On the one hand, in order to conserve the social, legislative and civil gains of the Revolution it was a matter of foiling all efforts to restore the *Ancien Régime*, and, on the other hand, to ensure these conquests through a constitutional framework that placed the interests of those without property outside the political pale. The defence of the Charter as a guarantee both against the nostalgic ambitions of the Ultras and the rising tide of social demands: the controlled liberalization of the press and the administration; representative government calculated strictly on the basis of the amount of tax paid, so as to exclude from any participation in politics those whose possessions did not guarantee an attachment to social stability: under the Restoration these were some of the main options in this programme, for which the group of Doctrinaires inspired by Guizot was the most active spokesman.

The fact that this general policy was strictly interpreted in the field of public assistance has been less often emphasized by historians.

The results of it were not marked by spectacular events, but it had long-term effects that are expressed in social-work policy right up to the present day. It concerns that movement whose philosophy was presented under the banner of 'philanthropy', namely, of a vast policy of subjugation of the poor, unfortunate and dangerous classes (see chapter 3). To recall it in a nutshell: at the very least, to keep the heads of those 'wounded by civilization' above water so that they would not resort to extreme solutions; at best, through an excess of morality and discipline to enmesh them in a tight network of surveillance so as to galvanize them to struggle energetically against misfortune. Thus, without resorting to overt violence, the policy was concerned with stifling the possible focuses of revolt, and even, if possible, of extinguishing them at source, taking preventive action through the inculcation of discipline.

If philanthropy is a policy, we must not be astonished that politicians attempted to carry out its programme. Guizot's career, particularly at the beginning, was one of the best examples of this interpenetration between the two. He struggled against the lack of responsibility of the Ultras insofar as general policy is concerned. This irresponsibility risked jamming the mechanisms of the new society and ending up either with a return to the archaic practices of the *Ancien Régime*, or in a social revolution. His struggle was backed by an effort to reform prisons, asylums, hospices and hospitals, and by an interest in the education of the poorer classes.

Yet Guizot's policy, and the current of opinion he represented was still a fragile one at the beginning of the Restoration. He seemed to be aware of this and redoubled his efforts as Director-General of Departmental and Communal Administration, launching at least one measure of assistance every month. But he held this strategic position for hardly a year. On 20 February 1820 the Duc de Berry was assassinated. Descazes (who had earlier begun to distance himself from the 'Constitutionals') fell, and Guizot resigned shortly afterwards. The second Richelieu ministry, and above all the Villèle ministry that succeeded it, unleashed a campaign of repression against liberal circles. The philanthropic tendency and the mental health movement were affected at the same time, which is an indication of their solidarity, and of the way in which their activities were perceived politically. The Duc de la Rochefoucault-Liancourt, 'the unoriginal patron of all the philanthropic movements on earth', as a police report put it,[27] had to give up or resign from several of his responsibilities.[28] The commission of the insane appointed by Descazes at the instigation of Guizot lost its powers and its work remained unfinished. The medical faculty was closed in 1822 as a result of a student riot. When it reopened, the chair of mental pathology that Royer-Collard occupied was abolished, and Pinel himself, despite his prestige, was dismissed. Esquirol, less politically marked, put his reforming ambitions on one side, left the Salpêtrière for Charenton, and joined up with the Society for Christian Morality.

This Society for Christian Morality is an essential link in the chain in following, on the political stage behind the scenes, the course of philanthropic ideas and the ripening policy of public assistance. Founded in 1821 at the time of the resurgence of liberal influence and (still) chaired by the Duc de la Rochefoucault-Liancourt, then in 1828 by Guizot, the Society brought together the main liberal members of the Opposition who shared the same 'social' aspirations (but who were not at all socialist). Protestant representation on it was considerable, such as the President of the Paris Consistory, Guizot and several of his friends, among them the father of Lafont de Ladebat, and some 15 pastors as against only two priests. The Catholic Church as a whole was on the side of the Ultras, of private charity, and supported the public assistance policy of the religious orders, which was modelled on the *Ancien Régime*; at this time the orders even regained the essential part of the ground they had lost. The Catholics in the Society for Christian Morality, on the contrary, were those philanthropists who defended 'public welfare', such as De Gerando, journalists and liberal politicians, and some enlightened bankers. Among these politicians could be distinguished numerous names who were to play a prominent role under the July Monarchy, and others, or the same ones, who took an active part in working out the law of 1838, such as De Gasperin, the Minister of the Interior who proposed it, Vivien, his rapporteur in the Chamber of Deputies, and Dufaure, the inspirer of the first Article of the law, which dominated its whole spirit.

This Society, ecumenical before its time, laid down in its statutes that 'The initiation of any discussion on points that divide the different branches of the Christian family shall be scrupulously avoided': it had something better to do. Its proper purpose was 'the application of the precepts of Christianity to social relationships'. In other words, private urges towards charity had to be replaced by the reasoned precepts of a healthful philanthropy, or, to put it in more modern language, a complete programme of social action, surveillance and controlled education, had to be developed, directed towards the poor and dangerous classes in society, instead of one that was content to dole out alms to them in extreme situations.

> We may add, gentlemen, that philanthropy, namely, the philosophical method of loving and serving humanity, is your banner, rather than charity, which is the Christian duty of loving and succouring one's neighbour . . . Charity is satisfied when it has comforted against misfortune; philanthropy can only be satisfied when it has forestalled it . . . The improvements made, the (philanthropists') work, far from stopping at this, *sooner or later are transformed into institutions.*[29]

In fact, most future institutions of public assistance, or reforms of the old ones, were brought to fruition in this circle, which, among others, included a committee for the moral improvement of prisoners, a committee for the placement of orphans, and a charity and welfare committee for matters relating to the insane, the sick, the indigent and public hygiene. The work of these committees was carried out in close cooperation with that of the Protestant Consistory, which at this time sponsored a society for the encouragement of primary education, later to inspire the Guizot law of 1833, and a friendly and mutual benefit society.[30] The connections between this militant philanthropy and politics were so close that Guizot was to recruit from among the cadres of the Society for Christian Morality most of the cadres for the Society 'God helps those who help themselves', which galvanized the Opposition in the preparation for the elections of 1828, and whose activities were to be enlarged into a focus for liberal and constitutional agitation. Hence the origin of the careers of a certain number of politicians under the July Monarchy.

There was coincidence in time between this political tendency passing over to the Opposition and the key event that conditioned the attempt at a return in strength of the conservative faction, namely, the assassination of the Duc de Berry in 1820. Yet still more significant was the strict coincidence in time between this withdrawal and the abandonment of the policy of assistance to the insane that seemed on the point of prevailing. Conversely, when the moderate liberals returned to power, they dealt with the most urgent business by suppressing the attempts at radicalization made in the July Revolution. Then they took up once more the question of the insane precisely at the point where Guizot had left off.

However, the situation had veered in two directions. On the one hand, the mental health movement had continued its underground progression on a threefold level: the conquest of the administrative direction of the hospitals, the decisive weight attached to medical certificates regulating admission to asylums, and the acknowledgement of medico-legal expertise by the courts (see chapter 4). But, conversely, a parallel system had progressively developed, backed by the other France, that of the conservative notables and the religious orders. It carried on the tradition of the 'charities' under the *Ancien Régime* and tended to deal directly with families, eliminating intervention by the public authority.

Thus Abbé Jaumet, not content with developing the Bon-Sauveur de Caen, which became one of the model asylums of the time, proselytized in the provinces, where, like Esquirol, he was invited to give his opinion on the construction of new institutions. Above all, it was Brother Hilarion who brought about an increase in the number of private asylums. He was a strange character, who had been treated for four years at Charenton; then in 1815 he retired into the Trappist order, where he read the biography of Saint-Jean-de-Dieu and decided to devote himself to the insane. He founded his first asylum – an 'agricultural and preparatory' one – at Piolec, and then in 1819 a second one in an old château of the Vaucluse. In 1829 he published a *Manuel de l'hospitalier et de l'infirmier*, which was probably the first of its kind.[31] Although dismissed from the order of Saint-Jean-de-Dieu, between several stays in prison for debt he increased his founding activities, setting up or reorganizing the asylums at Clermont-Ferrand, La Cellette, Leyme, Saint-Alban, Auch, Quimper . . .[32]

The activities of Brother Hilarion were only the most conspicuous aspect of a general process that installed a whole network of assistance. The cloak of private transactions provided facilities to preserve 'the honour of families' – and their material interests. If in the provinces the operation was carried on above all through the mediation of religious orders, in the large towns too there was a proliferation of private institutions, but these most usually had a lay director and pursued essentially the goal of profit. It will be recalled that in Paris Belleyme, the prefect, had issued his ordinance of 1828 in order to attempt to rectify the dangers resulting from the existence of over 200 private institutions, many of which took in insane or similar cases practically without any official control.

Faced with this ill-controlled development of a private sector, the interests of the central authority and the mental health movement overlapped. The latter's expansion was threatened, and its 'scientific basis' placed in jeopardy, by these parallel practices. It was one episode in the conflict between the 'enlightenment of science' and the 'spirit of charity'. The private sector, which was above all religious, developed an anti-rationalist and mystical conception of mental illness. Prayers were more effective than medical treatment. Such 'obscurantism' was attacked by the mental health specialists. There exists an abundant psychiatric literature of the time regarding the dangers of religious exultation in sustaining delirium: it was only if religion were reduced to its bare bones of moral precepts that it could be of use, but as a mere *auxiliary* of medicine.[33] Ferrus, in his capacity as Inspector-General, even called into question the practical role of nuns in the asylums and preferred the lay staff of the Salpêtrière. At the time of the discussions on the law of 1838 Brother Hilarion was accused (without being named) of 'not really having the use of his faculties' because he 'thought that, with the help of supernatural means and superstitious procedures that have no connection with those that Science prescribes, he will be able to cure mental illness'.[34] Through the defence of this 'scientific' base the mental health specialists fought for a monopoly in the problems of madness that they risked seeing elude them.

Moreover, for its part, the central administration, however respectful of private interests it may have been, could not allow practices of the *Ancien Régime* incompatible with a modern conception of the state to continue, or even worsen. The constitutional monarchical state had, moreover, been much more anxious to standardize its services of control than one would be led to believe from its 'liberal' label. Thus, in spite of numerous plans and attempts at administrative reform (upheld above all by the supporters of a return to the *Ancien Régime*) it never really turned its back on Napoleonic centralism. The bourgeois class that would prevail with the July Monarchy had an interest, if not in breaking, at least in controlling the symbiosis of the traditional family and religion, which sustained the power of the most conservative Notables. On the particular question of the insane, this preponderance of intervention by public authority in the transactions between clients, turned upon the relationship between the public and private sectors. To make psychiatry a true public service, namely, to give power to mental health specialists placed under the authority of the prefects, was to open up a path that would make madness, that explosion of private subjectivity, literally an 'affair of State'.[35]

The Compromise of the Law

From January 1837 to June 1838 the Chamber of Deputies and the Chamber of Peers constituted the stage on which the different matters at stake in a policy for mental health were confronted: the readjustment of the relations between the administration and justice, the legitimizing of a new, powerful medical authority, which is an episode in the struggle between rural and urban France, between the traditional notables and the bourgeoisie, between relationships in client networks and rationalized social relationships, between defence of family privacy against the intervention of the power of public authority . . . Over 965 pages of debates, of a somewhat remarkable richness, remain, which describe the pyrrhic victory of the mental health movement.

That movement had spared no pains: there were interventions in the lobbies, and spokesmen in the two Chambers. Mental health specialists, among them the most famous, Esquirol, J. P. Falret, Scipion Pinel, Ferrus, Londe, Adéodat Faivre, were extensively consulted by parliamentary committees and their advice often religiously followed. Esquirol, Falret and Faivre wrote red-hot pamphlets that were distributed to the deputies and served as works of reference in the discussions.[36] Their representatives in the two Chambers, particularly Dufaure and Calemard-Lafayette, intervened frequently in the debate and contributed to the transformation from top to bottom of the initial Bill put forward by the minister of the Interior, who, for his part, was inspired by a purely administrative logic and wished to give the essential prerogatives to the prefects. Thus 'a law on police and finance' became 'a law on welfare and public charity'.[37] The outcome, however, was a compromise laboriously negotiated at several levels, which obstructed as much as it ensured the possibility of future developments in mental health medicine.

The most clear-cut success of the mental health specialists, obtained thanks to the total support of the administration, emerged on the point that was apparently the most delicate: the elimination of justice from any *direct* role in the procedure for admissions. Here, the exchanges between medicine and the administration analysed above worked completely. The Minister of the Interior stated: 'Here is raised a fundamental question that epitomizes almost the whole substance of the law: as it has just been defined, must or can the shutting away of the insane person be subordinated to civil interdiction? The men of medicine reply unanimously: No. In reality, this subordination would be impossible; in principle, it would be iniquitous.'[38]

In spite of determined opposition, which came however from a minority, such as Isambert, the medical rationalization, repeated several times in the course of the discussions and backed unreservedly by the administration, silenced the scruples of the lawyers.[39]

A certain number of articles in the law established this sharing of authority between the prefect or his representatives and the doctor for legalizing the procedures for confinement in an asylum.[40] The judicial mechanisms thus ceased to be an active agent in the dynamics of detention. Whereas the procedure for interdiction had been the sole legal authorization, it could no longer be invoked save after the event, to verify externally whether the process had followed the rules. Thus the public prosecutor had to visit institutions for the insane regularly (article 4), and it was theoretically possible for a third party, the public prosecutor or the insane person himself, to appeal to the court if there were any presumption that illegal practices had occurred (article 29). In their implementation, these formal guarantees would reveal themselves to be somewhat fictitious. A magistrate could write: 'It is estimated that there are not one tenth of departments in which some of the persons mentioned in the law believe themselves obliged to visit the asylum once or twice a year[41].' Hence there arose a vast polemical literature concerning the question of arbitrary detentions.

Yet perhaps a mistaken meaning is attached to the word 'arbitrary'. Faced with the strong campaigns launched against them from 1860 onwards, the mental health specialists were able to challenge their opponents to present convincing examples of arbitrary detentions. And if one understands by this the cynical sequestration of a person known not to be ill, there were doubtless

few cases, at least in the public service. Yet it was the very relationship of what is arbitrary to what is legal that had shifted. The
regulated cooperation of medicine and the administration
henceforth guaranteed the legitimacy of the process, save for 'slip-
ups', such as hastiness, lack of perceptiveness when faced by
pressures from families, an error in diagnosis, etc. This is a further
reason for strengthening the authority of medical intervention, so as
to make it an act that is humanly and scientifically irreproachable:
'Here is revealed the importance of the functions of the doctor called
upon to pronounce whether an individual should be placed outside
the common law.'[42] 'His certificate affords the best guarantee of the
regularity of the administrative procedure';[43] it represents a
veritable 'medico-legal act'.[44] In fact, it can modify totally the social
status of an individual.[45]

Dufaure, who was one of the spokesmen for the mental health
movement during the debates in the Chamber of Deputies,
synthesized as follows the juridical implications of this legitimizing
of the new knowledge:

> At the time when the Civil Code was drawn up, it was considered that
> imprisonment – I do not say isolation – of the insane was a measure of
> last resort, at which one only arrived after interdiction.[46] Since that
> time skilful men have applied themselves to looking after these
> insane, inspired with admirable philanthropy, and the study of
> mental disturbances has convinced them of the disorders that the pro-
> cedure of interdiction might bring about in such sick people. On the
> other hand, they have recognized that, in almost all cases, isolation
> produced excellent results: *to isolate, and not to place under interdiction, are*
> *two new ideas that the law seeks to encourage and which, in my opinion, allow*
> *the Civil Code to be modified.'*[47]

The rock-solid alliance of the administration and medicine gave way
to a limping compromise concerning the nature of the 'special
institution'. If detention of the insane is assumed to operate for
medical reasons, it should be carried out in an entirely medical
environment. Renaudin, whose juridical sense was never at fault,
said so clearly: 'Detention is only legal in an asylum'.[48] The mental
health specialists were therefore logically led to attempt to extend the
recognition of their mandate as experts empowered to certify, by the
setting up of a complete service of public institutions. The asylum is
in fact not just any kind of institution, nor even a mere 'therapeutic

environment'. It is not satisfied with lodging its inmates, nor even with looking after them. Since the inmates are fulfilling a legal obligation in them, their presence in a hermetic environment defines for them, somewhat as prison does for those detained in it, a kind of legal status (absence of liberty and inability to exercise most civil rights, absolute dependence upon the authority of the institution, etc.) Such an institution should therefore be regulated according to strict rules and controlled by authorities provided with an official mandate. This, it appears, could not be realized save in institutions that are *both special and public*.

As to the special character of the institution, the mental health specialists carried the day. Despite pleas for mixed institutions (namely, the mixing of the insane with ordinary patients) made both on behalf of the interests of private clinics, the majority of which did not admit only the insane, and on behalf of families, who could better conceal the dishonourable character of mental illness when it was mixed with other forms of illness, the virtues of isolation had here too been recognized. For isolation represents not only the obligation for the insane person to break with his family and social environment, it is likewise his absolute separation from other patients and others in public care. Mental illness is not a sickness like any other, it is an anthropological *condition*, which requires to be treated in institutional conditions that are wholly specific: 'Last year's commission was unanimous on this point; after having listened for six weeks to the most well-known and most learned men in this kind of illness, no shadow of doubt whatsoever remained in our minds concerning the absolute necessity of a separate building for this type of illness.'[49] Thus at the very least there will be, in any institution that treats the insane, quarters rigorously separated off in which the 'special art' of mental health specialists can be deployed without outside interference.

The mental health specialist would have liked to have gone further. If the 'special doctor' is indeed a man whose 'position and learning confer upon him legal attributes that make him a direct and essential agent of the public authority',[50] he should exercise it in a public institution in which would be gathered together all the conditions and guarantees for carrying out such a mandate. The outline project of the government had not attached particular importance to this problem of the status of the institutions, which it was content to place under the control of the prefects. It was in the form of an amendment proposed at the beginning of the debates by Defaure that arose what was to become the main talking point in the discussions: the constitution of a complete network of institutions, directly emanating from the central authority, directed by a veritable corps of civil service doctors placed under the authority of the prefects. Calemard-Lafayette, a doctor close to the mental health specialists, gives the proposal its radical character:

> If the system presented for the first time by M. Esquirol in 1819 is still commended in 1834 by the skilful M. Ferrus, it is because it alone can lead to fruitful results. France is divided into twenty-six legal divisions, twenty-one military divisions, thirteen ecclesiastical divisions, and twenty forestry districts. You have central prisons; well, following the same principle, let us create public institutions for the insane. As to their number and siting, suffice for me to point out that the population must be taken into account: thus to each institution will be entrusted four to five hundred patients. For this, France must be divided into four sectors made up of four to six departments, in one of which would be organized the central institution.'[51]

But this was reckoning without the existence of a strong opposition in the Chambers, which linked care for making economies to respect for positions already acquired, in the name of the sacred rights of private property and of commerce, and the will to block a medical imperialism that would undermine once more the traditional rights of families.

First the financial argument, although behind this looms the conservative political context of this position:

> Institutions set up by the administration cost ten times as much as institutions set up by private individuals; above all, when it is a question of the insane, there are religious institutions that are run admirably, and which are satisfied with a modest payment for board, whilst institutions run by the administration maintain a staff that would be expensive for the whole department.[52]

The Marquis de Montalembert, after having strongly attacked Ferrus, who had questioned the competence of the nuns, clarified the background to the controversy: 'The most pressing argument that inclines me to fight the role of the central authority in these kinds of matters, [is that] they seem to fall within the province of the local authority, which knows better the advantages that religious institutions present'.[53] What exactly is meant? It is that local authorities and religious institutions promote a different policy on insanity, one which takes more account of the interests of families. Madness is a private matter (and a shameful one), which it is advantageous to gloss over so far as possible, by bringing to bear informal networks of connivence. To the mental health specialists who pleaded for a public system of assistance, the conservative majority in the Assemblies (and the strongest opposition was in the Chamber of Peers) opposed the principle of free choice: so far as possible keep the insane person within the family, at the very minimum be able to negotiate the type of institution in which he will be placed, so long at least as he has not caused a public scandal:

> It therefore seems to me that in M. Thénard's system [who takes up the proposals of the mental health specialists], the law is substituted completely for the family. I can well understand the action of the law when it is applied to individuals that the government causes to be arrested on the public highway because of their mental derangement, or those who threaten the public peace; it shuts them away in their own interest in institutions for the insane; nothing could be more natural. But for a family who has the misfortune to be afflicted through one of its members having a mental disorder – such a family has certainly the right to retain within it that member, if it has the means to do so . . . How could you wish to embrace the interests of the families more closely than they do themselves? . . . I believe that certain doctors, who see in it only the advantage that accrues to their art, who would like to treat everything on a grand scale, would be very pleased to have a large number of sick patients brought together in the same place. But, on the contrary, I believe that, in the interest of patients, it is much more useful to have a larger number of institutions each housing a smaller number of the sick . . . Yet, setting aside these theories, I say that it is impossible for the law to go so far as to remove from the families so innocent a freedom, and through which, by piling up numbers, one would act in a spirit of monopoly. This certainly presents no advantage either for the health of the patients or the good of the State . . . I therefore ask that the families be left every latitude and freedom in this respect.[54]

At the most, a public system should be instituted for the indigent poor, since, as another deputy makes plain,

they are the sole ones who, because of their very situation, can really
disturb the public peace . . . [But] does not the law go somewhat too
far when it applies several of its measures to those insane who are not
poor? . . . As for the insane who are not poor, . . . they are looked
after at home, where their relatives keep them confined, or they are
consigned to and shut away in special institutions for the insane . . .
But this detention takes place on the sole responsibility of their
relatives, the head of the institution, and the doctor treating them.
And is it indeed wise to call unnecessarily upon the administration to
assume a share of this responsibility?[55]

The controversy became lively because it had touched upon a
politically sensitive cluster of interests: the defence of the privacy of
families (naturally, families 'who are not poor') against the risk of
seeing snatched away from them, in the name of the law, one of their
members – and, in extreme cases, the possibility of subjecting this
private unit to administrative regulation. It ended in a dual compromise. Between the will of the mental health specialists to be
interventionist, and the concern of the most intransigent defenders
of the family to maintain the *status quo* and the ambiguous status of
'voluntary placement' – in so far as it differed from compulsory
placement – there half-opened up a breach that may have led to the
assumption of medical responsibility for family problems (see
chapter 6). Between the proponents of a uniform public service and
the defenders of absolute pluralism, guarantees and checks were
envisaged to associate private institutions with the general system.
The Dufaure amendment, which foresaw the establishment of one
asylum per department, became Article 1 of the law. Yet it was itself
amended in a way that emptied it of half its content: the departments
which did not possess asylums were not obliged to build them. They
could negotiate with public or private institutions in other departments or with private institutions in the same department. Private
institutions, if empowered to do so, could under the control of the
administration assume all the functions of public asylums. This was
a measure whose consequences were decisive for the application (or
non-application) in practice of the law. The law itself did not spark
off any decisive move to build public asylums. On the other hand,
the essential elements in the private system were continued. It was
not purely and simply maintenance of the *status quo*. But it was a
check to the ambition of mental health medicine to promote a

uniform organization that would exercise an absolute monopoly in the treatment of the insane.

If the central administration half abandoned the mental health specialists on this question of institutional form, it was because, in its eyes, this was not the main thrust of the law. On the other hand, after resolving to its advantage its conflict with the judiciary on the problem of admissions, by writing a new statute for the insane into the law it completed the project that it had been seeking ever since the Revolutionary era, that of taking the insane into guardianship.

In the penal sphere, the insane person was already absolved from all responsibility (Article 64). In fact, the criminally insane person was placed outside the common law: if he did not come to judgment, he could not be punished, but at the same time the duration of his detention in the asylum was indeterminate. Here also his status was wholly defined by his medical and institutional position. His possible discharge, which would be the equivalent to the end of a prison sentence, depended upon a medical assessment that had to be endorsed by the authority of the prefect, since his placement in the asylum was obligatory.

In the civil sphere, interdiction regulated the fate of the mad person by treating his person and property as that of a minor. But, in so far as interdiction was rarely applied, most of the insane in fact lacked any status at all. By the law of 1838, they were attributed one that was strictly defined by detention itself. Placement in an asylum entailed a novel mode of civil incapacity, that of 'provisional administration'. The detainee, being unable to manage his property, was provided with a 'provisional administrator' (generally, one of the members of the administrative board of the asylum), who could undertake acts to safeguard property, such as recovery of monies due, payment of debts, etc. (Article 31). The term 'provisional' signified the possibility of regaining civil autonomy without formality in the case of a cure: here again, it was the medical and administrative position that defined the status. The court, moreover, could appoint a 'personal "curator" ' for an individual not under interdiction who was placed in an institution for the insane, so as to see that his property was used in his best interest (Article 38). Finally, interdiction remained a possibility in the case of incurability, but it was not obligatory.

Jurists equated these measures with 'special incapacity'.[56] According to Demolombe, 'the law of 30 June 1838 introduced into the French Civil Code a modification in the condition of persons, a new form of incapacity, or rather, of semi-incapacity'.[57] The rapporteur of the law in the Chamber of Peers, for his part, considered that 'this form of administration will be analogous to the guardianship that is conferred on these same boards by the law of 15 Pluviôse, Year III, relating to foundlings'.[58] Thus the disciplinary analogy between the insane person and a child, which also regulated the whole organization of life in the asylum, found its judicial interpretation.

Finally, the law envisaged the financing of these measures of assistance. The insane poor were compulsorily taken over by the departmental and communal finances (Article 28). For the first time, therefore, a *right to treatment* was recognized. But, paradoxically, it was the countervailing element to the absence of any rights. Insofar as the insane person was humanly, civically and financially completely destitute, public charity necessarily assumed responsibility for him. This was the extreme case of an obligation with no reciprocity on the part of the person assisted.

'After all, it is only from 1838 onwards that the following combination was realized: the measure for placement + a determinate internal regime + [legal] incapacity + management of property + right to treatment within the framework of a special form of public assistance.'[59] But this was not a matter of merely adding together various elements. Or rather, these heterogeneous elements were irrevocably combined on the basis of the notion of detention, which constituted the matrix. The fact of detention of itself afforded this complete status. It sufficed for the sick person to cross the threshold of the asylum for him to become an *insane person:* this was entirely defined by a dependence that was indissolubly medical, institutional and legal.

The logic of the process of guardianship here arrives at its final term. In a society founded upon contract, the insane person is the one who escapes from any type of contractual relationship. But at the same time he ceases to offend against it, since this absence of rights constitutes his status. He submits to a unilateral guardianship at all levels of the network of public assistance: medical, institutional, and juridical. The concept of alienation is the synthetic expression of this combination of dependent elements. The notion of alienation is namely the product, the conquest, the 'medicalization' of the insane. 'To make madness a medical matter' consisted very exactly in instituting this complete status of guardianship. The Marquis de Barthélemey, the rapporteur before the House of Peers, summed up the whole movement as follows:

> Gentlemen, of all the illnesses that can beset humanity, the most afflicting is undoubtedly the one that deprives man of the use of his intellectual faculties. Born for society, the loss of his reason makes him incapable of fulfilling the mission that his destiny has imposed upon him; he ceases to be useful to his fellows and can become to them an object of fear. In this sad situation, where very often he is incapable of distinguishing good from evil, the just from the unjust, *the laws cannot form the rules for his behaviour. But, if he can no longer follow their prescription and be subject to their penalties, they should for that reason in no way cease to exercise their sway over him.* Special legislation must be enacted to cover him, and at the same time to protect society, his person and his possessions.[60]

This 'special legislation', which took the form of an exacting jurisprudence, represented however the first inroad made upon legalism. It constituted an assault upon the principle of the separation of powers. There was no longer, on one side, the administration, the transmission belt of the executive power and guardian of public order, and on the other, the magistracy, the guarantor of liberties because it possessed a monopoly of the decisions that could suspend that guarantee. A third power, the medical one, was legitimized and ensured a new balance between the two others. The sacredness of the principles of law gave way before the practical rationality that was represented by expertise.

That this mode of intervention was of a character that transgressed the principles of law did not pass unnoticed: 'We must acknowledge that the law is being profoundly innovatory as regards the situation of individual persons; it introduces, for individuals already a prey to insanity or threatened by it, a mode of procedure that exists in not a single one of our laws.' And the Comte de Portalis immediately insisted upon the necessity for strictly limiting the extent of such a dispensation: 'We accept this system, but we do so on condition that it is accompanied by the necessary precautions, so as not to diverge from the general system of our civil laws, and not to infringe the indispensable guarantees of individual liberty.'[61]

These 'precautions' (the supervisory role of the judiciary over the procedural regularity of the process of detention) were doubtless

hardly effective in their application. But, above all, they were inadequate from the point of view of principle. *The law of 1838 essentially
did not present a problem of juridical guarantees, because it posed the problem of
a change in the system and of the function of the juridical guarantee itself.*

In one sense the depiction of a purely contractual society is indeed
a myth: beneath the legal transactions and the regulated exchanges,
it is the involuntary acts of subjugation, the implicit norms and the
disciplines inculcated that make up the skein of real social relationships. But the problem – at least, one of the main problems – for
bourgeois society has been to reintroduce the traditional dependence
groups, and to develop new modes of domination, into a juridical
and administrative matrix that guarantees at the same time their
legal justification, their rational management, and their effective
control.

The law of 1838 doubtless represents the first clear and complete
success in the task of transmuting a system of given relationships of
authority into a system of legitimized and deliberate rules. In this
sense it can serve as a model for the analysis of the new processes for
'placing under guardianship' which, in contrast to former acts of
domination founded upon tradition and customary situations (that
'enchanted world of feudal relationships' of which Marx speaks, and
which of course still subsists in part), draw their justification from
knowledge and their effectiveness from their technical rationality.
Not that future developments were doomed to reproduce the rigidity
of the law of 1838. In this first stage, the intervention of medical
authority had practically only an impact upon the status of
individuals by imposing detention. It was a brutal demolition of
almost all the methods of control exercised over the frustrating and
costly procedure of sequestration. Yet when this near-identification
of the mental patient with the insane detainee was broken, the
function of medical expertise would also free itself from the
dichotomic logic it had begun to borrow from elsewhere. It would
continue to operate a kind of 'placing under guardianship' of a
technical and legal kind, but this would be able to assume forms that
were numerous and insidious in a different way.

6

Law and Order

In 1861, Dr Berthier, head doctor at Bourg-en-Bresse, a fairly typical representative of the silent majority of the new 'cadre' of mental health specialists, exclaimed, after undertaking a tour of the asylums of France:

> For our part, our task is almost accomplished. Our ideas, broadcast over the whole country, have to do no more than come to fruition. Let them depart, accompanied by charity and intelligence, to carry to all peoples our love of the beautiful and good. Auxerre, Avignon, Chambéry, Grenoble, Toulouse, Quatre-Mares, Marseille, Rennes, Rodez are there to speak for what we have been able to do; Paris is preparing to show in its turn of what it is capable, and we have every reason to believe that our capital will be worthy of its name, its rank and its glory. I have visited a large number of our French asylums, and I have always returned better for it. I propose to see them all, having the same goal: that of enlightening my judgement, rejoicing my heart, and improving the lot of those patients that Providence has entrusted to me.[1]

This exalted dithyramb is perhaps not free from underlying thoughts of publicity, or even of defensive reactions. The year 1861 is roughly the crucial date from when onwards mental health medicine began to be attacked on all sides: in its legislative monument, by the beginning of campaigns against arbitrary detentions; in its bastion of the asylum, by the opening of the debate on 'the different ways of treating the insane'; in its theoretical foundations, by the criticism of symptomatologies, through an organo-genetic movement inspired by the works of Morel upon degeneration. The mental health specialists closed ranks to prop up an edifice that was beginning to crack.

All the same, there is a paradox. This golden age of mental health medicine in a sense never truly existed in reality. The minimum requirement of article 1 of the law, of one asylum per department, would never even be realized. Let us as yet say nothing of the over-crowding, the moral and material misery in the asylums, the life of the psychiatrist lived in the midst of his failures, his horizons restricted by an isolation that matched that of his patients, the petty scandals, the petty calculations and petty profits. There was nothing to be cockahoop about.

Yet people like Berthier, who were perhaps not all simpletons, exulted. And above all, 130 years later, the old synthesis of the asylum still looms over the whole psychiatric landscape of France. Whatever the technocrats may say, an institution is not an undertaking whose success is measured by mere profitability. The asylum was astonishingly competitive, in its own way. A corpse, perhaps, it may have been, but how could it be got rid of? To understand the strange persistence within it of mental health medicine is also to be sensitive to the icy poetry of those cemetery-like laboratories where painstaking experimentation upon man was carried on in the shadow of high walls. It is also to show that there exists a symbolism of exclusion, of negative labelling, of stigmatization which, in its own way, could pay off as much as the positive programmes of resocialization and cure that served as cover for it.

Yet to isolate these dimensions would be to risk wishing to exorcise the lyricism of Berthier through another in just as doubtful taste. Thus we must spread out the net in all the directions in which the practice of mental health medicine reached out. But also we must understand what, through its very success, acted as a snare.

The Pseudo-application of the Law

The requirement by the mental health specialists that the whole territory should be covered by a uniform system of public institutions was, it will be recalled, disarmed in the very text of the law, through the option left open to departments to enter into agreements with existing public or private institutions. Moreover, the obligatory financing of assistance to the insane poor was not written into the central budget but had to be negotiated, in undefined proportions, by the departmental and municipal councils (article 28). Renaudin, a score of years later, regretted this, stating,

We are convinced that the State initiatives would have achieved in less time all the better results if they had been less disputed. There are few asylums which have not suffered from these disputes, and the gaps still observable in many of them bear the indelible imprint of that systematic hostility that, from the beginning, was declared by many departmental councils against the organization of the new service.[2]

Roguery, then on the part of the local elected representatives, but also competition from 'private industry', which 'attracts by offering a good bargain, whose significance is not being sufficiently investigated'.[3] The most significant point, however, is the fact that central government, whose persistence in pushing for a law has been noted, should have immediately lost interest in applying it effectively: not only by failing to take on the financing of it, but by commending to the departments a prudence to which they had no need to be incited. In the circular of 5 August 1839 applying the law, the Minister of the Interior made the following plain to prefects:

You will not lose sight of the fact, if it is desirable, – as I expressed in my circular of July 28, 1838, – that, although departments should consider the means available to set up special institutions that would doubtless be distinguished by wise administration and a wider development of the means for effecting cures, prudence demands that these new creations should not be voted upon before a well-considered examination of the department's financial situation. Amid all the emerging social needs, we must beware of overtaxing departmental expenses. Moreover, it is good not to lose sight of the fact that departmental institutions for the insane could not for the most part cover their expenses save to the extent that they received inmates from neighbouring departments: hence the consequence would be that over-duplication of these institutions would do mutual harm. Thus it is in no way to be desired that each department should burden itself with establishing and maintaining a special hospice devoted to the insane.[4]

Everything occurred as if the government lost interest in the practical application of this law 'of charity and humanity', once it had been voted, and the difficulties and juridical and administrative contradictions that motivated governmental interest formally resolved.

In any case, the passing of the law did not set in train any decisive drive towards the construction or even the refurbishing of asylums.

From 1818 to 1838, without any help from any central initiative, the situation nevertheless had already much improved (see chapter 4). From 1838 to 1852 only seven new asylums were established, of which only three represented really new creations. Almost everywhere the departmental councils carried out a patching-up operation, knocking down or building a few walls, restoring a few old quarters in the hospice in order to conform with the letter of the law, which required the separation of the insane from other sick persons. Above all, they haggled as often as possible about the least cost (the celebrated question of 'daily cost') with existing public or private institutions. Even in 1874, only 40 departments (out of 88) were provided with special institutions.[5]

It is true that the number of the insane that were 'assisted' had increased considerably. Yet, on the one hand, this progression was astonishingly regular, without ever marking new thresholds, at a rate of about 800 extra insane persons per year: 10,000 detained in 1834, 16,255 in 1844, 24,524 in 1854, 34,919 in 1864, 42,077 in 1874[6]: there is nothing in the statistics that allows one to identify specifically the effect of the law. On the other hand, this growth in the number of places available petered out in seeking to follow the increase in 'demand' – which, in fact, was the consequence of the crisis in rural society and the advance of urbanization. Even in 1872, the number of 'insane living at home' surveyed exceeded the number in asylums.[7] If public service in asylums was indeed the dominant model of psychiatric assistance, it had never enjoyed an absolute monopoly. The old practices of dealing with madness continued a more or less underground existence. For rich families, isolation within the domestic framework under the surveillance of servants, the old tradition of travel as a diversion, with or without an accompanying doctor, and, above all, direct negotiation with private institutions had all been perpetuated, as we shall see. For the poor, neighbourhood contacts, principally in the rural areas, ensured that numerous insane persons were taken in directly, particularly if they were not violent.

Faced with these limitations on their undertaking, the mental health specialists clearly rose up in protest. The campaign they led to denounce the dangerous character of the sick and ostensibly inoffensive was largely inspired by this motive. Thus there exists a whole literature upon idiots, in order to demonstrate that they were not so harmless as they appeared. But one thing or the other occurred:

either they were left to their own devices, or they came into, and swamped, the asylums. The overburdening of the services was a constant feature in the history of psychiatry. But with overburdening inevitably went lack of differentiation, and thus the impossibility of working out medical classifications, the halting of the techniques employed in mental health medicine, and, finally, the abandonment of the proclaimed therapeutic vocation of these institutions.

Through the problems of applying concretely (or not applying) the law, we therefore see a transformation of its goals. This was manifested in a paralysing effect on those technical clauses in it that might perhaps have made it a more 'medical' law. In particular, the preponderance of compulsory placements over voluntary ones in reality blocked the whole process inaugurated by the mental health specialists.

These two modes of admission did not, in fact, possess at all the same significance for the possibilities for development that they afforded mental health medicine. Compulsory placement is society's response to the most spectacular manifestations of mental disturbance. It goes back to the old idea of 'wandering abroad', or vagrancy, by the mad person. It relates most importantly to the 'violent insane' – and also the person who is indigent and/or without roots. Absence of means and any social network to support him exposes him to direct intervention by the public authority. Here the law is indeed a law 'of administration and police'. Above all else it aims at neutralizing a dangerous individual. It is only after the event that the doctor intervenes, when the detainee is considered as undergoing treatment in a special institution. It is an arrangement that most resembles the old 'king's orders'.

· The procedure for voluntary placement is much more subtle and leaves greater scope for medical intervention. The initiative for placement here lies with the family or those close to it, whose request is necessarily backed by a medical certificate. The institution's doctor must also endorse the diagnosis upon admission, so as to guarantee that sequestration is according to the rules. The measure of placement therefore rests upon cooperation between the family and medical authorities, with no direct intervention by the public authority. It can then take into account disturbances that have not yet reached the threshold where they emerge socially. Whereas compulsory placement trawls over the surface of the pathological, only scooping up a limited number of spectacular cases in the name of a conception of public order that lacks any subtlety, the procedure for voluntary placement allows it to fasten on to more discrete and so often more precocious and tenuous pathological manifestations. In this way there emerges the possibility of more frequent medical interventions, which can be more diversified, more subtle, and in the final analysis, preventive in their effect. Insofar as the origins of mental disturbance will increasingly be traced back to pathological states within the family, voluntary placement may offer the possibility of seizing it *in statu nascendi*, before it becomes objectified on the social scene, and *a fortiori*, in public, where only compulsory placement can function. We can see that this line traces out the path for future developments in mental health medicine. But hardly has it been traced out than the process was blocked.

The principle of a medical extension of the law rested upon one of its paragraphs (article 25, ss.2): 'Those insane whose mental state would not in any way compromise public order or the safety of persons shall likewise be admitted to them in the forms, circumstances and conditions that shall be laid down by the Conseil Général, upon a request made by the prefect and approved by the minister.' Every freedom in assessment was thus left to the departmental councils and to the administration. We can guess what use of it they would make. It is a position diametrically opposed to that of the mental health specialists, who were impatient to plunge into the breach:

> For our part, leaving aside the financial question, whose very great importance we realize, we would like admissions not to be limited in any way; in short, for us to be able to admit to institutions for the insane any individual, whether indigent or not, whose state of mental derangement has been ascertained, and who has come before the director in possession of the validating documents as required by law . . . In my view, the asylums should be open to the insane as are hospitals to ordinary sick people, namely, without hindrance and without limit.[8]

But the ministerial instructions had exactly the same restrictive meaning as when there was a question of creating new institutions: 'Undoubtedly, Prefect, the asylums set up or subsidized by the departments must not be opened up indiscriminately to anyone who presents himself to them as insane: such ease of access would give rise to the gravest abuses, and would compromise the department's finances.' 'The departmental councils,' the circular of August 14,

1840 makes clear, 'should in this respect be the first arbiters to be consulted'.[9] But they were arbiters who at the same time were an interested party, since they were the principal dispensers of funds.

Thus the number of compulsory placements had always swamped that of voluntary placements. In 1853, there were 80 per cent in Paris and, of the admissions over the year in the whole of France, they numbered 6,473 as against 2,609 voluntary placements.[10] This imbalance would still worsen, since certain departmental councils would prescribe ingenious arrangements so as to limit absolutely the number of admissions. Thus, 'the first duty of an administration that looks to its interests being so to regulate the admission of the insane to the asylum as to take in only those for whom the law authorizes compulsory detention, and thus to counter the rapid increase in the number of admissions', the council for the Meurthe department set up at the hospital in Epinal a sorting centre, so as to avoid steering towards the asylum at Mareville any save those insane who, 'have been recognized as dangerous to public morality or to the safety of persons and property'. A. Pain, whilst asserting that 'the insane are certainly the spoilt children of modern philanthropy', praised the procedure in these terms: 'We can only applaud the results coming out of this measure; in 1861 the figure for admissions had been 47; it went down to 16 in 1862 and 15 in 1863.'[11]

Faced with such practices, numerous mental health specialists fell into the habit of requesting compulsory placement for any patient for whom they wished to ensure access to treatment. It was a usage that would be perpetuated for a long time (it was only in 1938 that the conversion of compulsory placements into voluntary ones, upon medical opinion endorsed by the prefect, was authorized).[12] Haussmann denounced the 'universal tendency to declare dangerous even the most harmless demented in order to get local assistance provided free of charge, and also to certify the indigent state of these wretches. I have had to exercise much firmness in order to react against this double abuse'.[13]

Thus early on the situation was taken in hand once more by the administrators responsible, against a tendency on the part of the mental health specialists to get round the letter of the law in order to defend its 'medical' spirit. Yet, although inspired by humanitarian motives, this tendency on the part of the doctors did not favour –and this is the least that can be said – the liberalization of psychiatry. The supremacy of compulsory placement over voluntary placement maintained the almost exclusive linking of mental illness to the degree of danger. The asylum was in no way a hospital like any other, but the last resort for individuals that were everywhere rejected.

Thus, even before the 1860s, which, as we shall see, represent a turning point, one begins to read pessimistic reports on the situation of psychiatry:

> Today, as then [the author is referring to the situation before 1838], in most asylums a medical service is absolutely non-existent. The lot of the insane is alleviated, but nothing is done to cure them. They are brought together in buildings inadequate to house them. Confined to their rooms, they lack space and air. They are mixed up together instead of being divided into distinct categories, categories for which science has demonstrated the necessity. The insane mingle with the epileptics; there is a mingling of sexes, and of children with older people. The insane that are afflicted with chance or unsavoury illnesses have no separate quarters for themselves, and all this is true even for the most reputable asylums.[14]

Doubtless the author of this report, a Catholic Integralist, was somewhat hostile to the theses of the mental health specialists. Psychiatric literature proper wavered between the exultant tone of Berthier when he made his wondrous 'excursions' round the asylums of France, and the more measured tone of Renaudin, who termed the new legislation the 'institution that does most honour to French administration',[15] but inveighed against the obstacles, technical, administrative and financial, that impeded its full implementation. Thus we are justified in speaking, at the very least, of a pseudo-application of the law: it did not innovate as regards any new practices, it was content to sanction and coordinate previous procedures, and did not even mark a decisive stage in their development.

On Efficiency: Real, Administrative and Symbolic

Why then all these speeches made around the law, these discussions in the two Chambers spread out over a year and a half, and its function as a model, inspiring legislation in most of Europe? It may have been because the law had not to be 'truly' applied to meet its purpose: to resolve formally the juridical and administrative contradictions that gave rise to it, to provide a cohesive pattern in which medicine and the administration could cooperate together in managing technocratically a particularly thorny problem. It is in this precise sense that Renaudin could state:

> Blessed with 25 years' experience, after having been prepared for by the work of illustrious specialists, the legislation of the insane is among that of which the French administration has every right to be proud, and foreign countries have made numerous borrowings from it. Revitalized daily by the wisdom and vigilance of the higher administration, it now truly constitutes a science.[16]

Why was this so? 'The services for the insane rest upon an idea that, at first defended by Pinel, Fodéré and Esquirol, has ended up by becoming one of government.'[17] Falret went still further: 'We believed that these arguments and proofs, resting upon general principles for legislation concerning the insane, had not lost their value and topicality: *that they were applicable to every age and in every country and were as ineradicable as mental derangement itself.*'[18]

A naive form of Substantialism? Not if this permanence, this 'ineradicability' of insanity is understood in terms of the *administrative and medical* dimensions of its management, as they have been established above (see chapter 5). The theoretical conceptions of mental illness could be modified, and Falret, who himself contributed to promoting such changes, was sufficiently logical to be aware of this. Nevertheless, 'principles' for the assumption of responsibility of mental illness existed, where (a) medical knowledge of the nature of madness, and (b) what society insists upon in the management of the insane come together. Falret's position expressed less an 'eternal' state of medical knowledge and rather an awareness of the complicity, which was illustrated throughout the history of mental health medicine, between the medical position, faced with madness, and the administrative position. In this sense history has not proved him wrong, at least for a century. The *content* of medical knowledge may have changed fairly profoundly; the *stance* of the doctor faced with the problem of madness has rarely diverged from this solidarity with the requirements of managing it.

One can then understand that the law might have modified things little in practice, and yet transformed the nature of the rhetoric of

those responsible. This had been done without having to refer back
to some vague function of the 'ideology', as opposed to the 'reality'.
The ideology has reality, or rather there is an effectiveness peculiar
to a certain type of rhetoric that also transforms the world, because it
works upon that specific dimension of 'what is capable of being
administered', the importance of which we are trying to establish
here. After 1838 various criticisms, occasionally profound, of the
new arrangements were made very rapidly. We find hardly any
longer the type of rhetoric of catastrophe that deplored the absence
of a *system* for the insane, which juridical, institutional and financial
contradictions were preventing from being realized. The indisputable success of the law of 1838 was that it was able to respond
simultaneously to all these requirements. As Daumezon said,[19] it
was a 'grouping of variable elements with a fixed content', on the
basis of a status of detention, and it enunciated unified and coherent
prescripts for the assumption of responsibility. In other words, after
1838 problems remained. But there were no longer open contradictions and ambiguities. Madness continued to cause difficulties. It
had ceased to be a challenge. This formal reconciliation of adver-
sarial elements, which shifted them around and produced their real
and economical solution, was realized at all levels:

• on the legal plane, by legalizing the detention without interdiction of the insane – even if the guarantees of a judicial verifi-
  cation *a posteriori*, carefully provided for on paper, remained
  inoperative;
• on the administrative plane, by defining the precise attributions of
  the different authorities responsible for admissions – even if real
  coordination between them left room for arbitrary action;
• on the institutional plane, by bridging the disparity between
  places of detention (prisons, beggaries, hospices, hospitals,
  private clinics) – even if the apparent uniformity of the 'special
  institution' cloaked concrete realities as different as the public
  asylum, hospice quarters, and private institutions under the
  somewhat nebulous control of the administration;
• on the financial plane, by designating an obligatory procedure for
  financing the expenses of the indigent through the communes and
  departments – even if these authorities generally carried out their
  obligations with such ill-will that they made the asylum the most
  wretched environment for the most wretched.

We are therefore justified in saying, without any finality, that it was *necessary* for the law to exist, even if its implementation remained largely imaginary: the principle of reality is not at all the same for the managers and those they manage. At the margin, the fact that the insane derived no advantage from the existence of the law (which is not entirely exact) would not in any way invalidate its administrative 'excellence'. This is doubtless not a paradox peculiar to this particular law. However, here a sleight of hand was carried out across and through the linkage with medicine: the medical label allowed a formal reconciliation of real antinomies. This is precisely what provides a social mandate for mental health medicine.

Yet what of the peculiarly medical effectiveness, the therapeutic aspect? To answer such a question we would need to be able to assess the effective results of that 'moral treatment' which was thought at the time to constitute the essential element in the therapeutic activities of the asylum. This is a difficult undertaking, in which a few statistics, which are disputable, are of little help. What we can glimpse of this aspect is not encouraging. But above all we must perhaps understand that here also the benefits of 'assumption of responsibility' are not measured solely in terms of positive results, assessed as rates of cure. There can be a symbolic effectiveness of the functioning of the institution which projects the contrary image of the therapeutic effectiveness proper.

Moral treatment takes on meaning – we have already insisted upon this – in the framework of a vast analogy with pedagogy, which makes the asylum a reformatory of a special character. 'In effect, institutions devoted to the treatment of madness have most connexion with reformatories . . . We must not forget that the insane are older children, always ready to avoid the discipline and the regime imposed upon them.'[20]

'Older children' they are, above all because they reveal the greatest distance from the norms one wishes to reinculcate in them. Pedagogically speaking, the sole originality of moral treatment is not that it really innovates in the means brought into play – since these merely adopt once more a range of disciplinary techniques – but it has to double in intensity their coercive character. Whereas normal education takes over from socialization in the family, the deep gulf that madness evinces demands a redoubling and intensification of pedagogical effectiveness: uprooting from the social and family framework, transplantation into a special environment, maximization of disciplinary techniques. In this allegedly consists that 'special, laborious form of education through which the doctor attempts to reform, and in some way to reconstitute, the mind of the sick person'.[21]

Thus there is a 'reconstitution', and not merely new grafts on the base of a rational nature. Behind this project lies a kind of constructionist Utopia: the pedagogy of the asylum entails the application of a veritable reconditioning programme in advance of its time. By controlling all the environmental variables, by constantly applying a cohesive set of rational means to staunch all the breaches through which disorder is manifested, a normalized profile will be rebuilt in its entirety for the sick man, 'for external order reveals internal order, and we have said that the latter is the highest expression of the reason, which one must cause to prevail over madness'.[22] Thus it is a very strongly imposed maieutic, but one justified by the size of the gap that has to be bridged in order to restore the reasonable nature in man. Muscular authoritarianism, far from being in contradiction to the humanism proclaimed by the first mental health specialists, is its instrument. The philosophy of moral treatment shares without a shadow of doubt in the pedagogical optimism of the Enlightenment.

Yet it also represents the point of application where that optimism can come up against its limits. Madness is not merely a world shrouded in prejudices, errors, or excesses of passion that rational means could dispel without trace. This is because the difficulty of the task to be accomplished would justify in advance a 'reasonable' failure rate. Also an increasingly acute awareness of the distance that madness maintains between itself and reason has progressively developed during the whole process of its becoming a medical matter. It signifies a slow transformation in the conception of what is pathological, which took place over more than half a century.

A whole trend of thought first directly applied the optimism of the Enlightenment to the problem of madness: the latter was a mere error of judgement that would be eliminated by the progress of thought, pathology would retreat as civilization developed and would be definitively dispelled by it.[23] The positions of the mental health school had been conquered in part by combatting this tendency: madness marks a graver rupture than a mere derangement of the judgement or a pure excess of passion. For example, Falret stated: 'Experience bears witness to the fact that one must not treat mental illnesses as mere aberrations of the feelings or errors of the intellect. Reasoning has only very limited power to rectify the sick disturbances of the understanding.'[24] Nevertheless, the mental health specialists remained midway in this criticism of intellectualism. The condition for the application of moral treatment is that the insane person should retain a basis of reason that can be restored by judicious means: 'The art of seeking how to impart a different direction to the excluding will of the insane, of reasoning with them and making them feel their dependence, assumes that their reason has not gone completely astray.'[25] The 1874 report would say also: 'But the majority [of the insane] in most cases know perfectly when they are doing wrong, and there would be no moral treatment or discipline possible if this were not brought home to them'.[26]

But – and this is the third stage in this process – the discussions about monomania (see chapter 4) uncover a pathological nucleus that cannot be at all amenable to a rational pedagogy. This pessimism will be accentuated through the series of investigations of degenerescence, constitutional perversions and organic deficiencies, etc.

Concerning this issue, which is vital because it qualifies the relevance of the pedagogical analogy on which moral treatment rests, the asylum occupies an ambiguous position. It keeps, if one may say so, both irons in the fire. A paradoxical pedagogical machine, it proposes explicitly to effect a cure. But its characteristics already display the opposite features to those of a normal education system, lending themselves to overturning the progressive character of learning, through the negative example of failure:

- Negative selection as against positive selection: entrance into the system, instead of being a promotion, consummates a situation of decadence for one deprived of the attributes of reason;
- A reverse reckoning of the duration of the stay in the institution: whereas a pupil increases his objective chances of success depending on his length of education within the school system, the length of stay in the asylum increasingly compromises the chances of rehabilitation of the insane person;
- A reverse labelling of the institutional affiliation: whereas the pupil participates in the prestige of the school (and all the more so the 'larger' it is), the insane person bears the dishonouring stigma of his passage through the asylum;

- The contrasting significance of 'leaving': expulsion from the institution of schooling means for the pupil being consigned to the outer darkness, and he becomes attached to the negative pole of the duality 'culture-barbarism'; on the contrary, the insane person who has been cured joins once more the positive pole of the normal-pathological antinomy.

The functioning of the pedagogy of mental health medicine does not therefore only depend upon the cumulative logic of the acquisition of knowledge and know-how, through which the pupil progresses along a quantitative scale that goes at least from lack of culture to more culture. It can also be discerned in the logic of symbolic exclusion, negative labelling replacing the acquisition of culture.[27] One can thus understand that the patent failure of this pedagogical undertaking, viz., the incurability of the sick person, can bring about one of its profoundly significant outcomes. The insane person who dies insane in a lunatic asylum, after a long life as an insane person, has displayed in his destiny all the negative characteristics of mental disturbance. He symbolizes, with the perfection of a tragic character, the exclusion of madness from society and humanity. If anything can dissuade a person from madness it is indeed this vision of the life of the insane, that is to say, the life made for the insane in those asylums where, however, they are, so it is said, given all the help of science and all the resources of philanthropy.

Thus in all circumstances the system wins. Doubtless it occasionally cures, and that is all to the good: so many individuals who are returned to the sway of reason. Is this frequent, or is it rare? This is perhaps not the main question. In any case, it is not the sole question. For to the failures themselves can be attached a more subtle pedagogical meaning, and one that can perhaps serve better as example: they state the price it costs to transgress the norms.

The asylums, those ponderous buildings set down on the outskirts of towns, thus also dominate a moral landscape. Social consensus emerges reinforced through maintaining in this way on the margin of the community an image, both discrete and spectacular, of the fate of those who have failed. Down to their very architecture and geographical siting, the asylums, like the prisons, enclosed but visible, imposing but tucked away, common in form but majestic in their austerity, assume this function of both concealing and displaying the unavowable.[28]

It is not a chimera, or if it is, it operates universally. In each region there exists a popular saying that expresses, in a form mingled with derision and horror, the vividness of this perception: 'to come back from Charenton', 'to be ripe for Charenton' – what one would not, it is said, wish one's worst enemy.

The associates of Pinel, the great philanthropist, were thus not content to cleanse the surface of the body social by ridding it of those undesirables, the mentally ill. They also mounted guard on the frontiers of reason and madness. In order to do this, their principal need was not to cure, nor even always to shut away. Even if the insane were few, they taught everybody how good and prudent it was to be normal. It is perhaps a symbolic effectiveness, a social fancy, if you will, but one which must not be ruled out of account in understanding also the kind of supra-historical longevity of the asylum form.

The Paradigm of Detention

The most burdensome legacy of the law of 1838 was doubtless, however, the way in which it blocked possibilities for expansion in mental health medicine. It is indisputable that logistic problems largely contributed to the half-hearted application of the law as regards concrete achievements, and to turning the asylum into a negative model. This nevertheless does not justify our contrasting, with the psychiatrist historians, a medical Utopia inspired by generous motives with the egoism of the administration and the political authorities, or the indifference and even hostility towards insanity felt by the population as a whole. A certain number of 'blockages' arose through this 'medical' law, and because of its terms, such as the relationship of compulsory placements to voluntary ones. The medical sphere as related to the asylum received a negative investment. Yet, above all, these 'blunders' in its application, and this functioning of the asylum as a contrasting negative phenomenon, reveal a central contradiction, written into the very heart of the law. This is none other than the fundamental ambiguity within which mental health medicine was trapped in the first half of the nineteenth century.

It will be recalled that one of the matters at stake in the discussion on the public or private nature of the caring institutions had been the defence of 'the honour of families'. But this position of family privacy as a sanctuary in the face of an external controlling authority was even more directly threatened by the danger that might be presented by a mental health medicine endowed with powers of decision, working on its own criteria as to who should be detained:

> Your honourable colleague supposes that you will go and snatch from the bosom of his family a man who has the misfortune to be afflicted by a mental derangement, who is being looked after by his family, an insane person who is not wandering abroad and consequently does not compromise public safety. Well, I ask whether it is this right of snatching just such an unfortunate person from the devout care of his family that it is intended to establish? In that case I shall vote against all those articles from which might be induced such an extension of the rights of the administration. I therefore ask for it to be clearly understood that the rights of the administration shall not be invoked against the insane as much, but only insofar as they compromise public safety.[29]

Here also there was compromise, since the law was not content with detaining by compulsory placement those 'insane persons who compromise public safety', i.e. very often the indigent, or at least those who had already broken from any family controls. It foresaw the possibility of medical intervention within families, which even its most intransigent defenders did not desire. This intervention was through the procedure for voluntary placement. Yet this strange appellation of 'voluntary' for a placement as constraining for the insane person as the other form, meant that here in principle the family retained its freedom to call in the mental health specialist or to refuse his assistance. The outcome was that the family would preserve the right to deal itself with an insane person, even if dangerous, provided that it could neutralize the effects of his behaviour upon public order.[30] It could also ask for the discharge of the insane person, even against medical advice (article 14). But, if the institution doctor was not in agreement, he could request the prefect to change voluntary into compulsory placement (same article 14), and the insane person was then subject to the common regime. An unequal compromise was thus made between the three authorities – family, administrative and medical – who vied for control of the insane person. The introduction of the medical partner complicated the old institution of 'family prisoners', whereby the family appealed directly to the public authorities to request them to assume responsibility for any of its members that were uncontrollable (see chapter 1). But the type of autonomy with which the new mechanisms were equipped, the extent to which the medical diagnosis was sovereign or remained subject either to the agreement of the administration or the family, remained ill-defined. At one time the medical authority served to cover the orders of the prefect, at another it legitimated a demand, for which the initiative remained with the family.

As at the time of the debate on the public or private nature of the special institution (see chapter 5), the mental health specialists would have liked to go beyond this halting compromise. If it were really a matter of illness, the medical diagnosis should be the governing element in assessing how the entire course of the mentally ill person's life should proceed. Thus Lisle, whilst remaining within the framework of the contrast, 'compulsory placement – voluntary placement', proposed to impose the obligation on the prefects to detain compulsorily not only all those individuals whose state of mental derangement would compromise *public safety imminently*, but also all those reported to him as *having clear signs of madness*, and over whom their families would not or could not exercise sufficient supervision.[31] Medical expertise would thus have of itself a constraining value: imposing intervention by the public authorities, it would strip the family of all its rights. A little later, in one of the more fully developed plans for reform of the law of 1838, Theophile Roussel sought to go even farther. In the residual power of families to object to medical and administrative intervention, he denounced 'the great gap in the law' and wished to 'extend the authority and working of the law to the domicile of the insane person, even to his domestic hearth',[32] – but he immediately deplored the fact that 'predominant opinion' shrunk from such a bold procedure.

Undoubtedly the majority of mental health specialists were in advance of this 'predominant opinion'. They anticipated the possibility of a new mechanism of control that would be able to penetrate the family and assume responsibility for those whom it had failed to socialize. At the margin, a plan emerged in outline that made this family structure the privileged target for medical intervention: to treat the family itself and/or, at individual level, the mechanisms that relate to bad socialization in the family, – this represented almost the entire programme for future 'progress' in mental health medicine, including psycho-analysis.

But until the end of the century these views were only prospective, and this, it appears, for two sets of reasons. On the one hand, the problem of social control was not yet such that it had to employ such subtle strategies. We are still within the dominant framework of legalism: objective definition of a system of rules and correction of failure to observe them by authority and coercion, rather than by an overlapping set of norms and prevention of their infringement by persuasion and manipulation. The time for 'soft' technologies had not yet come in the asylums, any more than it had in prisons, factories, barracks or schools. In particular, if it is true that a considerable part of these new strategies would entail action upon the family, which was both a target and a transmitter of normalizing authority, such a policy for families supposed a complex set of conditions that had not yet been realized.[33]

On the other hand, and above all, the objective mechanisms of mental health medicine, as they had been fixed by the law of 1838, rendered them incapable of carrying through an interventionist programme outside the asylum. One is tempted to say that the victory of mental health medicine was too magnificent: in succeeding in bringing about the 'medicalization' of madness, the law of 1838 imposed upon it conditions which sterilized any possibilities of future development. 'One is mad or one is not mad', the Minister of the Interior interjected into the discussion[34]: this was more than a tautology, or rather it was a tautology at the foundation of mental health medicine. An insane person was not solely a sick person, even a mentally sick person, he was someone who *must be detained*. Conversely, a sick person not subject to detention was not properly speaking a mentally ill person, or in any case he was not affected in practice by any psychiatric intervention technique. *To intervene was to detain.* The legislation instituted this law of all or nothing: one was mad or not mad, one was detained or not detained, one was subject to mental health medicine or one was not. As late as 1865, Raynier and Beaudoin would have no other expedient for defining an insane person save to identify him with the legal measure that had decreed his placement:

> The insane person is an individual of either sex who, presenting psychical disturbances that have been duly established, whether temporary or lasting, dangerous or not, has been the subject of a placement order as defined in the law of 1838. The discharge of the person concerned in conformity with the legal procedures puts an end to the character of mental illness proper.[35]

There is the crossing of a line: from one day to the next, one became insane by virtue of being placed in a special institution; from one day to the next, one ceased to be so, by being discharged from it. There was no means of dissociating the psychical condition of the sick person from the administrative and legal position that defined detention. Hence flowed consequences that were ruinous to any coherent medical programme: activities such as prevention or post-cure follow-up, which would show themselves increasingly essential, had no proper status medically, because they could find no place in this dichotomous functional model. Likewise, the possibility of intervention within families was rendered fruitless from the outset. To conquer this field of activity henceforth the placement of the disturbing element must be procured: the family link must be broken. Splitting the family in this way, this procedure precludes any plan for treating it, i.e. by intervening *within* the family structure *in vivo*.[36]

Such a Substantialist definition of mental illness already lagged behind the medical knowledge of the time. In the discussions on the law of 1838 itself, reference was made to pathological manifestations that could not be subsumed under this conception of the legally insane person. 'One cannot consider as insane within the meaning of the law all persons inflicted with a complaint that changes the use or exercise of their intellectual faculties.'[37] But all those psychical disturbances that had already been recognized – 'brainstorms, outbursts of delirium, fits of hysteria that disturb the reason and cloud the intelligence'[38] – ran the risk of falling outside the field of mental health medicine, whose acknowledged sphere of action began and ended with detention. Likewise, the discussions on monomania (see chapter 4) have shown that the mental health specialists not only perceived dimensions of the pathological other than those of 'classic' mental illness, but even devoted an essential part of their ambition to planning how to assume responsibility for them. But faced with the monomaniacs (and soon the host of perverts, psychopaths and abnormal people, etc.) they were to be set an impossible task, – either to shut them all away, or to let them carry out their 'misdeeds' in freedom. This was the paradoxical consequence of this so much elaborated and yet so very rigorous definition of the insane person. It ran the risk of leading one to categorize, *a contrario*, as perfectly normal all the psychopathological profiles that did not come within this matrix of detention. This implication was clearly unacceptable to mental health medicine, anxious to realize its 'mission' in its entirety and, in order to do so, having to conquer new territories. Yet, to annex these still unploughed fields, it would have to break up the framework of the asylum.

However, to shatter the paradigm of detention was to risk effecting the disorientation of the whole mental health system: its legislation, the framework in which it was exercised, the theoretical foundation of its knowledge, the conception of treatment . . . This explains why, for over a century, very few mental health specialists had the heart to attempt it: 'The law of 1838 had achieved in this matter a kind of success: from elements very diverse at the beginning, it had built up the notion that henceforth will prevail absolutely for most of those in France who tackle the problem of assistance to the mentally ill.'[39] It was that very 'success' that had closed upon it like a trap.

This inner contradiction will thus condition the whole history of mental health medicine. There were, as it were, two faces to the law, or rather, it opened onto two opposing areas between which it acted as a kind of interchange. From the outside it filtered those who were liable to come within the ambit of mental health medicine. The filter was rigid and, in the end, sterilizing; it bid fair to paralyse the whole system, in spite of the leeway hinted at in the difference between compulsory placement and voluntary placement. Yet, if the mental health specialists were for a long while so insensitive in their practices to the danger of paralysis, it is because in exchange the law opened up to them, from the inside, within the asylum, an almost absolute kingship. The implementing ordinance of 18 December 1839 laid this down in article 8: 'The medical service, in everything concerning the physical and moral regime, good order, and medical and personal discipline of the insane, is placed under the authority of the doctor, subject to the internal regulations mentioned in the preceding article.'[40] Once he had respected a few minimal administrative requirements, the doctor disposed of a practically unbounded authority: 'An institution for the insane is a small State under protection, having its own world, laws, habits, customs and language. Essentially monarchical, its governance in no way admits any sharing of power, which might lead to a source of harmful conflict.'[41]

More than imaginary power, it was a matter of the real exercise of sovereign power for which contractual societies scarcely any longer provided the opportunity. Even under the *Ancien Régime*, the freedom of the administrator in a closed institution was limited by the authority which had made the placement and which decided also the type of regime ('under restraint', 'half under restraint', and 'at liberty') and the duration of the stay. Now it was the organization of the entire daily life of the patient that depended upon the 'quarters system' described by Parchappe[42] and analysed by Goffman[43]: the patient progressed or regressed in the hierarchy of services by virtue of a 'medical' judgement that in fact very often depended upon the docility he demonstrated towards the rules and values of the institution. As for length of stay, this depended largely upon the doctor, through the dual procedure of compulsory or voluntary placement: he it was who requested discharge from the prefect in the first case, or who, on the contrary, could request the change from voluntary to compulsory placement, if the family sought discharge against his advice – and his judgements were almost always endorsed by the prefect. If it was not a matter of a life-and-death right, it was at least one of taking away or restoring freedom, of suspending all the civil guarantees that citizens 'normally' enjoy, and this for an indefinite period.

How could the psychiatrist give up the direction of this 'phalanstery' of a new kind? 'The insane assembled in an asylum should, we have said, to a certain extent realize a Utopia of the phalanstery, unrealizable anywhere else, in which the work of each individual serves to contribute to the welfare of all.'[44]

Thus the asylum set itself up as at least an approximate realization of the perfectionist daydreams of the social reformers that flourished at the time (Cabet, Fourrier, the attempts to set up anarchist agricultural communes, etc.) It was a curious reversal, whereby the most concerted efforts for the subjugation of men appeared as a model for attempts at libertarian enfranchisement. On this basis an abundant psychiatric literature relating to *work* was developed, which we shall pass over here, in order not to burden unduly our argument. It is a path that led to modern therapy through ergonomics. The ideology of moral treatment provided an immediate rationalization for attempts to make the asylum economically profitable. Work, as the learning of order, regularity and discipline (soon it would be said to be 'resocializing'), would increasingly constitute the axis upon which moral treatment turned. The 'secondary benefits' of an economic order would evidently be welcome.

For example, Berthier presented as follows a dual rationalization for therapeutic work:

> The original and basic aim of work in our institutions is to amuse, to institute regularity, to keep occupied, for, in Franklin's phrase, he who does nothing is close to doing evil. It is only as an afterthought that the economic idea arose . . . What at the beginning had been only a means of recreation and discipline thus became, by a happy extension, a precious budgetary resource.[45]

Yet another happy coincidence! One could draw up a typology of this psychiatric literature upon work, depending on whether it laid the stress upon the one or the other of these poles. But, whether it was inspired by a care for 'moralization' or by profitability, or by both, the reference to Benjamin Franklin and the 'spirit of capitalism' provided the key to it.

This medical justification for the over-exploitation of the sick would determine the most odious aspects of the organization of asylum life: blackmail exerted over the patient by meting out or withholding little privileges, shutting away for life 'good patients' whose free labour is indispensable to the economic balance of the institution, etc. Such practices have recently been denounced. They maintained a kind of autarchic Utopia, according to which 'this little absolute government' could itself meet all its needs. Thus Baron Haussmann's technocratic spirit, in advance of its time, conceived a plan of financial balance for the asylum based on the dual concepts of the inmates' labour and the admission of a judicious number of paying patients.[46] Only the self-reproduction of this system was not ensured, because sexual relations were strictly forbidden. Nevertheless, recruitment to it was always guaranteed.

This is not a mere administrator's daydream (moreover, it appears that Haussmann was no daydreamer). Psychiatrists were broadly asssociated with it, showing once more in this way how much they clung to their mandate as responsible managers. More generally, they identified themselves with 'this organization formed *de novo* and presenting an irresistible force for cohesion that ends sooner or later by overcoming all obstacles'.[47] How could they have done otherwise, since it did no more than increase their own power?

Thus the mental health movement, in its majority, would be led to think of its possibilities for development *through the mere quantitative growth of the asylum model.* Even if this programme had been followed – which it was not, for the administrative and financial reasons given earlier – it was condemning itself to leaving out the qualitative dimensions of the pathological, whose proportions, compared to those 'cases' that depended upon detention, were to reveal itself each day ever greater.

The model of the asylum thus in turn conditioned a kind of ideal model of the psychiatric patient: indigent, dangerous or incurable, exhibiting great spectacular episodes in his mental history. This would be the basis for the practice of mental health medicine, and, all in all, its privileged raw material. Through its mere description we can realize to what extent it is limited. A psychiatry for the poor, but also a poor psychiatry, which is forced to 'select' its subjects on the basis of essentially negative criteria: those who are farthest removed from medical concerns, those who have most chance of. being classed as incurable, those who are the poorest both in money and 'insight' (sic: the word is in English in the French text-*trans.*) in being able to reward the doctor for his pains. The latter must already have been dreaming of the *Yarvis syndrome.*[48] In any case he must have observed with regret the rise of 'the slightly mentally deranged', a whole clientele richer, more interesting, more rewarding and more numerous, which he was going to have to abandon to private or university practice.[49]

Private and Public

Doubtless there existed on the fringes of the system a few regulations that somewhat softened the distorted nature of its rigid workings. First, the model type of asylum patient previously depicted as firmly installed is indeed an ideal type: there most certainly existed others, medically and socially more 'interesting', within the public service. But it is above all the embryo of a private sector that began to drain off another type of population. Already a complex organization existed for this purpose, although the information that we possess on how it really functioned is fragmentary.

In the first place, there was the now forgotten institution of those in public asylums who were paying inmates. Only the indigent could benefit from free care. But other patients might pay an amount per diem, thus falling into three or four categories whose privileges increased according to the price paid for board and lodging.[50] If the bottom class differed very little from the 'common regime', in the top one, those of the insane who were well off could even have their own servants. This phenomenon was by no means negligible, even from the purely quantitative viewpoint. In 1874, out of 40,804 inmates shut away in 'special institutions' (excluding private clinics), the Inspectors-General Constans, Lunier and Dumesnil reckoned there were 5,067 insane who were not on the common regime.[51]

These inmates helped to ensure the institution's financial equilibrium. But they also benefited from a more personalized system. To what extent did their 'clinical treatment' differ from that of the common run of inmates? It is difficult to answer this with any certainty, for hardly any detailed documentation upon the question exists. But it is very probable that these facilities were to draw into the asylum groups whose social as well as pathological characteristics differed from those of the indigent.

The flexibility of the regime was even more marked in private clinics that specialized in the treatment of the insane. The same report of 1874 noted 25 of these in 1872. At that time they included 1,632 inmates, almost always with less than 100 per institution.[52] They also comprised various categories.[53] Certain of them had been founded by mental health specialists, and not the least famous among them: Esquirol's clinic near the Jardin des Plantes, transferred later to Ivry, which he directed with Mitivié, his brother-in-law; the clinic at Vanves founded by Falret and Voisin; and another in Paris directed by Brière de Boismont . . . A certain number of mental health specialists divided their activities in this way between the public and private sectors. Others such as Pinel's nephew, Casimir, who owned and ran the Château Saint-James at Neuilly, devoted themselves entirely to the private sector. Finally, other institutions belonged to private individuals, but employed resident doctors or consultants, such as the Pension Belhomme, where Pinel already 'filled in' before the Revolution, or the Maison Blanche, in which Guy de Maupassant was nursed.[54] Doubtless this was a lucrative business, since the boarding charge at Esquirol's clinic amounted to 6,000 francs a year, a figure to be compared with the daily amount payable for the common regime in public asylums – between 1 franc and 1.25 francs. (6,000 francs was also the annual salary of a medical director of a first category asylum).

There existed also a third type of institution whose function was difficult to define because of a lack of documents: the private institutions that did not specialize only in the treatment of the insane. It is known that there were many of these – some 200 in Paris. They did not come under the law of 1838, and thus in principle could not admit the insane. But – as is still the case today – a few of them were to admit a certain number of insane from good families, avoiding labelling them as such. Above all they were to draw from among the well-off classes of society some of the less severe pathological cases that did not come within the ambit of insanity as narrowly defined in the law of 1838.

Finally, the mental health specialists were frequently to fill the role of consultant among their equals: members of the administrative board of the hospitals or of the departmental Council, contacts in high society, etc., who could ask their advice when a member of the family or one closely connected displayed signs of mental disturbance. This represents the beginnings of the building up of private psychiatric practice, the history of which has apparently not been written.[55]

What may have been the impact of this private system upon the public? Casimir Pinel, who moreover was both judge and participant in this matter, did not hide his preferences: 'In spite of the grandiose buildings, the good administration and a learned medical direction, from the very fact that their mission was to take in the poor, the public asylums could not, when the option was open to them, come up to the private institutions.'[56] However, setting aside this competition, which was nevertheless limited since the two systems did not target the same population, the private sector may have served as a model, which the fact that certain mental health specialists had both types of practice underlines. Philippe Pinel himself depicted Esquirol's clinic in a particularly eulogistic fashion: 'In Dr Esquirol's institution, so well-reputed, and deservedly so, each insane patient has a servant exclusively at his service, who always sleeps near him, and even in his bedroom when it is judged necessary.'[57]

It is during family visits or on walks that Dr Esquirol skilfully applies moral treatment, when madness is abating, or during convalescence. He gives comfort to this one, encourages another, chats with a melancholic patient, and seeks to dispel his chimerical illusions . . . As soon as the insane patient gives unequivocal signs of convalescence, he is admitted to sit at the common table with the doctor . . . They meet together for lunch, and to play billiards or certain other games; some part of the evening is spent in a vast drawing-room, where music is enjoyed, and when no impediment can be foreseen, the convalescent patient is allowed to walk with his servant in the Jardin des Plantes or go for a drive in the country.[58]

Psychiatry goes in for 'pilot experiments' (cf. today 'the 13th Arrondissement experiment', or La Borde's clinic) which often serve as a cloak for a general situation that is far less brilliant. Would moral treatment have, in doctors' eyes, enjoyed such credibility if it had not been thought out, at least in part, as seen through this miniaturized 'prism'? Was it not a bold extrapolation – or an advantageous rationalization – to transplant it as such into the ever more populous asylums?[59]

Moreover, it is not only for moral treatment that this model may have come into play. Thus we learn, from chance reading (for there exist no specific sources concerning private institutions) that 'the institution founded by Mitivié and Esquirol at Ivry, and particularly the quarters reserved for the violent, which were newly built, served for a long while as a model for specialist doctors and architects, and was the starting point for the improvements that since that time have been made to the building of asylums for the insane.'[60]

So far as we can judge, the embryonic existence of a private sector must therefore have played a more important role than it is generally stated to have done in the overall balance of the system. It allowed the richest to escape from the misery of the common regime. From among these well-off classes, it must have welcomed 'clinical treatment cases' that were less rigorous than those presented by the common run of the asylum population: doubtless these were the less dangerously insane, presenting symptoms that resembled more neurotic disturbances. Finally, it provided organizational 'models' and treatment schemes that helped to cover the great misery of the public asylums modestly with a veil.

Casimir Pinel thus contrasted the public asylums, in which 'it is above all upon hygiene and exact discipline that one must count', and the clinics, in which, 'having only to look after a small number of patients, the doctor, aided by one or two assistants, can very easily exercise direct and continual action over them; in other words, he can bring to bear upon them all the hygienic influences, as well as the form of treatment termed 'moral'.'[61] This is doubtless true. But the skill of the mental health specialists consisted in making those 'hygienic influences' and disciplinary requirements that determined the mass treatment of the insane poor an integrating, and even the essential part, of moral treatment itself. And this is independent of whether or not there existed certain differences between these collective disciplinary forms of treatment and a more personalized intervention. Falret went so far as to make this disparity, which is explicable as a *class* difference between the groups for which responsibility was assumed, represent a time-lag in relation to knowledge:

> Moral treatment can be divided into general or collective treatment, and into individual treatment . . . If science were more advanced, individual treatment might well occupy first place . . . In the present state of our medical knowledge, collective treatment is our most precious resource. Individual treatment, set up as an exclusive system, would, unless care were taken, lead to the negation of any general rules in therapy, and to the negation of all science; thus transforming Science into an art, the patient would be abandoned to all the whims of instinct or to the inspiration of the moment[62]

In contrast, collective treatment 'is applicable to all patients, since it attacks tendencies that are common to everybody'.[63] This hesitation is significant: what has just been presented as the quasi-superiority of collective treatment now appears as a deficiency in knowledge: 'We have wished you to carry away the reassuring conviction that, if the special science that we follow is unfortunately not very advanced on an individual basis, at least we possess a few effective principles for general treatment that have been applied successfully in the best run asylums in every country.'[64] Naturally, the real reconciliation – which allows one to be 'reassured' – is of a social and political order: personalized care for those who pay for it, mass regimentation of the mass of the poor. 'Liberal' medicine and collective medicine – all is for the best in the best possible of worlds. For the common herd, 'the sight of general submission prepares for individual obedience',[65] whilst the rich person already begins to renounce his subjectivity through a dyadic relationship. This double standard is the one which mental health medicine has always operated. We know that we have not yet emerged from this regime, which ranks psychiatric and psycho-analytical practices as class practices.[66] But their complementary nature is today concealed by psycho-analysis, under rationalizations more subtle than those of Falret.

The rectifications and even the models that the beginnings of a private type of practice brought to the general system were thus not negligible. However, they remained marginal. The centre of gravity of psychiatric activities remained indeed, and by a long chalk, the asylum, the hospital for the poor, the completely and the chronically mad, a sphere entirely dominated by the rigid constraints of detention. This is what accounts for both the extraordinary permanence and the fragility of the synthesis of the asylum. It has survived throughout the history of psychiatry as 'the good form', in the Gestaltist sense of the term. In so doing it has dazzled the gaze of its protagonists in two ways.

Already in the world of detention the systematic nature of the coherence provided by the asylum inspired a kind of morbid rationalism that served to mask the real situation, which became more and more degrading. Overcrowding, material misery, absence of therapeutic activities, daily violence, etc. – these were, so to speak, sublimated by a rational, near-delirious rhetoric concerning the benefits of isolation, the medical rigour of the classifications, the effectiveness of moral treatment . . . It has been a long-lasting, dogmatic slumber on the part of the psychiatrist, who has continued to think of himself as a doctor whereas he was no longer any more than the guardian of the asylum order, that immense cemetery that has swallowed up thousands of despairing lives.

Outside the asylum also, the domination of the asylum form has left without any recognized status a whole host of practices through which mental health medicine could just as well, and doubtless better, have satisfied its ambitions. Yet we have seen that the extra-hospital inputs of psychiatry were practically contemporaneous to its success in the asylum. But they would be forced to develop, if not clandestinely, at least as subordinate to those on whose behalf the law of 1838 arrogated official legitimacy.

7

The Transition: From the
Golden Age to the *Aggiornamento*

All in all, we have attempted to reconstitute the workings of a machine. We have shown how the arrangement of the parts of the asylum complex and the intertwining of its various strands produced a certain number of effects: it conquered for itself a market, promoted its agents and selected its patients, categorized modes of behaviour, worked at the texture of an institution, traced out frontiers and established bridgeheads with other authorities, etc. Its next task would be operate the same mechanisms both for installing and dismantling the present-day machinery. It is therefore a subject that, even if it resorts to history, is not properly speaking of an historical order. Its realization does not entail following at every stage the chronology that has led to the present-day metamorphosis.

However, the novelty of the present-day situation in psychiatry has slowly disengaged itself from the furrows dug by the former organization. Innovations that are apparently the most unexpected represent so many attempts to escape from former contradictory positions. It is in this exact sense that the pre-history and history of mental medicine are necessary conditions for understanding the modern situation. It is not even certain that an alternative that would completely do without the former asylum complex can even today be conceived. In any case, this is the legacy on which it would have to be built. Thus, at the very least, we must disentangle the main strands in its decomposition and recomposition that lead to the present-day organization of the psychiatric landscape.

The First Cracks

As early as 1864 Jules Falret wrote:

> The law of 1838 and the asylums for the insane are being attacked on
> all sides. In the press, in books, at scientific congresses, one seeks to
> combat principles that have served as the basis for our asylums for
> sixty years. It is proposed to overturn everything, destroy everything,
> and what is desired is nothing less than a radical reform both of ideas
> and of the reality. A veritable crusade has been preached for some
> years against the present-day organization of institutions for
> the insane by men not lacking in heart or conviction, but who do
> not know these patients sufficiently well. This tide, which is mount-
> ing every day, threatens to invade everything and accomplish a
> veritable revolution in the principles that have guided doctors and
> administrators in asylums for the insane since the beginning of this
> century.[1]

From 1860 onwards there did indeed appear a series of criticisms
that, although not concerted, focused simultaneously on each and
every one of the elements in the synthesis of mental health medicine.

1 The law

The law of 1838 was welcomed with marked favour when it appeared;
for twenty years, it was unreservedly praised, and several foreign
powers borrowed from it. About 1860 a sea-change occurred in the
public; strong criticisms were directed against this law, which had
been ratified by public opinion. To respond to desires that were
insistently expressed, the government set up in 1869 a commission
entrusted with the task of investigating what reforms could usefully be
introduced.[2]

This was the first of a good score of plans for reform, whose cycle
is not yet complete, since, at the time when this book is appearing,
the Commission on Liberties of the National Assembly has taken up
the problem once more. It is indeed a tricky question, but one from
which, upon examination, some lessons can be drawn.

The problem arose through the denunciation of arbitrary
detentions. It represented an attempt at revenge by a judiciary
brutally dispossessed by the 1838 law. But there was also a political

background: the press, muzzled under the Second Empire, sought out indirect targets through which to assail the absolutism of the regime. Thus the first affair concerned a certain person called Sandron, detained at a time when he was said to be ready, through compromising letters allegedly in his possession, to implicate an important personage who had recently rallied to the Empire.[3] Was he a dangerous persecuted person turned persecutor, or a political opponent that had been silenced? Clearly, however, it was not a conflict of the Left against the Right. Shortly afterwards a nurse from the asylum at Châlons-sur-Marne launched a petition that denounced 'medical omnipotence that is exercised without any serious controls'. However, the enquiry, or what the medical health specialists report of it, discovered that the nurse had allegedly been put up to it by the hospital chaplain. It was a fresh episode in 'religious obscurantism' versus the 'light of Science'.[4]

However, the Senate took the petition seriously and appointed a commission of enquiry, but in 1867 its rapporteur absolved the law of 1838.[5] Nevertheless, the opposition took up the question again, and a first proposal for the revision of the law was placed before the Chamber of Deputies in 1870 by Gambetta himself. It was not to succeed, because of the events that would bring about the fall of the Empire. The problem was that none of the proposals that followed would succeed either, however much their adjournment was caused by events.

The first attempt at revision was, however, one of the most daring. In contrast to most of those that were to follow, it was not content with asking for the reinforcement of judicial authority. It proposed the constitution of a veritable board, to have the power to decide absolutely upon admissions.[6] It also contained violent attacks against 'the bitter resistance of mental health medicine, which made the law, which applies it and which lives on it'. 'Allow the mental health School to elevate to the dignity of a principle of jurisprudence this aphorism that can be of far-reaching consequence: madness is only visible to the eye of the specialist. Then say, what Frenchman is sure not to have to sleep this evening at Charenton?'[7]

It is not useful to go into the detail of the successive plans for revision. Almost all were characterized by their juridical nature. It was a question, in all their technical variations, of making the judicial authority once more an *active* partner in the process of selection. This juridical criticism gave rise sometimes to violent accusations against the mental health school. But the condemnation of arbitrariness concentrated the attention of those that attacked it. What was sought was an unchallengeable set of *guarantees* that should be written into the text of the law and should rectify the shift in power that the legislators of 1838 had endorsed under the pressure of the mental health specialists. Broadly speaking, one can therefore interpret these polemics as so many attempts on the part of the judiciary, and the legalist tendencies that supported it, to take their revenge upon 1838.

Faced with these accusations, the position of the psychiatrists was remarkably uniform in its defence of the law – naturally, in the interests of the patients. We recall Falret's opinion, for whom the clauses of the law were 'applicable in all times and in all countries, as ineradicable as insanity itself'.[8] With the passage of time, certain mental health specialists allowed some refurbishing of the detail, some minor technical adaptations relating solely to the conditions of its application. But the law itself remained excellent 'in its principle'. About this no discordant note whatsoever emerged:

> Let us not weary of stating that madness creates for him who is affected by it entirely exceptional conditions. . . . The law of 1838 is good: if there have been abuses, and M. de Bosredon was able to say that not a single one had been detected by the commission, it is because the law has not been rigorously carried out. It answers the needs of modern society, it protects the individual through the precautions that it has built up around admissions, and through the facilities it has given for discharges. The legislators that prepared it, the Chambers that accepted it, wished the idea that there was a sick person to be treated and cured to prevail everywhere. By leaving to the doctor the right to decide what was useful and opportune, they have given the French medical body proof of their high confidence, of which it has always shown itself worthy.[9]

Thus there was a dialogue of the deaf, which arose because the problem was still seen from the wrong end of the opera-glasses: to reinforce the legal guarantees for the *application* of the law. Only extremists such as Garsonnet[10] called into question its *principle*: 'A strange matter: we have allowed mental health medicine to make a law, but we have not thought of asking it whether it had the knowledge to do so . . . In the end, what is the law upon the insane? Nothing other than mental health therapy raised to the level of an institution; when the therapy has been judged, one will have judged the law.'[11] But it was only from the twentieth century onwards that criticisms began to take into account this relationship between legislation and the problem of the nature of mental health illness. A certain number of psychiatrists realized then that the law imposed too narrow a definition of insanity, and the question of its revision opened up an internal debate inside the movement.[12]

2 *The institutional mechanism*

The criticism of the institution from the outset cut deep into the structure of mental health medicine, for it was more internal, and revealed contradictions that began to surface in daily practice.

A discussion was opened up at the meeting in July 1860 of the Medico-Psychological Society[13] concerning the celebrated agricultural colony at Gheel in Belgium, which, since the Middle Ages, had admitted insane people in a state of semi-liberty, under the responsibility of peasants who kept them. The Society decided that a delegation would go to Gheel, and Jules Falret read their report at the meeting on 30 December 1861. It was a fine monument to mental health ethnocentricity: 'One is really stupefied and fearful at seeing the peasants allow the insane to move freely among their families, their female domestics and children, and entrusting them with weapons and tools . . . The feeling that is predominant at Gheel . . . is one of really exaggerated confidence in the insane and in their harmless character.'[14] 'Even from this viewpoint of the general treatment exercised by local authorities and individuals, the total absence of order, rules and discipline, to which all mental health doctors have attached real importance, must be considered a very regrettable gap in the internal organization at Gheel.'[15]

However, since he had to acknowledge that there were hardly any untoward happenings, Falret could not completely condemn the arrangements. He therefore concluded by emphasizing the analogies between the agricultural colony and the asylum, and recommending the reinforcement of medical control:

Gheel has not been able, and will not be able to improve, save by drawing closer to the enclosed asylums. The latter, in their turn, will be unable themselves to improve save by progressing prudently and slowly along the path to liberty . . . Gheel has more to gain by drawing closer to the asylums than the latter have by drawing closer to Gheel.[16]

But the discussion was resumed in 1864. This time the pretext was the reading of a paper by an obscure provincial doctor, who was not even a specialist in mental health, but who praised the little farm-cum-asylum, with few medical overtones, at Leyme, where the insane allotted to work in the fields enjoyed a certain freedom. The discussion lasted a full year, and the principal representatives of the mental health school intervened in it, progressively widening the scope of the debate. The general tendency was always to censure the author of the paper for his naivety and his ignorance of the principles of mental health medicine. But muted anxieties surfaced. In particular, Morel intervened vigorously, stressing the overcrowding and above all the lack of differentiation in the services provided:

> These institutions have become entirely inadequate. But this is still not the most serious matter in a situation that is already so deplorable. Not only are we swamped by the numbers of insane, but also by categories of sick people who could be cared for in ordinary hospitals and hospices . . . Idiots, imbeciles, cretins and epileptics – in other words a host of the socially useless – tend to flood into the asylums, where they settle in, taking up the places of the really insane.[17]

However, this was a minority opinion. Significantly, it was a foreign doctor, Mundy, who developed a new 'family system', which he wanted to see replace that of the asylum: 'Family life supervised by a doctor, regulated freedom and optional open-air work, these are therefore the main features of the new system.'[18] He was not listened to. Moreover, he toned down his thoughts before the learned assembly. In a work published immediately afterwards he denounced 'those frightful dens in which the unhappy insane are destined to incurability and death'.[19] And another doctor, French this time, but who was not a psychiatrist, asserted in 1864, in order to support the petition to the Senate against the law of 1838, that the asylum rendered the condition chronic, and killed.[20] These are extreme opinions that remain, like criticisms of the law on Garsonnet's lines, marginal standpoints. On asylums Jules Falret held the perennial position, strictly the corollary to the one concerning the law defended by his father:

> A radical reform would be a retrograde step, and not a step forward. After many attacks launched from all sides, the asylums for the insane will still remain standing, because they respond to social and medical needs that are for all times and places. Whilst they will change and successively improve, they will remain founded on the same general principles, which are in reality related to the true needs of the insane . . . Other modes of assistance will never be more than ancillary and complementary, clustered around the main system that is represented by enclosed asylums.[21]

However, the canker was in the apple. Looking more closely, from these first criticisms of institutions during the 1860s two positions emerge (three, if one counts that of the traditionalist supporters of the *status quo*). There was technical criticism of isolation, which sought to make the ways in which it was applied more flexible. Thus Moreau de Tours gave a positive judgement on Gheel, which he saw as a means of improving the asylum structure, giving it, if it may be so expressed, room to breathe, by attaching to it a system of agricultural colonies. And, behind this institutional modification what the aim was to render the principles of mental health medicine more flexible, faithful to their true spirit:

> Need we therefore shut away absolutely the insane in order to isolate them? The two terms are far from being synonymous in their grammatical sense; they are even less so in their scientific connotation. To isolate an insane person is to break utterly the habits amid which madness has arisen, to remove him from places, things and persons that are not entirely alien to the disturbances of his mind . . . At Gheel, all these conditions are faithfully fulfilled. The places where the insane person lives, the individuals with whom he comes into daily contact, the tasks he performs, the leisure pursuits – everything is new to him. He is in no way cut off from every social contact, and he cannot fail to form, in the society of which he has become a member, impressions that can provide a most felicitous distraction from his delirious ideas.[22]

This was properly a reformist position. It went back on those interpretations of the doctrine that were too exclusive, that were caricatures of it, such as the complete identification of isolation with detention within a confined space. But, adapted in this way, the institutional mechanism remained the adequate instrument for the therapy of insanity. On the same basis, one could therefore establish more flexible distinctions, for example, between a recent onset of madness and the chronic state, between the insane capable of work and those who are not, etc. Linas was of the same opinion: 'In so many respects (discipline, supervision and isolation) [the asylum] is particularly suitable for madness that is recent, acute or paroxysmic. Beyond this, it is notoriously inadequate and imperfect.'[23] This was a more nuanced position, but not in contradiction with that of Jules Falret: the extension of the asylum to agricultural colonies, and even to placements in a family – since this idea was also beginning to appear – remained faithful to the spirit of the system.

However, at the same time was born the suspicion that the asylum might not be that 'medicized area' conceived of by Pinel and his successors. It was no mere chance that it was Morel who, within the school, took up the most critical position regarding the institution. To make the asylum a 'medicized area' supposed a homogeneity in mental illness in the classification of which only sub-species of insanity were separated out (see chapter 2: Pinel's Technology). Now, a profound upheaval in the very conception of mental illness undermined this representation of an order that was indissolubly spatial (distribution over the hospital area), and theoretical (the nosographical classifications). If the concept of insanity was exploded, the asylum ran the risk of merely housing together heterogeneous groups, the sick and the 'socially worthless' of all kinds. It was in danger of becoming a new version of the former Hôpital Général, in which medical effectiveness would be lost when faced with a lack of differentiation between these groups, whose sole common feature would merely be that they were shut away.

3   The theoretical code

We have insisted (chapter 3) on the expedient through which, from the beginning, the mental health school had elaborated its reactive and psychogenic conception of mental illness, disregarding researches into clinical medicine. Clearly the distance between a 'psychological medicine', a term that became more and more derogatory, and a general medicine that was increasingly assured of keeping a 'scientific' monopoly had only grown wider. The uneasiness that had been felt since the foundation of the school grew during the 1850s.

A certain number of mental health specialists tried, as a first step, to escape from the dilemma between moral and organic causes, and that between description of the symptoms and the search for the source of illness, by establishing the intelligibility of the illness through its *evolution* and no longer through the *description* of its symptoms. Thus in 1852 Lasègue isolated the persecution delirium.[24] J. P. Falret and Baillarger both discovered at the same time, in 1854, what became known as 'circular' and 'dual form' madness.[25] These nosographic groupings were not content to describe a symptom or even a cluster of symptoms. They made each symptom a *sign* that, together with other signs, referred back to a *hidden* intelligibility of the illness, displayed over time. Thus one passed from a symptomatology, a mere descriptive phenomenology, to a *semiology*, through which the illness acquired both a meaning that underlay its external manifestations and a potential for evolution.

A further step could be taken if this underlying meaning and evolution were attached to an objective cause. This was the transition of semiology to *aetiology*, which was realized in Morel's conception of degenerescence. Lasègue said of him: 'His pathology relates far less to the phenomenology than to the genesis [of the illness], it is more enquiring than descriptive. In this lies the superiority of his talent. . . . Morel resolutely embarked upon this voyage of discovery and devoted the best part of his work to the *potentially insane.*'[26]

Phenomena of degenerescence were sickly deviations from the normal type of humanity that were transmitted through heredity. They could have various causes, and Morel's plan for the *Traité des dégénérescences* was drawn up in accordance with this diversity: various forms of intoxication, influences of the social environment and heredity, acquired or congenital infirmities . . . But once it had a hold, the illness followed its course and was handed on to the descendants, until the line died out.

It is less important here to evaluate in itself this theory of degenerescence, which, particularly through Magnan, was to exercise a decisive influence on the future of psychiatry, than to be conscious of the upheaval it caused in relation to the concept of

mental illness that prevailed up to that time. Buchez, opening a
great debate upon the idea that was to take up eight meetings of the
Medico-Psychological Society from 12 November 1860 to 27 May
1861 pointed out from the beginning that this 'pathogenic' conception clashed with the custom of 'classifying the forms of madness
according to the symptoms'.[27] And as Morel made plain in the
discussion: 'The predisposition, the determining cause that triggers
off that predisposition, finally the succession and transformation of
pathological phenomena, which engender and command one
another in turn, determine according to a genesial or pathogenic
procedure the place that the individual should occupy in the
nosological pattern.'[28] The intelligibility of the illness was no longer
given through the grouping together of its symptoms, but by
reference to a hidden causality.

Morel's discovery was, moreover, only the manifestation that had
the most repercussions in a general transformation of the conception
of mental illness that the more inventive of his contemporaries
promoted, each in his own fashion.[29] Thus Marcé's *Traité pratique des
maladies mentales*, published in 1862, takes as its starting point a
criticism of Esquirol's symptomatological classifications and a
discussion of Morel. He proposed to conceive of madness as an
illness (the title of *Traité* was already significant, compared with the
classic conception of mental illness), seeking as the basis of each one
of its manifestations a 'special and constituent' defect: 'I do not
hesitate to state that any method founded mainly on psychology
must be utterly rejected . . . If one seeks to use it as the point of
departure for a study of madness, one will certainly go astray,
wandering along murky paths remote from any practicality.'[30]

At the beginning of the twentieth century, when organicism had
triumphed, G. Ballet's *Traité de pathologie mentale*, which was thought
authoritative, summed up the theoretical movement that, in his
view, had led to the pathogenic conception he defended, seeking
morphological or histological defects:

> Some (Pinel, Esquirol, Guislain and, to a certain extent, Griesinger,
> Baillarger and Marcé) have confined their gaze to the external
> physiognomy of the syndromes, and have grouped these together
> more or less artificially, without worrying sufficiently about the
> causes and the evolution of the various disturbances: their classi-
> fications are too exclusively symptomatic, or rather, related to

syndromes. Others, and these are above all the more modern writers (Morel, Magnan), on the contrary have tried to take into account, when constituting the types and nosological groupings that they have accepted, the aetiology and the development of mental illnesses . . . However imperfect, for example, Morel's classification may have been, it is indisputably very superior to that of Pinel and Esquirol[31]

These are perhaps value judgements which we do not have to endorse as such. But they indicate the decisive shift that had been implemented in comparison with that first 'social psychiatry' studied in chapter 3. The 'theoretical' conception of mental illness no longer directly presided over the social phenomenology of the illness. Conversely, it tended to draw closer to the common core of medicine, whose organicist tendencies were more marked. This is the perspective in which Morel consciously placed his own work: 'I have followed my dominant idea, which was to link mental illness to general medicine more firmly than has been done up to now.'[32] And, in a discussion devoted to the concept of 'no restraint', namely, a practical problem that calls into question the traditional conception of moral treatment, he sets out the enlargement of the definition of mental illness that has resulted from his operation: 'I have written a whole book in order to broaden the study of the special causes of mental illness, adding to this a study of the causes of the intellectual, physical and moral degenerescence of the human species.'[33] Indeed such a transformation of the 'scientific' conception of mental pathology could not fail to have profound repercussions upon practice.

4 Technology

Perhaps a disputable, but enlightening image might be: moral treatment forms a kind of disciplinary triangle that joins together doctor, patient and institution. It is the hierarchical and regulated relationship between these three poles that constitutes its dynamism and explains the effectiveness ascribed to it. An all-powerful personality imposes his reasonable will upon one that is utterly deprived, by means of institutional stages that are designed to reflect back and multiply that power: subordinate staff, regulations, timetables, regulated activities, etc. It is therefore comprehensible that the modification of at least two of the elements in this triad, the institutional set-up and the conception of the patient and the illness, profoundly upsets this system.

Viewed from this modification of the pathological conception, and therefore from the patient's viewpoint, at first sight it would seem that the transformation of the 1860s should have led to the abandonment of moral treatment. If it were true that such treatment supposed the educability of a man, even a madman, the set of notions progressively substituted for a disorder of the mind produced directly by controllable external influences – such as an inner perversity, hereditary tendencies or organic defects – such substitution should correspondingly reduce the sphere of application of a rational technology. A prognosis of incurability should replace the hope of returning the insane person to reason through active intervention to eliminate the pathological processes.

A tendency to do this effectively existed, but upon it another tendency was superimposed, one that aimed, for its part, at profoundly transforming moral treatment itself and at shifting the field where it was practised outside the asylum. Morel's phrase cited above, which explains his theoretical intention of promoting a stronger medical approach, ends up in expressing this will to universalize moral treatment: 'I have followed my dominant idea, which was to link mental illness to general medicine, *and to cause to emerge from this study a more fruitful and more universal application of moral treatment.*'

In what did this change consist? Up to now, according to Morel, society had merely proceeded to a 'defensive prophylaxy' by shutting away dangerous and sick people and treating them with more or less effectiveness in an enclosed environment. 'It must carry out a *preserving prophylaxy* by trying to modify the intellectual, physical and moral conditions of those who, on various counts, have been separated from the rest of mankind; before sending them back into the social environment, it must, so to speak, arm them against themselves so as to diminish the number of relapses.'[34]

Prophylaxy thus set out to 'fight the causes of illnesses and forestall their effects'.[35] The programme of the science of mental health in this way linked up with that of physical and moral hygiene. It spilled over into unsuspected possibilities, and, at the extreme limit covered the whole social scene: 'We can conceive that the goal to be reached in the application of therapeutic and hygienic means has been singularly enlarged. Indeed we are no longer in the presence of one man in isolation, but of a society, and the power of the means of action will have to be proportionate to the importance of the goal.'[36]

However, if society as a whole was thus the horizon for preventive intervention, it was very plainly its points of weakness, the centres of disorder and misery, that were targeted as a priority. It was above all to a 'moralization of the masses' that mental health medicine was to contribute, by assisting the assumption of responsibility for 'those broken-down classes in society who hardly glimpse the upward movement of the higher classes and who cannot attain to it if they are abandoned to their own resources'.[37]

It was certainly not by chance that Morel built his conception of degenerescence upon the observation of the over-exploited proletariat of the Rouen region and of the wretched surrounding agricultural population (he was head doctor of the asylum at Saint-Yon). But it was no chance either that he wrote to the Senator (who was also the Prefect) for the Seine-Inférieure department to offer his services and suggest to him a veritable plan for the surveillance of the most wretched groups in the population:

(1) What is the morality of the inhabitants of a given environment . . ., the number of illegitimate children, the number of assaults against persons and property . . ., the number of suicides, the extent of prostitution, the figures for natural and accidental deaths, etc.? (2) What is the state of food and hygiene among the inhabitants? (3) What is the state of primary education in each one of our communes? . . . (4) Above all, what is the proportion of drunkenness, and in what quantities are alcoholic drinks consumed? . . . In many cases it is necessary to penetrate inside families, to see at close quarters the manner in which the inhabitants of a locality live, to acquaint oneself with the state of their physical and moral hygiene. This is, as is easily understood, a delicate task, and one which cannot be suitably performed save under the aegis of the authorities. I do not believe that there is any other way in which we can arrive at the moral statistics for this important department, and thus provide the authority with useful documentation on the causes for the increase in number of the insane and on the most appropriate hygienic and prophylactic means of preventing such a great infirmity.[38]

This was an extraordinary extrapolation of the medical function. The doctor in his asylum was imprisoned within too restricted a framework, often reduced to impotence because he intervened too tardily, on too small a scale, upon material that was hardly any longer amenable to his action. Yet even the preponderance of incurables should not lead to pessimism and even less to abandoning the will to intervene medically: one had to know how to shift the point at which this intervention was applied.

> Everything induces us to get out of the false position in which we have been placed, and not to remain inactive spectators of so many causes destructive of the human species. We have to prove, whatever the difficulty of the situation, that medicine, far from being struck with impotency, as some of its detractors claim, can still become for society a valuable means of salvation, in spite of the predominance of incurable cases. It alone can evaluate effectively the nature of the causes that bring about the various kinds of degenerescence in the human species; to it alone appertain positive indications of the remedies to be employed.[39]

This awesome extension of the medical role represented at the same time a profound transformation of the way in which it was practised. The doctor would no longer be the exclusive agent, as he was in the asylum, nor even the direct operator in the actions in which he participated. He would be able to advise, inspire and enlighten all the decision-makers, all those whose professional function and/or position in the social hierarchy called them to exercise political acts over the masses: 'Its claim is not to set itself up as an exclusive mediating force; it invites the participation in this task of regeneration of all those to whom is entrusted the welfare and destiny of the people, all those who possess the means of realizing the plans for improvement that medical science submits to their examination.'[39a]

Very precisely, this anticipated the functions that the proponents of preventive psychiatry sought to realize through claiming a voice in all those places where decisions about the community are made.[40] Let every committee have its consultant psychiatrist, let every assembly refer to the opinion of the competent specialist. We can see that the function of expertise was about to dissolve, but by conjuring up the old Platonic dream of the philosopher-king. We must remember – as Plato's *Republic* demonstrates – that such Utopias flourish only in class societies. Also – our own society shows us this – it is there too they are realized. In another text Morel asks, 'Why would it be impossible to extend to the outside world what is done in our asylums?'[41] Alas, it is this that we also must ask.

The transformation of the theoretical basis of mental illness produced a contrasting and dual effect. On the one hand, the pessimistic prognoses dictated by organic aetiology, the increase in the number of the incurable, the appearance of the ineducable, closed in upon the darkness of the asylums. They were vast cemeteries of the dead where referral to medical science became increasingly a farce. On the other hand, a boundless field for medical intervention opened up: prevention, prophylaxy, detection . . ., the doctors offered their services and increased in number. They wished to be present on all those sectors of the front where a danger of disorder might emerge. For these new activities Morel kept the label of 'moral treatment', which to him 'seems a felicitous term',[42] because of its reference to a 'moral law', which doubtless flattered his sensibility as a onetime seminarist. It is doubtful whether he was right in this, for the term 'moral treatment' is deeply rooted in the classic tradition of the asylum. But the word is less important than the thing. We have not yet finished with dealing with what, under other names and in the last analysis, was a strategy of guardianship.

Thus the hiatus, so very embarrassing in the previous period, between the strategies of subjugation of the 'philanthropists' and the technology of the asylum (see chapter 3) seemed capable of being bridged. But it was on condition that medical practice cast off from its privileged moorings in the asylum. There was a long road to travel before this could be accomplished.

The Double Line of Reconstitution

Contrary to a common conception of the history of psychiatry, it is thus not in recent times (in 1945, or about 1960 with the 'sector') that a deep crisis in the traditional organization broke out. In the 1860s not only had none of these elements been spared,[43] but connections between these different criticisms were coming to light. Thus Morel called into question both classical nosographies, through degenerescence, the lack of internal differentiation within the asylum institution and its rigidity, which blocked the possibility of acting outside it, as well as absolute confidence in the classic techniques of imposing discipline, since he himself rallied to

Conolly's idea of 'no restraint'. For psychiatry, the question was therefore not one to which historical events, through their unexpected character, generally gave rise. It was the opposite: why had this change taken so long? And even, had it really happened? We shall not answer this here by propounding a mere formula. We shall only sketch the outline of the argument, which will be expanded elsewhere.

I

From the criticisms raised in the 1860s, attempts at reform tended to take two *divergent* directions. This cleavage broke the fragile synthesis of the medical and social strands established by mental health medicine in its golden age (chapter 3). By emphasizing the maladjustment between practices within and outside the hospital, it postponed for a long time the possibility of working out a new *overall* organization.

The first measure was devoted to reconstituting the asylum sector in order to make it a *truly* medical one. In short, it was a matter of taking up anew the operation carried out three quarters of a century earlier for the Hôpital Général. This was because the asylum was beginning to be perceived in the same way as was the Hôpital Général by the first mental health specialists: lack of differentiation and overcrowding reintroduced a confused mixing of people, and the juxtaposition of heterogeneous categories of detainees. The consequence was the same: the impossibility of treating medically groups unless they represented different classes of illness, since at the most the sole feature they shared was that they were shut away.

Yet, in order to reconstitute groupings that could be treated separately, a start had to be made by transplanting a certain number of patients elsewhere. The asylum had to be rid of the chronically ill, the senile, the poor – who still managed to get in – the epileptics, the alcoholics, the criminally insane, etc. Thus, in the end, scientific medicine had to be dissociated from public assistance, keeping only the 'truly ill', who could then be treated intensively.

This tendency gave rise to a certain number of practical initiatives, from the off-loading of the chronically insane from the Paris region to provincial asylums, to the creation of family agricultural colonies in the centre of France at the end of the nineteenth century and the opening of special sections for male epileptics

(Ville-Evrard, 1892) and female epileptics (Maison-Blanche, 1910), and for the criminally insane (the Henri-Colin Service at Villejuif, 1910).[44] It also inspired plans for the general reorganization of public psychiatric assistance, limited at first to the Paris region, such as Haussmann's new plan in 1860 for the siting of asylums,[45] the later more ambitious one as in the Sérieux report of 1903,[46] or the Toulouse plans.[47] It was an inspiration that led to the setting up of the 'free services' in the psychiatric hospitals, the development of neuro-psychiatric services in the medical faculties, down to the present-day tendency to attach the new 'sectors' to ordinary hospitals. These attempts corresponded to a desire to 'medicalize' in the technical sense of the term: mental illness was seen as an illness almost like any other, which had to be treated by means that were, as far as possible, comparable to those of ordinary medicine, in places that resembled, as closely as possible, the hospitals that treated other illnesses. It was therefore breaking with the 'special' character of asylum practices and placing psychiatry once more within the mainstream of medicine.

But these reforms were forced to operate in a *selective* manner: they rejected from the medical sphere all those who could be treated as 'true' patients, and therefore could not be admitted into highly specialized institutions. The duality between medicine and public assistance was thus continued in a mixture of institutions: on the one hand, specialized services, on the other, 'minding' institutions. Such a formula could not therefore provide a unified solution to the set of problems covered by the label of 'mental derangement'. It also presented disadvantages for a strategy of expansion in mental health medicine: through inability to treat all groups needing assistance according to a more exacting medical pattern, it had to abandon them to other authorities capable of assuming responsibility.

A second line of reconstitution tended, on the contrary, to break up the privileged relationship between psychiatric practice and the hospital. It was no longer a matter of 'medicalizing' the asylum, but, at the extreme limit, of not using it, and instead directly intervening in those areas where madness emerged – in non-medical institutions such as the school, the army and the family . . . It was the line that strove for prevention, prophylaxy and detection. Here the institutional set-up was minimal – for instance, a dispensary sited in the city. The nature of the intervention was also profoundly changed. It was less a matter of curing than of preventing, of assessing the

dangers, of detecting anomalies, of testing aptitudes. It was also less
a question of acting upon the individual than of modifying the
environment by programmes of hygiene that were not necessarily
linked to medicine. The medical function had exploded. The
specialist was less visible and yet everywhere present. But also the
type of group for which responsibility was assumed was profoundly
transformed, both quantitatively and qualitatively. There is an
astonishingly modern note about the criticism made in Toulouse by
one of the opponents of this line, a mental health specialist in the
classic mould:

> He dreams of a Federation of psychiatric republics in which the
> commonality of citizens would be examined on a conveyor belt
> system, at the beginning of their principal activities, by the army of
> prophylaxis specialists, large- and small-scale guidance counsellors,
> sexologists of every kind, specialists in suicide, in head colds, in car
> driving and statistics, – in short, by all the sub-products of 'noölogy'
> born or to be born from its creative imagination.[48]

Was there an opposition between a technically oriented medicine
and a social medicine? This dichotomy, as we shall see, was too
widely drawn. Behind these procedures for intervention there was
also a technical medical pattern, that of the fight against tuberculosis
and venereal diseases, under the general heading of the struggle
against 'social scourges'. Nevertheless, it was indeed the unstable
unity of mental health medicine as the first 'social medicine' that
was being broken up. There was a somewhat frustrating, and
already halting synthesis between the technology of the asylum, a
nosographic classification insufficiently distinguishable from a social
phenomenology of disorder, and a plan for public assistance of the
'philanthropic' kind (see chapter 3). This synthesis had less
resistance to a scientific, medical model (which had become more
exacting) because the institution of the asylum that served as a
matrix for all these practices became blocked. In this synthesis, the
unity of mental health medicine ran the risk of being lost. In its place
emerged a bipolar system: on the one hand, work on preselected
groups treated in the hospital, and on the other, the activities of
prevention, selection and assessment, with very weak institutional
support.

The divergence between these two lines, the fact that in spite of
efforts to blend them together, in Toulouse about 1920, and that

they tended each to become systematized independently, explains to a large extent the lapse of time that separated the first criticisms of the asylum system from the discovery of a new *global* formula. Very precisely, the 'sector' represented the effort to reconcile these strands, to rediscover that unitary inspiration of the early psychiatry, whilst at the same time taking into account the requirements of the work outside the hospital. This effort was the work of doctors within the 'framework' of the psychiatric hospitals, who were the heirs of the old mental health specialists, and was against the wishes of the 'university' doctors. This preliminary note is made here merely to suggest how understanding the historical lines of development can help to unravel present-day imbroglios.

II

However enlightening this may be, such a hypothesis cannot, however, account for the whole process of transformation of mental health medicine. Or rather, there is still the risk that these modifications will be interpreted as the *internal* evolution of the mechanisms of psychiatry, whereas at the same time they represent the change in *relationships* with the other authorities, and, beyond this, with the set of practices for control and normalization. A change in the problems of mental health medicine occurred where these two series of 'internal' and 'external' transformations came together.

As we have seen, the reforms in justice and administration effected at the end of the eighteenth and in the first half of the nineteenth century do not constitute, as regards mental health medicine, an external decor which a scrupulous stage producer would use as a backcloth in order to provide a frame for the evolution of his character. Nor is psychiatry content to 'answer' on its own behalf for 'difficulties' arising from the outside. The *internal* structure of its responses depends upon these 'external' requirements. For example, the intrinsic nature of the admission certificate is that of a 'medico-legal act', as Renaudin terms it, constructed from nothing in order to resolve the problem of the new sharing of authority between the administration and justice. Likewise, the concept of monomania has no meaning if it is not related to a specific judicial scenario, etc. What arises in the history of mental health medicine must therefore be reintegrated into any reconstitution of the set of practices of normalization, of which the medically linked process of guardianship represents but one element – yet, it is true, one that is more and more predominant.

Take, for instance, the transformation of moral treatment into a therapeutic relationship. Leuret's paradox will be recalled. Leuret was the doctor who pushed the coercive nature of moral treatment to the limit, undertaking a veritable struggle against the insane person's delirium in which almost all assaults, physical violence, dissimulation and lies were permitted. But he was also the one who best adjusted his method to the particular case, carrying out long individual therapeutic sessions, pursuing indefatigably the patient until he had caused him to admit the vanity of his delirium. The framework of Leuret's practice does not allow us to decide exactly what it owes to the asylum structure. Occasionally we indeed have the feeling that Leuret was somewhat handicapped by having to act in these impersonal places, within the overpowering atmosphere of the asylum. Moreover, the most original features of his practice could only exceptionally be exercised, through lack of time, since he was also responsible, as head of the service, for the treatment of hundreds of the insane.

The distinction that Falret drew between individual moral treatment and collective treatment (see chapter 4) betrayed the same ambiguity. Did it arise from, as he said, a disparity in knowledge, or from the conditions of asylum practice? Doubtless from both. The most likely hypothesis is this: the model for the therapeutic relationship as one of guardianship was constituted in the asylum. It could be constructed because the power relationship from which it was constituted rests upon institutional supports. It was installed in it almost exclusively in the form of collective treatment, because in this way it best corresponded to the true 'social mission' of the asylums, frequented above all by the poor, and in which hundreds of the insane were entrusted to the responsibility of one doctor alone. However, the overloading of the psychiatric institution counteracted these massive regulations that were supposed to treat all the detainees. Moral treatment died in the asylum, but a flexible structure emerged from this all-enveloping one. Already, Morel had attempted prophylactic intervention. Moral treatment (let us now say 'the therapeutic relationship') kept certain essential features of its asylum matrix. The relationship still functioned according to a fundamental disparity between two personalities, one of whom had power and authority and represented the norm. However, the objectively visible grounds for these privileges had vanished. This had consequences: first, the relationship was thereafter more flexible, more mobile, easily transposable, and in practice transportable anywhere. Secondly, the ever-implied violence was more discrete, and at the margin, invisible. It was true that moral treatment had indeed changed. Proof of this lay in the fact that the term disappeared, and that many did not recognize its features – above all, those who carried out the therapeutic relationship in the form of 'liberal' practices. In the private consulting-room there was very little objective backing left for the old relationship between doctor and patient, and in any case there was no shower above the doctor's couch. But, particularly if one believes the effectiveness of the symbolic, is it so outrageous a hypothesis that there can also be a violence of interpretation?

A change in the location of moral treatment thus entailed a transformation of its archaic features into sophisticated mechanisms. But through this transfer, the conditions for placing into guardianship were near to becoming comparable to those of taking out a contract. A *contract of guardianship* would be as wondrous an invention as that which stupefied the Marquis de Barthélemey when he 'became aware' of the reconciliation, through therapeutic isolation, between the harshness of humanity, the interests of society, and those of the sick person. We shall see that this is what psychoanalysis has promoted. But the acclimatization in France of behaviour modification, the rearrangement of the living environment into a space for continuous surveillance in certain kinds of 'sector', the techniques for examination and assessment of performance from birth to death, etc. inaugurated other procedures, more or less subtle, for assumption of responsibility, and which were so many means for taking into guardianship. The process of guardianship whose origins we have followed here was then relaunched in a different orbit.

In order to draw up this new chart of dependent relationships, we may have to break away from that Gallocentricity that has perhaps appeared to inspire this present work. Indeed, apart from the fact that familiarity with the French historical situation was easier to acquire, the ponderousness that would have ensued from the simultaneous examination of other national situations in the nineteenth century would not have been compensated by any substantial gain in new facts. The maladjustment between former control

apparatuses, the reorganization of justice, the rationalization of the
administration, the beginnings of unbridled urbanization, the
unblocking of the labour market, etc., have imposed on the different
Western nations a restructuring of public assistance policy that has
given rise to simular formulas. But the violence of the crisis that was
opened up in France by the Revolution hardened these antinomies
and made explicit what was at stake, right up to the 'solution' of the
law of 1838, whose value as an exemplar was perceived by all contemporaries.[49]

Although the concept of the 'sector' is exportable, as they say, just
as Concorde is, the function as a model of the French situation is
today less plain. Thus one also seeks elsewhere, and especially in the
United States, elements that will relate the transformations in
mental health medicine to that 'outside world' worked on by
psychiatry, and which turn out also to be its 'inside world'.

Why indeed did these dependency relationships, established so
irrefutably for the situation in the nineteenth century, vanish so
abruptly as to place the new ' "psy" function' in a position
completely outside the social sphere? Have the present-day techniques been made more autonomous, the theoretical classifications
more refined, or the institutional arrangements more sophisticated?
This is doubtless true: the fine simplicity of the nineteenth century is
no longer to be found. Are dominance relationships in contemporary
society more complex, and do we lack the necessary perspective to
objectify them? Doubtless this is so: thus we will assist ourselves by
using the model that the analysis of a less confused situation has
allowed us to construct.

However, this must be done with prudence. If the former policy of
public assistance appears to us today to be somewhat naive, it is
because it still states explicitly what its function is to obliterate: the
difference between classes. Is it permissible to quote a song by
Théodore Borel as the typical and ideal expression of this attitude?

> O you rich, you will sleep in peace,
> You and your capital,
> So long as beggars have a loaf of bread
> In which to stick their knife.

Not only does one no longer write in such a vein, but one no
longer proceeds in such a way. There are no longer beggars or rich

men, but social partners who share the benefits of expansion. The new 'social work' thus breaks the ties that public beneficence maintained formerly with charity. Such beneficence *assisted* the impoverished groups by marking the visible signs of their dependence, thus reproducing the cleavage between classes. Now it is a question of *aiding each and all* of the partners – naturally in accordance with each one's place in society – to remain in the production and consumption cycle by reproducing the socio-economic structure *in its entirety*. One can then understand the political interest in modes of control that do away with discontinuities and cobble together principles that are objectively opposed, in order to sustain a continuity in qualitative differences.

Mental health medicine and its model of detention represented the 'medicalized' version of the conception of public assistance through segregation. The techniques of community relationships correspond to a 'participatory' conception of integration. They assume that the dichotomy of the normal and the pathological has been broken down, as well as the separation between the areas where 'assumption of responsibility' takes place, just as, on the social plane, the split between the classes must be outmoded. The best minds apply themselves to this.

Just as the analysis of the functions of the asylum does not imply a desire to return to penitentiaries, the intention here is not systematically to refute those who innovate in this way. Nor, moreover, is it to underestimate the qualitative importance of the shift that they effect. On the contrary, one would wish to show the somewhat dizzy possibilities that these new strategies open up – and thus also, to do justice to the novelty of the techniques that back them up.

If, however, such a procedure still carries with it the risk of reductionism, it is one that must be run. The rhetoric of autonomy of the specialism is a monotonous one. For its part, it takes few risks, and it strengthens the good conscience of the professionals: psychiatry progresses increasingly towards the realization of its true therapeutic vocation, the unconscious opens access to a different scenario in which what is at stake is no longer connected with social and political destinies: the doctor is a neutral actor who deals with technical problems, etc. It is also a vain rhetoric, unless it develops the potential for intervention of the competent specialist. It is therefore understandable that the latter is eager to retain it. It is his right to do so. It should also be a right to try out another procedure corresponding to a totally different intention, one of demystifying the viewpoint of the specialism and technical competence. This procedure would also begin to take the measure of the proliferation of specialists, this increase in the number of experts who, even when they say they are giving up any plan to cure (which, moreover, has never been a crime), assess, select and 'normalize' under the cover of their competence. It is to continue, after others and with others, to circumscribe these less visible strategies whose power of domination has become a power of manipulation. For the power grows because it remains concealed.

From the paradigm of detention to generalized intervention, from muscular paternalism to the symbolic violence of interpretation: we shall attempt to describe this metamorphosis, without the double advantage available here of having used historical material and having waited for the death of those who produced it.

Appendix A

Law of 30 June 1838 Concerning the Insane

Title I Concerning Institutions for the Insane

Art. 1 Each department is required to possess a public institution especially intended for the admittance and care of the insane, or to negotiate for this purpose with a public or private institution either in the department or in another department. The contracts agreed with public or private institutions must be approved by the Minister of the Interior.

Art. 2 Public institutions for the insane are placed under the direction of the public authority.

Art. 3 Private institutions for the insane are placed under the supervision of the public authority.

Art. 4 The prefect and the persons specially delegated for this purpose by him, or by the Minister of the Interior, the president of the law-courts, the king's prosecutor, the justice of the peace, or the mayor of the commune, are required to visit the public or private institutions for the insane. They shall receive the complaints of the persons therein, and shall on their behalf obtain such information as is needful in order to ascertain their position. Private institutions shall be visited, on days not previously laid down, at least once a quarter, by the king's district prosecutor. Public institutions shall likewise be visited at least once every half-year.

Art. 5 No person may direct or start a private institution for the insane without the authorization of the government. Private institutions devoted to the treatment of other illnesses may not admit those suffering from mental illness unless the latter are placed in entirely separate quarters. For this purpose these institutions must be specially authorized by the government, and shall be subject, as regards the insane, to all the obligations laid down in the present law.

Art. 6 Public authority regulations shall determine the conditions on which shall be granted the authorizations stated in the preceding article, the cases in which these may 'be withdrawn, and the obligations to which the institutions so authorized shall be subjected.

Art. 7 The internal regulations of public institutions devoted, wholly or in part, to the care of the insane, shall, insofar as the arrangements relate to that care, be submitted to the Minister of the Interior for approval.

Title II **Concerning Admissions to Institutions for the Insane**

Section 1 Voluntary placements

Art. 8 The heads or those responsible for public institutions, and the directors of private institutions devoted to the insane, may not admit a person suffering from mental illness if there is not handed to them: (1) A request for admission containing the names, occupation, age and residence both of the person formulating the request and of the person on whose behalf it is made, together with a statement of the degree of kinship, or, failing this, of the nature of the relationship existing between them. The request shall be in writing and signed by the person making it, and, if he cannot write, shall be made to the mayor or superintendent of police, who shall give it legal form. Heads of institutions, or those responsible, or directors, must, on their own responsibility, assure themselves of the identity of the person who has formulated the request, when that request has not been made to the mayor or superintendent of police. If the request for admission is formulated by the guardian of a person under interdiction, he must provide, in support of the request, an extract from the judgment of interdiction. (2) A doctor's certificate of the mental state of the person to be admitted, giving particulars of the illness, and attesting to the need to have the person undergo treatment in an institution for the insane, and to have him detained. Such a certificate shall not be accepted if it has been made out more than fifteen days before being handed to the institution's head or director; nor if it is signed by a doctor attached to the institution, nor if the doctor signing it is a relative by blood or marriage, to the second degree inclusive, of the head or proprietor(s) of the institution, or of the person causing the admission to be made. In cases of emergency heads of public institutions may dispense with the requirement for a doctor's certificate. (3) The passport or any other document attesting to the identity of the person to be admitted. On an admission form there shall be listed all the documents produced, and this shall be sent, within twenty-four hours, with a certificate of the institution's doctor and a copy of the one mentioned above, to the Prefect of Police in Paris, to the prefect or sub-prefect in the chief town of the department or the district, and to the mayors in other communes. The sub-prefect or the mayor will immediately forward them to the prefect.

Art. 9 If placement is made in a private institution, the prefect, within three days of receipt of the form, shall appoint one or several doctors to examine the person named on the form, in order to investigate his mental state and to report immediately upon it. To them he can add any other person that he shall designate.

Art. 10 In the same space of time, the prefect shall notify through the administration the names, occupation and residence both of the person admitted and of the person who has requested the admission, and the reasons for his placement: (1) to the king's prosecutor of the district in which the person admitted has his residence; (2) to the king's prosecutor of the district in which the institution is located. These conditions shall apply to both public and private institutions.

Art. 11 Fifteen days after the placement of a person in a public or private institution, there shall be submitted to the prefect, in accordance with the last paragraph of article 8, a fresh certificate from the institution's doctor; this certificate shall confirm or rectify, if needs be, the observations made in the first certificate, mentioning the return in greater or lesser frequency, of attacks or acts of insanity.

Art. 12 In each institution there shall be a numbered register countersigned by the mayor, in which shall be entered forthwith the names, occupation, age and residence of the persons placed in the institutions; the statement of the judgment of interdiction, if it has been pronounced, and the name of their guardian; the date of placement, the names, occupation, and residence of the person, whether a relative or not, that requested it. There shall likewise be recorded in this register: (1) the doctor's certificate, attached to the request for admission; (2) those certificates that the institution's doctor must despatch to the authorities, in accordance with articles 8 and 11.

The doctor shall be required to note down in this register, at least once every month, the changes that have occurred in the mental state of every patient. The register shall also record discharges and deaths. It shall be submitted to those persons who, in accordance with article 4, have the right to visit the institution when they present themselves at it for this purpose; after having completed their visit, they shall put in the register their mark, signature and observations, if any are required.

Art. 13 Every person placed in an institution for the insane shall cease to be detained in it as soon as the institution doctors have declared, in the register foreseen in the preceding article, that a cure has been effected. If a minor or one placed under interdiction is involved, notice of the declaration by the doctors shall be given at once to the persons to whom it has to be made, and to the king's prosecutor.

Art. 14 Even before the doctors have declared a cure to have been effected, every person placed in an institution for the insane shall likewise cease to be detained therein as soon as his discharge shall have been requested by one of the persons designated hereafter, namely: (1) the trustee named for the carrying out of article 38 of the present law; (2) the husband or wife; (3) failing any husband or wife, their immediate forbears; (4) if there are no forebears, the descendants; (5) the person that signed the request for admission, unless a relative has declared himself against that person making use of this power without the assent of the family council; (6) any person authorized for this purpose by the family council. If, as a result of an opposition notified to the head of the institution by one authorized to do so, demonstrating that there is disagreement, either among forbears or descendants, the family council shall decide. Nevertheless, if the institution doctor is of the opinion that the mental state of the patient might compromise public order or the safety of persons, notice of this shall be given in advance to the mayor, who may immediately order a temporary postponement of the discharge, on condition that it be referred within 24 hours to the prefect. This temporary postponement shall cease unconditionally after 15 full days, if the prefect has not, within this space of time, given orders to the contrary, in accordance with article 21 hereafter. The order of the mayor shall be recorded on the register kept in compliance with article 12. In cases involving minors or interdiction, the guardian alone can request discharge.

Art. 15 In the 24 hours following discharge, the heads, others responsible, or directors of institutions shall give notice to those officials designated in the last paragraph of article 8, and shall inform them of the name and residence of the persons who have withdrawn the patient, his mental state at the time of discharge, and, so far as possible, the name of the place to which he shall have been conveyed.

Art. 16 The prefect may at all times order the immediate discharge of persons placed voluntarily in institutions for the insane.

Art. 17 In no case can a person under interdiction be handed over to anyone save his guardian, or a minor save to those under whose authority he is placed by the law.

Section 2 *Placements ordered by the public authorities*

Art. 18 In Paris the Prefect of Police, and in the departments the prefect, shall order mandatorily the placement in an institution for the insane of any person, whether under interdiction or not, whose state of mental disturbance might compromise public order or the safety of persons. The orders of the prefects shall give reasons and must describe the circumstances that have made them necessary. These orders, as well as those made in accordance with articles 19, 20, 21 and 23, shall be recorded in a register similar to the one prescribed in article 12 above, all of whose stipulations shall apply to individuals mandatorily detained.

Art. 19 In case of imminent danger, attested to by a doctor's certificate of where it is of public notoriety, the superintendents of police in Paris, and the mayors in other communes, shall order, with respect to persons afflicted with mental disturbance, all temporary measures necessary to be taken, on condition that they are referred within the space of 24 hours to the prefect, who shall take decisions upon them without delay.

Art. 20 The heads, directors, or others responsible for institutions shall be required to despatch to the prefects, in the first month of each half-year, a report drawn up by the institution doctor on the condition of every person detained in it, concerning the nature of his illness and the results of treatment. The prefect will pronounce upon each case individually, and will order his continued stay in the institution or his discharge.

Art. 21 With respect to persons whose placement is voluntary, and in the case where their mental state might compromise public order and the safety of persons, the prefect may, on the lines laid down in the second paragraph of article 18, grant a special order, so as to prevent such persons being discharged from the institution without his authorization, unless it is in order to be placed in another institution. The heads, directors, or others responsible are required to comply with this order.

Art. 22 The king's prosecutors shall be informed of all orders issued under articles 18, 19, 20 and 21. These orders shall be notified to the mayors where persons subject to placement reside; the mayors shall immediately inform their families. A report on this shall be made to the Minister of the Interior. The various notifications prescribed in this present article shall be made in the form and within the space of time laid down in article 10.

Art. 23 If in the interval that elapses between the reports prescribed under article 20 the doctors declare, in the register kept in compliance with article 12, that discharge may be ordered, the heads, directors or others responsible for the institutions shall be required, under penalty of being prosecuted in accordance with article 30 hereafter, to refer the matter immediately to the prefect, who shall decide upon it without delay.

Art. 24 Hospices and civilian hospitals are required to admit provisionally those persons who may be sent to them in accordance with article 18 and 19, until they are moved to the special institution designed to receive them, according to the terms of article 1, or in the course of the journey made to reach it. In all communes where hospices and hospitals exist, the insane may not be lodged save in such hospices or hospitals. In place where they do not exist, the mayors must provide for their lodgings, either in a hostelry or in a building hired for this purpose. In no case may the insane be conveyed with those under sentence or accused of a crime; nor may they be housed in a prison. These stipulations are applicable to all those insane directed by the authorities to a public or private institution.

Section 3 Expenditure on the services for the insane

Art. 25 Those insane whose placement has been ordered by the prefect and whose families have not requested their admission into a private institution, shall be conveyed to the institution belonging to the department, or the one with which an arrangement has been made. Those insane whose mental state would not in any way compromise public order or the safety of persons shall likewise be admitted to them, in the forms, circumstances and conditions that shall be laid down by the Conseil Général (Departmental Council), upon a request made by the prefect and approved by the minister.

Art. 26 The transport expenses of persons directed by the authorities to institutions for the insane shall be decided by the prefect, upon a memorandum submitted by those responsible for their transportation. The boarding costs, maintenance and allowances of persons placed in hospices or public institutions for the insane shall be regulated in accordance with a list of charges laid down by the prefect. The maintenance, boarding and allowance of persons placed by the departments in private institutions shall be fixed according to agreements made by the departments, in accordance with article 1.

Art. 27 The expenditure set out in the preceding article shall fall to the persons being admitted; in default, it shall fall to those from whom sustenance may be required in accordance with the terms of articles 205 ff. of the Civil Code. If a dispute arises concerning the obligation to provide sustenance, or about its quantity, the matter shall be decided by the competent court of law, at the request of the administrator designated to carry out article 31 and 32. The recovery of the sums due shall be pursued and effected through the administration for registration and for estates.

Art. 28 In default, or in the case of an insufficiency of the resources set out in the preceding article, the expense shall be met out of the special percentage added, by the finance law, to the normal expenses of the department to which the insane person belongs, without prejudice to the support of the commune in which the insane person is domiciled, upon a basis proposed by the Conseil Général (Departmental Council), upon the advice of the prefect, and approved by the government. The hospices will be limited to an indemnity proportionate to the number of insane whose treatment or maintenance was their responsibility, and who might be placed in a special institution for the insane. In case of dispute, the prefectoral council shall decide.

Section 4 Arrangements common to all persons placed in institutions for the insane

Art. 29 Any person placed or detained in an institution for the insane, his guardian, if he is a minor, his trustee, any relative or friend, may, at any time, appeal to the court of law in the place where the institution is situated. The court, after proceeding to the necessary verifications, may order, if needs be, the immediate release of the insane person. The persons that asked for the placement and the king's prosecutor, on his own authority, may appeal to procure the same end. In the case of interdiction, this demand may only be formulated by the guardian of the person under interdiction. The decision shall be given upon a mere request, in chambers and without delay; no reasons at all shall be given. The request, the judgment and the other acts to which the appeal might give rise will be sealed by stamp and debited. No requests, no appeals addressed either to the judicial or administrative authorities may be suppressed or delayed by the heads of institutions, without their being liable to the penalties set out in Title III below.

Art. 30 The heads, directors or others responsible may not, without being liable to the penalties laid down in article 120 of the Penal Code, detain a person placed in an institution for the insane when his discharge has been ordered by the prefect, under the terms of article 16, 20 and 23, or by the court, under the terms of article 29, nor when that person falls under the cases set out in article 13 and 14.

Art. 31 The administrative or supervisory commissions of hospices or public institutions for the insane shall exercise, for those persons not under interdiction that are placed in them, the functions of provisional administrators. They shall designate one of their members to fulfil them; the administrator so designated shall proceed to the recovery of sums due to the person placed in the institution and to the discharge of his debts, shall grant leases that may not exceed three years, and may even, under a special authorization granted by the president of the civil court, cause moveable property to be sold. The sums arising either from the sale or from other recovery acts, shall be paid directly into the account of the institution and shall be employed, if needs be, to the profit of the person placed in the institution. The bursar's security shall provide the guarantee for such funds, taking precedence over credits of all other kinds. Notwithstanding, the parents, husband or wife of the persons placed in institutions for the insane that are managed or supervised by administrative commissions, those commissions themselves, as well as the king's prosecutor, may always have recourse to the provisions laid down in the following articles.

Art. 32 Upon the request of the parents, husband or wife, or that of the administrative commission, or upon the intervention by virtue of his office of the king's prosecutor, the civil court of the place of domicile, may, in accordance with article 496 of the Civil Code, appoint, in chambers, a provisional administrator for the property of any person not under interdiction who has been placed in an institution for the insane. This appointment shall only take place after discussion within the family council and after the king's prosecutor has arrived at his conclusions. It shall not be subject to appeal.

Art. 33 The court, upon the demand of the provisional administrator or at the request of the king's prosecutor, shall designate a special mandatory charged with the legal representation of any individual not subject to interdiction and placed or detained in an institution for the insane who may be engaged in a judicial action at the time of his placement or against whom an action may later be brought. The court may also in cases of emergency designate a special mandatory in order to bring, in the name of the same individuals, an action concerning moveable or immoveable property. The provisional administrator may in both cases be designated as special mandatory.

Art. 34 The provisions of the Civil Code concerning the causes that dispense with guardianship, that concern the exclusion and the depriving of the rights of guardians, are applicable to the provisional administrators appointed by the court. Upon the demand of the parties concerned or upon that of the royal prosecutor, the judgment that appoints the provisional administrator may at the same time place upon his property a general or special mortgage to the limit of any sum determined in the said judgment. The king's prosecutor must, within fifteen days, register this mortgage with the Mortage Record Office; it shall date only from the day of registration.

Art. 35 In the case where a provisional administrator shall have been appointed through a judgment pronounced, the notifications of the judgment to be made to the person placed in an institution for the insane shall be made to the said administrator. The notifications to be made at the place of domicile may, depending on circumstances, be annulled by the courts. There is no dispensation from the provisions of article 173 of the Commercial Code.

Art. 36 In the absence of a provisional administrator, the president of the court, at the request of the principal party, shall entrust a notary with representing persons not subject to interdiction placed in institutions for the insane, in matters concerning inventories, accounts, distribution of property or liquidations in which they are concerned.

Art. 37 The powers conferred by virtue of the preceding articles shall cease as of right as soon as the person placed in an institution for the insane is no longer detained therein. The powers conferred by the court by virtue of article 32 shall cease as of right after the expiry of a term of three years; they may be renewed. This provision is not applicable to provisional administrators who are assigned to persons maintained by the authorities in private institutions.

Art. 38 Upon the demand of the person concerned, or one of his parents, husband or wife, or a friend, or upon the intervention on his own authority by the royal prosecutor, the court may appoint, in chambers, by a judgment not subject to appeal, not only the provisional administrator, but also a personal curator, for every individual not under interdiction placed in an institution for the insane. He shall see to it that: (1) the income of the insane person is used to improve his lot and hasten his cure; (2) the said individual shall be restored to the free exercise of his rights as soon as the situation permits. The curator may not be chosen from among the heirs presumptive of the person placed in an institution for the insane.

Art. 39 The acts performed by a person placed in an institution for the insane, during the time that he has been detained there, without interdiction being pronounced against him or embarked upon, may be subject to legal action for reason of dementia, in accordance with article 1304 of the Civil Code. The ten years during which an action for nullity shall run, in regard to the person detained who has subscribed to such acts, from the date of the notification of them being made to him, or from the date he has had knowledge of them after his final discharge from the asylum; and, with respect to his heirs, the date at which notification shall have been made to him, or the knowledge they shall have had of them, since the death of their perpetrator. When the ten years have already begun to run against him, they will continue to run against his heirs.

Art. 40 The public authority shall be heard in all matters concerning persons placed in an institution for the insane, even when they are not under interdiction.

Title III   General Provisions

Art. 41 Contraventions of the provisions of article 5, 8, 11, 12, the second paragraph clause of article 13, articles 15, 17, 20, 21 and of the last clause of article 29 of the present law, and of the regulations laid down in article 6, that may be committed by the heads, directors or others responsible for public or private institutions for the insane, and by the doctors employed in such institutions, will be punished by a period of five days to one year in prison, and a fine of from 50 to 3,000 francs, or by either of these penalties. article 463 of the penal code may be applied.

Appendix B

Chronology and the Law of 30 June 1838

Since the division into chapters does not follow a strict chronology, the principal historical facts evaluated and which led to the passing of the Law of June 30 1838 on the insane have been placed here in their order of appearance.

	PUBLIC ASSISTANCE AND CONTROLLING AUTHORITIES	MENTAL HEALTH MEDICINE
1784	Circular of Bréteuil, Minister of the King's Household, regulating and limiting the use of *lettres de cachet.*	
1785	Royal Ordinance reorganizing beggaries.	Special quarters for the insane are planned for each beggary. J. Colombier and F. Doublet, *Instruction sur la manière de gouverner les insensés et de travailler à leur guérison dans les asiles qui leur sont destinés.*
1788	Plan by Tenon for the reorganization of the Paris hospitals. Royal Ordinance prescribing the development of charity workshops for the poor.	Tenon recommends that special quarters be reserved for 200 incurable insane in a new hospital for 1,000 injured and fever patients that is to be built at Sainte-Anne.

1790	Law of 27 March concerning the abolition of *lettres de cachet*. Beginning of the work of the Committee on Begging of the Constituent Assembly, presided over by the Duc de La Rochefoucault-Liancourt. The Constituent Assembly decrees that public assistance to the poor is a national duty and plans the nationalization of hospital property. Beginning of vast roadworks in Paris to occupy the poor. Reorganization of criminal justice. Elected juries. Cabanis, *Observations sur les hôpitaux*.	Article 9 of the law of 27 March: persons detained on account of dementia will be questioned by judges and examined by doctors, and if they are classified as insane, treated in hospitals. Law of 24 August which 'entrusts to the vigilance of the municipal authorities untoward happenings that might be occasioned by the demented or furiously insane left at liberty, or by evil and ferocious animals'. Enquiry into the condition of the insane requested by the Deputy-Governor of Hospitals. A commission of the Committee on Begging, with La Rochefoucault-Liancourt, likewise visits the institutions in Paris where the insane are shut away.
1791	Setting up of the Committee of Public Assistance of the Legislative Assembly, presided over by Tenon. It succeeds the Committee on Begging and contains a majority of doctors. Institution of family courts. Closure of the workshops for public works for the poor of the Paris area. Abolition of the privileges and exemptions enjoyed by hospices and hospitals. Abolition of the corporations and the prohibition of workers' coalitions.	The law of July 21 renders liable to criminal penalties 'those who allow to wander abroad the demented or furiously insane, or evil and ferocious animals'. Report by Cabanis to the department of Paris on 'the state of the female insane detained in the Salpêtrière'.

1792	Suppression of the religious orders. The 'Rapport sur l'organisation générale des secours publics et sur la destruction de la mendicité', by B. d'Airy, places the emphasis on home assistance and envisages departmental institutions for the detention of incorrigible beggars.	Pinel is appointed to Bicêtre. Charenton is closed.
1793–1794 (Year II of the Republic)	New Declaration of the Rights of Man and of the Citizen, Art. XXII: 'Public assistance is a sacred debt, and it is for the law to determine its nature and how it should be applied' (29 May). The nation assumes responsibility for poverty-stricken orphans and abandoned children (28 June). Law of 24 Vendémiaire, Year II: the elaboration of the idea of a 'public assistance' domicile as a condition for participation in that assistance, and transformation of beggaries into departmental institutions for the suppression of begging. The law of 22 Floréal, Year II, decrees the registration of the indigenous poor in 'the great book of national welfare' and grants the option of public assistance at home. 'No more alms, no more hospitals'. (Barère) Institution of a corps of para-medical officers paid by the state. Law of 23 Messidor, Year II: the property of hospitals is put up for sale as the property of the nation.	Law of 24 Vendémiaire, Year II: 'Those at present detained by reason of insanity, and who are maintained at the expense of the nation, shall be transferred to new institutions of detention and shall continue to be a charge upon the authorities.'

Year III	After Thermidor, on 9 Fructidor Year III, the Convention postpones the sale of hospital property.	As part of the foundation of the Paris School of Medicine, Pinel is appointed Assistant Professor, and then Professor.
Year IV	Report by Delecloy on 'the organisation of public assistance' that criticizes the work of the Revolutionary assemblies and puts forward the principle of privatization of public assistance and of making it a matter for the communes. Abolition of family courts.	
Year V (Directory)	The Directory decides that hospital property sold off as property of the nation shall be replaced (16 Vendémiaire, Year V). Nuns begin to install themselves once more in hospitals and hospices. Law of 7 Frimaire, Year V: charity bureaux with limited and local resources replace the registration of the indigent poor on the national welfare list. Installation of administrative hospital commissions (Law of 16 Vendémiaire, year V). These confirm that hospital assistance is a matter for the community (but they will be placed under the control of the sub-prefects in Year VIII).	The Directory re-opens Charenton for the treatment of the curable insane. Beds for insane patients at the Hôtel-Dieu, as well as in the 'small institutions' which admitted the incurable, are done away with. Pinel is appointed to the Salpêtrière.
Year VIII	The Constitution of Year VIII lays down principles for the political, judicial and administrative reorganisation of France, the spirit of which is later defined by Guizot (*Histoire*	

générale de la civilisation en Europe, Lecture XV, Brussels, 1839): 'Administration, from the most general viewpoint, consists of a set of means designed to cause the imposition, in the most prompt and surest way possible, of the will of the central authority on all sections of society, and to ensure the return, under the same conditions, to the central authority, the forces of society, either in men or money.' Appointment of prefects.

Year IX	Setting up of the General Council for the administration of hospices of Paris. Setting up of special criminal courts, particularly for judging vagrants.	Pinel, *Traité médico-philosophique sur l'aliénation mentale.*
Year X		Esquirol joins Pinel at the Salpêtrière.
Year XI	Reappearance of the 'Société de charité maternelle', founded before 1789 by a group of philanthropists.	Pinel is appointed consultant physician to the Emperor and is awarded the Legion of Honour in the following year.
Year XII	Civil Code. Re-establishment and development of the Ministry of General Police.	Civil Code, Art. 489: 'The adult person who is habitually in a state of imbecility, dementia or raving madness must be placed under interdiction, even when his condition is marked by periods of lucidity.' Art. 509. The person under interdiction has the same status as a minor as regards his person and property. The laws concerning guardianship of

Year XIII	Members of the charity bureaux and hospice commissions are appointed by the Minister of the Interior upon the advice of the prefect.	minors shall apply to the guardianship of those under interdiction.
1806		Renovation of Bicêtre and Salpêtrière. Opening of treatment wards.
1808	Imperial decree on the abolition of begging. Institution of a beggary in every department. Organization of the Imperial 'Université', which establishes a monopoly in public education. Code of Criminal Investigation.	Circular of the Minister of the Interior reiterates the necessity to place the insane under interdiction.
1809	Re-establishment of the religious orders and private foundations.	
1810	Penal Code. The decree of 3 March 1810 recognizes the practice of administrative internment and legalizes the existence of state prisons for 'persons detained without it being fitting for them to be brought before the courts or to be set free.'	Penal Code, Art. 64: 'There is no crime or offence committed when the accused was in a state of dementia at the time of the action, or when he has been contrained by a force that he was unable to resist.' Arts 475 and 479 are adapted from Laws of 24 August 1790 and 21 July 1791.
1811	The decree of 19 January 1811 prescribes the setting up of a hospice in every district ['arrondissement'] for abandoned children.	
1813	Institution of 233 central prisons.	Circular of the Minister of the Interior ordering prefects to undertake an enquiry into the position of the insane.

1814	Plan for the establishment of regional asylums by the Napoleonic administration. Foundation of the first of them at Mareville, near Nancy.	
1817	Esquirol starts a clinical course for mental illnesses at the Salpêtrière.	
1818	Report of Esquirol to the Minister of the Interior: *Des établissements consacrés aux aliénés en France et des moyens de les améliorer.*	
1819	Circular of Decazes, Minister of the Interior, setting out the organization for a system of special institutions for the insane. Article on 'Monomania' by Esquirol.	Guizot is appointed director of the Department and Communal Administration and prepares a programme of reforms in the various fields of public assistance. Foundation of the Royal Society for the improvement of prisons.
1820	The medical commission appointed by the Minister of the Interior to organize a service for the insane interrupts its work.	Fall of Guizot and seizure of power by the Ultras after the assassination of the Duc de Berry. Baron de Gerando, *Le Visiteur du pauvre.*
1821		Foundation of the Société de morale chrétienne under the presidency of the Duc de La Rochefoucault-Liancourt.
1822	Pinel is not reinstated in his professorship at the Faculty of Medicine.	
1822–1830	Foundation of private asylums (Brother Hilarion).	Development of private system of assistance under religious control.

	Relations between the philanthropic movement and the liberal constitutional opposition in the Société de morale chrétienne.	Polemics regarding monomania and psychiatric expertise before the courts.
1825		Bayle, *Nouvelle doctrine des maladies mentales.*
1827		Annotated translation by Esquirol of Hoffbauer, *Traité de médecine légale.*
1828		Circular of the Prefect of Police of Paris regulating the rules for private health clinics.
1829	Creation of the *Annales d'hygiène publique et de médecine légale.*	
1831	Tocqueville goes to the US to study the penitentiary regime.	
1832	Reform of the Penal Code. Mitigating circumstances.	
1833	Guizot Law on elementary education.	Enquiry by the Minister of the Interior into the situation of the insane.
1834		Report of Ferrus to the Conseil Général for the insane: *Des aliénés.*
1835		The Minister of the Interior submits the question of the insane for deliberation by the Conseils Généraux.
1836	Parent du Chatelet, *De la prostitution dans la ville de Paris,* and *Hygiène publique.*	Ferrus is appointed Inspector General of the services for the insane.

	The finance law of 1836 puts expenditure on the insane under the variable expenses of the departments.	
	The Conseil d'Etat prepares a Bill.	
1837	Abortive Parliamentary debate on penitentiary reform.	Beginning of the discussion of the Law on the Insane in the Chamber of Deputies.
1838	L. Moreau Christophe, *De la réforme des prisons en France basée sur la doctrine du système pénal et le principe de l'isolement individuel*; also, C. Lucas, *De la réforme des prisons*.	Esquirol, *Des maladies mentales considérées sous les rapports médical, hygiénique et médico-légal*.

Notes

Introduction

1. Ministère de l'intérieur et des cultes, *Législation sur les aliénés et les enfants assistés*, vol. I, Paris, 1880, p. 1.
2. U. Trélat, *La folie lucide*, Paris, 1861, p. 320.

1 The Challenge of Madness

1. G. Ferrus, *Des aliénés*, Paris, 1834.
2. Cf. H. Derouin, A. Gary, F. Worms, *Traité théorique et pratique de l'assistance publique*, Paris, 1914. Cf. also Gasperin (Minister of the Interior). *Rapport au Roi sur les hôpitaux, les hospices et les services de bienfaisance*, Paris, 1837.
3. In this exposition a strictly chronological order has not been observed. See Appendix B, in which principal events are recalled chronologically, whether they are strictly speaking medical or concern the general complex of problems relating to public assistance.
4. Cf. P. Sérieux and M. Trenel, 'L'internement des aliénés par voie judiciaire sous l'Ancien Régime', *Revue historique de droit français et étranger*, Series 4, 10th year, July-Sept, 1931; P. Sérieux, 'L'internement par ordre de justice des aliénés et correctionnaires sous l'Ancien Régime', ibid., Series 4, 11th year, July-Sept, 1932.
5. Cf. P. Chatelin, *Contribution à l'étude des aliénés et anormaux au XVIIè et XVIIIè siècle*, Paris, 1923.
6. Cf. P. Sérieux and L. Libert, *Les lettres de cachet, 'prisonniers de famille' et 'placements volontaires'*, Ghent, 1912.
7. Cf. A. Joly, *Du sort des aliénés en Basse Normandie avant 1789*, Caen, 1869.
8. Cf. C. Paultre, *De la répression de la mendicité et du vagabondage sous l'Ancien Régime*, Paris, 1906.

9. Quoted in P. Sérieux and L. Libert, 'Le régime des aliénés en France au XVIIIè siècle', *Annales médico-psychologiques*, 1914, II, p. 97.
10. The Breteuil Circular, March 1784, quoted in F. Funck-Bretano, *Les lettres de cachet à Paris*, Paris, 1903, p. XLIV.
11. Des Essarts, 'Folie, fureur, démence', *Dictionnaire universelle de police*, Paris, 1787. vol. IV.
12. A. Tuetey, *L'assistance publique à Paris pendant la Révolution, documents inédits*, vol. III, Paris, 1898, p. 368.
13. Des Essarts, 'Folie'.
14. In 1789 Des Essarts made a very significant self-criticism: 'In April 1789, re-reading this article, which was written in 1784, I must add that the nation expresses the wish that this part of the administration should be abolished, or at least modified, so that the liberty of citizens is ensured in the most inviolate fashion.'
15. Decree quoted in J. C. Simon, *L'assistance aux malades mentaux, histoires et problèmes modernes*, Thesis, Faculty of Medicine, Paris, 1964.
16. Cf. M. Foucault, *Histoire de la folie*, Paris, 1961, vol. III, ch. 2, 'Le nouveau partage'.
17. Cf. P. Goubert, *l'Ancien Régime*, vol. II, *Les pouvoirs*, Paris, 1973.
18. Quoted in F. Funck-Brentano, *Lettres de cachet*, p. XXXIII.
19. Cf. for example, Sérieux and Libert, 'Le régime des aliénés; 'Un asile de sûreté sous l'Ancien Régime', *Annales de la Societe médicale de Gand*, June 1911; A. Bigorre, *L'admission du malade mental dans les établissements de soin de 1789 à 1838*, Thesis, Faculty of Medicine, Dijon, 1967.
20. Quoted in Funck-Brentano, *Lettres de cachet*, p. XLV.
21. Ibid. Unless stated to the contrary, the passages in the quotations given in italics denote the present author's emphasis.
22. Quoted in Tuetey, *L'assistance publique*, vol. I, p. 200.
23. Documents in ibid., vol. III, pp. 229–38.
24. M. Foucault, *Surveiller et punir*, Paris, 1975.
25. Cf. C. B. Beccaria, *Traité des délits et des peines*, Fr. trans., Lausanne, 1976.
26. 'Opinion de Cabanis, député de Paris, sur la nécessité de réunir en un seul système commun la législation des prisons et celles des secours publics', *Corps législatifs, Conseil des Cinq-Cents*, 7 messidor an VI, p. 6.
27. Quoted by Sérieux and Libert, *Les lettres de cachet*, p. 51.
28. Cf. J. Donzelot, *La police des familles*, publication due shortly.
29. Paultre, *De la répression*.
30. Quoted in F. Dreyfus, *Un philanthrope d'autrefois. La Rochefoucault Liancourt*, Paris, 1903, p. 173.
31. 'Opinion de Cabanis' p. 3.
32. Cf. J. Imbert, *Le droit hospitalier de la Révolution et de l'Empire*, Paris, 1954, p. 26 ff. For an analysis in greater depth of the relationships

between the new policy of public assistance, the right to work, and the real state of the labour market, see chapter 3 of this book.

33. F. Dreyfus, 'Le vagabondage et la mendicité dans les campagnes', in *Misères sociales et études historiques*, Paris, 1901.

34. For the sake of completeness it should be added that the fiction of the contract only applies within the framework of national sovereignty, and for citizens only of the nation state. International policy is the authorized exercise of violence, at the opposite pole to contract. Likewise, beyond their frontiers the liberals have no scruples at being protectionist if their interest so dictates. Colonial policy invented on its own behalf one and even several statuses of guardianship for the native inhabitants. These latter normally pay by the loss of their autonomy for the advantage of being placed under the guardian authority of the civilizing power.

35. *Législation sur les aliénés et les enfants assistés*, vol. I, p. 3.

36. P. Pinel, *Traité medico-philosophique sur l'aliénation mentale*, 2nd edn, Paris, 1809, p. 202.

37. J-J. Rousseau, *Discours sur l'origine et les fondements de l'inégalité parmi les hommes*, Paris 1754, Pléiade edn, vol. III, p. 156.

38. Cf. the commentary of J. Derrida, *De la grammatologie*, Paris, 1967, p. 247 ff.

39. Report cited in its entirety in Tuetey, *L'assistance publique*, p. 489–506.

40. Just as it inspires the analogy of the poor person and the child. See chapter 3.

41. Circular of Portalis of 30 Fructidor, Year XII, quoted in: G. Bollotte, 'Les malades mentaux de 1789 à 1838 dans l'oeuvre de P. Sérieux', *Information psychiatrique*, 1968, no. 10, p. 916.

42. Quoted in M. Gillet, *Analyse des circulaires, instructions et décisions émanées du ministère de la justice*, Paris, 1892, no. 1559.

43. E. J. Georget, *Considérations médico-légales sur la liberté morale*, Paris, 1825, p. 38.

44. G. Delangre, *De la conditions des aliénés en droit romain et en droit français*, Paris, 1876.

45. *Législation sur les aliénés et les enfants assistés*, vol. I, p. 2.

46. Ibid., vol. II, p. 14.

47. Ibid., vol. II, p. 72.

48. Bernard d'Airey, *Rapport sur l'organisation générale des secours publics*, Legislative Assembly, 13 June 1792, pp. 86–7.

2   The Rescue of the Totalitarian Institution

1. Cf. J. Colombier and F. Doublet, *Instruction sur la manière de gouverner les insensés et de travailler à leur guérison dans les asiles qui leur sont destinés*, Paris,

1786. The second part, 'Treatment', written by Doublet, set out the various remedies for the different kinds of madness.

2. Cf. A. Tuetey, *L'Assistance publique à Paris pendant la Révolution, documents inédits*, I, p. 237.

3. Jean Wier, *De l'imposture et tromperie des diables, des enchantements et sorcelleries*, First French edition, Paris, 1570, p. 6.

4. Cf. P. Sérieux, L. Libert, 'Le régime des aliénés en France au XVIIIè siècle', *Annales médico-psychologiques*, p. 215.

5. J. Colombier, F. Doublet, *Instruction sur la manière de gouverner les insensés*.

6. J. E. D. Esquirol, 'Des établissements consacrés aux aliénés en France et des moyens de les améliorer', (Mémoire présenté au ministère de l'Intérieur), *Des maladies mentales*, Paris, 1838, vol. II; G. Ferrus, *Des Aliénés*, Paris, 1834.

7. J. Colombier, F. Doublet, *Instruction sur la manière de gouverner les insensés*, p. 11.

8. Ibid., p. 5.

9. De Montlinot, *Etat actuel du dépôt de mendicité de Soissons*, Paris, 1781, p. 27.

10. Quoted in C. Paultre, *De la répression de la mendicité*, p. 414.

11. J. Colombier, F. Doublet, *Instruction sur la manière de gouverner les insensés*, p. 10.

12. J. Tenon, *Mémoires sur les hôpitaux de Paris*, Paris, 1788, p. 303 ff.

13. Cf. P. Carette, 'Tenon et l'assistance aux aliénés à la fin du XVIIIè siècle', *Annales médico-psychologiques*, 1925.

14. Quoted in F. Dreyfus, *Un philanthrope d'autrefois. La Rochefoucault-Liancourt*, p. 178.

15. C. Bloch and A. Tuetey, *Procès-verbaux et rapports du Comite de mendicité*, Paris, 1903, p. 762.

16. J. Tenon, *Mémoires*, p. 393.

17. J. E. D. Esquirol, 'Des établissements' vol. II, p. 398.

18. Quoted in Tuetey, *L'Assistance publique à Paris* vol. I, Paris, 1895, p. 237.

19. Cf. B. de Gerando, *De la bienfaisance publique*, Paris, 1839, p. 487 ff.

20. J. S. Mercier, *Tableau de Paris*, Paris 1783, vol. XIII, p. 174.

21. Cf. Paultre, *De la répression de la mendicité*.

22. Cf. L. Lallemand, 'L'assistance médicale au XVIIIè siècle', *Bulletin des sciences économiques et sociales du Comité des travaux historiques et scientifiques*, special issue, 1895.

23. Abbé Baudeau, *Idées d'un citoyen sur les besoins, les droits et les devoirs des vrais pauvres*, Paris, 1765.

24. Quoted in L. Lallemand, 'L'assistance médicale'.

25 Des Essarts, 'Hôpitaux,' *Dictionnaire de police*, cf. also: De Gerando, *De la bienfaisance publique;* F. E. Fodéré, *Essai historique et moral sur la pauvreté*

des nations, Paris, 1824; C. Granier, *Essai de bibliographie charitable*, Paris, 1891.

26. J. Michelet, *Histoire de France*, Paris, 1880, vol. XV, 21.
27. Tellès-Dacosta, *Plan général d'hospices royaux*, Paris, 1789, p. 4.
28. M. de Mirabeau, *L'ami des hommes*, Paris, 1774, pt 2, p. 349.
29. In the numerous literature on the subject published in the last years of the *Ancien Régime*, cf. Abbé de Reclade, *Traité des abus qui subsistent dans les hôpitaux*, Paris, 1786; R. L. D'Argenson, *Considérations sur le gouvernement de la France*, Paris, 1784; J. Howard, *Etat des prisons, des hôpitaux et des maisons de force*, Paris, 1788; Tellès-Dacosta, *Plan général*; P. S. Dupont de Nemours, *Idée des secours à donner aux pauvres malades dans une grande ville*, Paris, 1786.
30. Cf. A. R. J. Turgot, ' "Fondation" de l'*Encyclopédie*' in *Oeuvres*, ed. Schelle, Paris, 1824, vol. I, p. 584 ff. See also the commentary on this article and the evaluation of its influence in A. Monnier, *Histoire de l'Assistance dans les temps anciens et modernes*, Paris, 1856, p. 449 ff.
31. Cf. Tenon, *Mémoires*.
32. Cf. C. P. Coqueau, *Essai sur l'établissement des hôpitaux dans les grandes villes*, Paris, 1787, p. 142.
33. Lallemand, 'L'assistance médicale', p. 3.
34. Abbé Baudeau, *Idée d'un Citoyen*, vol. I, pp. 64–5.
35. Cf. Bloch, Tuetey, *Procès-verbaux*; and Dreyfus, *Un philanthrope d'autrefois*.
36. B. Barère, *Premier rapport fait au nom du Comité de salut public sur les moyens d'extirper la mendicité dans les campagnes et sur les secours que doit accorder la République aux citoyens indigents*, 22 Floréal, Year II.
37. M. Rochaix, *Essai sur l'évolution des questions hospitalières de l'Ancien Régime à nos jours*, Saintes, 1959.
38. Cf. Imbert, *Le droit hospitalier de la Révolution et de l'Empire*, Paris, 1954.
39. CF. J. B. Bô, *Rapport et projet de décret sur l'extinction de la mendicité, présenté à l'Assemblée Nationale au nom du Comité des secours publics*, n.d. (the report was read to the Convention).
40. Cf. M. Foucault, *Naissance de la clinique*, Paris, 1963; J. P. Peters, 'Le grand rêve de l'ordre médical en 1770 et aujourd'hui', *Autrement*, no. 4, (winter 1975–6); see also chapter 3 of this book.
41. Bloch, Tuetey, *Procès-verbaux*, p. 396.
42. Quoted, ibid., p. 394.
43. Cf. Rochaix, *Essai sur l'évolution*.
44. Lebon, quoted in Imbert, *Le droit hospitalier*. p. 78.
45. J. B. Delecloy, 'Rapport sur l'organisation des secours publics', *Convention nationale*, Session of 12 Vendémiaire, Year IV.
46. Ibid., p. 2.
47. Ibid., p. 4.

48. Ibid., p. 3.
49. Ibid., p. 6.
50. Ibid., p. 3.
51. Ibid., p. 6.
52. Ibid., p. 6.
53. Ibid., p. 8.
54. Delecloy appears also to play down another important 'social problem' whose ambiguous position in this context has already been noted: that of vagrancy and begging. His plan envisaged the transfer of the funds of the institutions for beggars to the new prisons, as if these latter could assume all the tasks relating to obligatory detention. We know that the Napoleonic administration remedied this laxity by making the re-installation of institutions for beggars an essential element in its mechanisms for the maintenance of order. But the decree of 1808 was also very badly applied. There was hesitation between a public assistance policy of *laissez-faire* and one of authoritarianism. Napoleonic centralization and the administration of assistance by the 'notables' and the clergy under the Restoration represent the two opposing options possible in the framework of the same 'liberal' policy. In fact, behind these hesitations can be found employment policy fluctuations, and diverging opinions on the social value of work (see chapter 3).
55. P. J. G. Cabanis, 'Quelques principes et quelques vues sur les secours publics', in: *Oeuvres complètes*, vol. II, Paris, 1823, pp. 201-2.
56. Cabanis, *Observations sur les hôpitaux*, Paris, 1790, p. 18.
57. Ibid., p. 7.
58. Cabanis, 'Quelques principes', p. 203.
59. Ibid., p. 203.
60. Cabanis. Report quoted without the name of the author in: Tuetey, *L'Assistance publique à Paris*, vol. III, p. 489 ff.
61. Ibid., p. 489.
62. Title II, Article 4 of the plan for new regulations, ibid., p. 502.
63. Ibid., p. 494.
64. Ibid., p. 502.
65. Foucault, *Histoire de la folie*, p. 459-63.
66. To point out certain continuities, let us also recall that the father of Cabanis was an intimate of Turgot, who introduced the young Cabanis into the circle of Mme Helvétius. Cf. 'Notice historique et philosophique sur la vie, les travaux et les doctrines de Cabanis', by L. Piess in his Introduction to the third edition of the *Rapports du physique et du moral de l'homme*, Paris, 1844.
67. Cf. G. Bollote, 'Les châteaux de Frère Hilarion', *Information psychiatrique*, Jan. 1966.

68. R. Semelaigne, *Les grands aliénistes français*, vol. I, Paris, 1894, p. 94.

69. Cf. Foucault, *Histoire de la folie*, vol. II, ch. I, 'Le fou au jardin des espèces'.

70. Doublet, 'Traitement qu'il faut administrer aux différentes espèces de folie', in Colombier and Doublet, *Instruction*, pt II.

71. On the contrary, the comparison with what occurred elsewhere at the same time indeed shows that it was this systematization of *relationships* between the elements of psychiatric practice that ensured the advances made by the French School during the first half of the nineteenth century. For example, in England the establishment by Tucke of *The Retreat* follows the same 'philanthropical' line. But Tucke was not a doctor. His practices were met head-on by the medical establishment, whilst at the same time attracting laymen, the 'lay' reformers of assistance. Hence arose a dangerous cleavage between the aspirations of good-hearted souls and the attractions of scientification, which English specialists in mental health medicine would have great difficulty in bridging in order to succeed in reinstating moral treatment as a medical technology. With Pinel, the synthesis was effected at the outset; he was a doctor who, by his practices, imposed a solidarity of knowledge, of authority, and of a place in which to exercise it, the hospital. These three dimensions, none of which was new, operated change by the fact that they are presented together. (Upon the situation in England at the same period cf. A. T. Scull, 'From madness to mental illness', *Archives européennes de sociologie*, 1975, no. 2).

72. P. Pinel, *La médicine clinique*, 2nd edn, Paris, 1804, 'Avis sur cette seconde édition', pp. XXIX–XXX.

73. Quoted in Bloch, Tuetey, *Procès-verbaux*, p. 598.

74. In contrast to the previous situation, described in these terms by La Rochefoucault-Liancourt after his visit to the Salpêtrière in 1790:

> The air in the old rooms is foul, they are small, the yards narrow, everything is in a state of abandonment as painful as it is inconceivable. The mad women who are chained (there are a large number of them) are mixed with those who are peaceful; those who are in the throes of rage are under the gaze of those who are peaceful: a spectacle of contorsions and fury, the shouting and incessant yelling prevent any means of resting for those that may need it and make outbursts of this horrible disease more frequent, more strident, more cruel and more incurable. In short, no gentleness, no consolation, no remedies exist therein.
>
> (Ibid., p. 624).

75. P. Pinel, *Traité médico-philosophique sur l'aliénation mentale*, 2nd edn, Paris, 1809, pp. 193–4.

76. Ibid., pp. 194–5.

77. Ibid., p. 5.
78. Ibid., pp. 198–9.
79. H. G. Mirabeau, 'Des lettres de cachet et des prisons d'Etat', *Oeuvres*, vol. I, Paris, 1820, p. 264.
80. Ibid., p. 264.
81. Pinel, *Traité médico-philosophique*, 'Plan général de l'ouvrage', pp. 6–7.
82. Ibid., p. 7.
83. Ibid; Preface to 2nd edn, p. IV.
84. Pinel follows the text above with: 'Thus for those suffering from such infirmities there are needed public or private institutions subject to standard internal rules.' (Ibid., p. V).
85. Cf. P. Sérieux, *Le quartier d'aliénés du dépôt de mendicité de Soissons au XVIIè siècle*, Paris, 1914.
86. P. Dunod, *Projet de la Charité de la ville de Dôle*, Paris, 1698.
87. Pinel, *Traité médico-philosophique*, p. 225.
88. M. Foucault, *Surveiller et punir*, Paris, 1975.
89. Cf. the presentation of *Asiles*, by E. Goffman (Fr. trans., Paris, 1968).
90. E. Goffman, *Asiles*.

3   The First Social Medicine

1. A. Corlieu, *Centenaire de la faculté de médicine*, Paris, 1896. In this pamphlet are to be found the timetable and programme of the different courses given at the Paris School of Medicine, which became a faculty after the Napoleonic reorganization of 1808. Pinel's course had nothing to do with mental health.
2. Cf. R. Semelaigne, *Quelques pionniers de la psychiatrie française*, Paris, 1930, and *Médecins et philanthropes*, Paris, 1912; cf. also A. Moret, *Notices bibliographiques*, Paris, 1894; A. Ritti, *Histoire des travaux de la société médico-psychologique*, Paris, 1913.
3. U. Trélat, *De la constitution du corps des médecins et de l'enseignement médical*, Paris, 1828.
4. A. Ritti, 'Eloge d'E. Renaudin', in *Histoire des travaux de la Société médico-psychologique*, p. 122.
5. E. Regnault, *Nouvelles réflexions sur la monomanie homocide*, Paris, 1830, pp. 5–6. (Author's emphasis).
6. C. Lasègue, 'Notice nécrologique sur J-P. Falret', *Archives générales de médecine*, 1871, vol. I, p. 487.
7. Ibid., p. 488.
8. Ibid., p. 490.
9. P. Pinel, *Nosographie philosophique ou la méthode de l'analyse appliquée à la médecine*, Paris, 1800, Introduction to the first edition, pp. VI–VII.

10. Pinel, *Traité médico-philosophique*, p. 136.
11. Pinel, *Nosographie philosophique*, p. X.
12. Cf. G. Rosen, 'The Philosophy of the Ideology and the Emergence of Modern Medicine in France', *Bulletin of the History of Medicine*, 1946, vol. XX.
13. Pinel, *Traité médico-philosophique*, Introduction to the first edition, p. IX.
14. Foucault, *Naissance de la clinique*.
15. Cf. F. J. Broussais, *De l'irritation et de la folie*, Paris, 1828.
16. X. Bichat, *Recherches physiologiques sur la vie et la mort*, Paris, 1868, p. 72-3.
17. E. G. Georget, *De la folie*, Paris, 1820, p. 245.
18. Ibid., p. 246.
19. Ibid., p. 258.
20. Ibid., pp. 155, 160.
21. A. L. J. Bayle, *Nouvelle doctrine des maladies mentales*, Paris, 1825, pp. 8-9.
22. A. L. J. Bayle, *Traité des maladies du cerveau et de ses membranes*, Paris, 1826, p. 498 ff.
23. Cf. G. Rosen, *Madness in Society*, London, 1968, ch. IX, 'Patterns of Discovery and Control in Mental Illness'.
24. L. Lunier, 'Recherches sur la paralysie générale progressive pour servir à l'histoire de cette maladie', *Annales médico-psychologiques*, 1849.
25. M. J. Baillarger, 'De la découverte de la paralysie générale et des doctrines émises par les premiers auteurs', *Annales médico-psychologiques*, 1850.
26. J. Falret, *Recherches sur la folie paralytique et les diverses paralysies générales*, Paris, 1853. For the whole of this discussion cf. Rosen, *Madness in Society*.
27. F. Leuret, *Du traitement moral de la folie*, Paris, 1840, p. 1.
28. Cf. for example, M. Parchappe, 'De la prédominance des causes morales dans la génération de la folie', *Annales médico-psychologiques*, 1843, vol. II.
29. Constans, Lunier and Dumesnil, *Rapport sur le service des aliénés en 1874*, Paris, 1878.
30. H. Girard, 'De l'organisation et de l'administration des établissements d'aliénés', *Annales médico-psychologiques*, 1843, vol. II, p. 231.
31. Pinel, *Traité medico-philosophique*, p. 154.
32. The expression is used by L. Bonnafé, 'De la doctrine post-esquirolienne', *Information psychiatrique*, vols. I and II, April and May 1960.
33. F. E. Fodéré, *Essai médico-legal sur la folie*, Paris, 1824, p. 124.
34. J. P. Falret, 'Du traitement général des aliénés', in *Des maladies mentales et des asiles d'aliénés*, Paris, 1864, p. 686.

35. H. Girard, 'Compte rendu sur le service des aliénés de Fains en 1842, 1843, 1844, par Renaudin', *Annales médico-psychologiques*, 1846, vol. VIII, p. 143.

36. Esquirol, 'Mémoire sur cette question: existe-t-il de nos jours un plus grand nombre de fous qu'il n'en existait il y a quarante ans?', in *Des maladies mentales*, vol. II, p. 742.

37. Constans, Lunier and Dumesnil, *Rapport sur le service des aliénés en 1874*, pp. 1–9. Cf. also, L. Lunier, *De l'influence des grandes commotions politiques et sociales sur le développement des maladies mentales pendant les années 1869 à 1873*, Paris, 1874.

38. M. J. Baillarger, 'Note sur la fréquence de la folie chez les prisonniers', *Annales médico-psychologiques*, 1844, vol. IV, p. 77.

39. Falret, 'Considérations générales sur les maladies mentales' (1843) in *Des maladies mentales*, p. 62.

40. Falret, 'Du traitement général des aliénés', in *Des maladies mentales*, p. 680.

41. E. Renaudin, 'L'asile d'Auxerre et les aliénés de l'Yonne', *Annales médico-psychologiques*, 1845, vol. V, p. 242.

42. Leuret, *Du traitement moral*.

43. Just as the general and the individual treatment of madness represented two varieties of moral treatment (cf. Falret, 'Du traitement général des aliénés', pp. 682–3, and my chapter 4), the use of openly coercive means by Leuret, or the benevolent paternalism of most psychiatrists during the first half of the nineteenth century, were two extreme procedures of a single strategy for imposing discipline that supposed a basic disequilibrium between patient and therapeutist, and the absolute malleability of the former by the latter. Cf. R. Castel, 'Le traitement moral, thérapeutique mentale et contrôle social au XIXè siècle', *Topique*, no. 2, Feb. 1970.

44. M. Parchappe, *Rapport sur le service médical de l'asile des aliénés de Saint-Yon*, Rouen, 1841, p. 11.

45. J. P. Falret, 'Du traitement général des aliénés', p. 685.

46. Ibid., p. 698.

47. F. Voisin, *Du traitement intelligent de la folie*, Paris, 1847, p. 10.

48. Romans de Coppins, in: *Mémoires qui ont concouru pour le prix accordé en 1774 par l'Académie de Châlons-sur-Marne*, Châlons, 1780, p. 327.

49. Cf. J. Donzelot, 'Espace clos, travail et moralisation', *Topique*, no. 3, May 1970.

50. C. P. Coqueau, *Essai sur l'établissement des hôpitaux dans les grandes villes*, Paris, 1787, p. 142.

51. Ibid., p. 13.

52. A. R. J. Turgot, 'Fondation', in *Oeuvres complètes*, Paris, 1920, p. 208.

53. Cf. Turgot, 'Instruction sur les moyens les plus convenables de gouverner les pauvres', ibid.

54. Cf. F. Dreyfus, *Un philanthrope d'autrefois, La Rochefoucault-Liancourt*, Paris, 1903.

55. With the exception of the relapsed incurable, for whom idleness was a moral choice. It was mainly for them that all the Revolutionary Assemblies prescribed 'repressive institutions', the successors to the beggaries, which were to constitute, with asylums and prisons, the only institutions preserved from the old totalitarian complex of institutions.

56. Foucault, *Histoire de la folie*, p. 430. Cf. also K. Polanyi, *The Great Transformation*, Boston, Mass., 1963.

57. Cabanis, 'Quelques principes et quelques vues sur les secours publics' in: *Oeuvres* vol. II, p. 229.

58. J. P. Brissot (de Warville), *Théorie des lois criminelles*, Paris, 1781, p. 75.

59. B. d'Airy, *Rapport et projet sur l'organisation générale des secours publics*, présenté à l'Assemblée nationale le 12 juin 1792, p. 7.

60. J. B. Bô, *Rapport et projet de décret sur l'extinction de la mendicité*, présenté à la Convention au nom du Comité de secours publics, pp. 4–5.

61. Cf. the discussion on the right to subsistence and the right to work on the occasion of Barère's presentation of Article 23 of the 1793 Constitution, in *Archives parlementaires*, first series, no. 63., p. 110ff., session of 22 April 1793. We know that the Convention, being aware of the risk that its initiatives might go beyond the bounds, and wishing to keep them within the limits of bourgeois law, voted unanimously to condemn any attack on the principle of private property. Cf. A. Monnier, *L'assistance dans les temps anciens et modernes*, Paris, 1856.

62. B. Barère, *Premier rapport fait au nom du Comité du salut public*, 22 Floréal, Year II.

63. T. Duchâtel, *De la charité dans ses rapports avec l'état moral et le bien-être des classes inférieures de la société*, Paris, 1829, p. 185.

64. Ibid., p. 343.

65. Ibid., p. 233.

66. In 1842 there were 1,800 religious institutions, with 25,000 nuns, as against 27,000 on the eve of the Revolution. Cf. Discours d'Isambert à la Chambre des députés, *Le Moniteur*, 19 May 1842.

67. F. Schaller summarizes this tendency as follows: 'To guarantee assistance is to encourage vice, dissipation and disorder; in the language of economics, it is to institute a premium to the prejudice of the economy, wise calculations and, finally, prudence in marriage.' (*Un aspect nouveau du Contrat social*, Neufchâtel, 1950, p. 41).

68. Coqueau, *Essai*, p. 29.

69. For the systematic analysis of this policy of philanthropy, cf. Donzelot, *La police des familles*.

70. De Gerando, *Le visiteur du pauvre*, Paris, 1820, pp. 9–10.

71. For the readjustment of the equilibrium between impersonal relation-

ships in exchange through an emotive link stimulated by charity itself, cf. De Gerando, *Le visiteur*, p. 10 ff.

72. Baron C. Dupin, *Bien-être et concorde des classes du peuple français*, Paris, 1840, p. 40. Dupin, a member of the Institut de France and a peer of France, was one of the first specialists in the harmonization between classes. He carried on his philanthropic work indefatigably by writing several works. But he was also the inspirer of numerous moves to educate deserving workers, such as the schools of Arts et Métiers. It was an indication of his strong position in the philanthropic movement that it was he who gave the eulogy of the Duc de La Rochefoucault-Liancourt at the Institut.

73. De Gerando, *Le Visiteur*, p. 39.

74. On philanthropy as a new technology of need, cf. Donzelot, *La Police*.

75. Foucault, *Naissance de la clinique*; cf. also above, chapter 2.

76. Peters, 'Le grand rêve'.

77. Cabanis, *Du degré de certitude de la médecine*, third edition, Paris, 1819, p. 147.

78. Cf. E. H. Ackernecht, 'Hygiene in France, 1815–1848', *Bulletin of the History of Medicine*, vol. XXII, no. 2, March–April 1948.

79. Prunelle, *De la médecine considérée politiquement*, Paris, 1818, p. 29.

80. A. Bouchardat, *Rapport sur les progrès de l'hygiène en France*, Paris, 1867, p. 49.

81. Prospectus, *Annales d'hygiène publique et de médecine légale*, no. 1, January 1829, p. V.

82. Ibid., p. VI.

83. Cf. G. Caplan, *Principles of Preventive Psychiatry*, Boston, Mass., 1963.

84. P. S. Thouvenel, *Sur les devoirs du médecin*, Paris, 1806, p. 10 (Thouvenel joined the Société de morale chrétienne, whose role would be seen in the development of the mental health movement under the Restoration, and would publish *Eléments d'hygiène*, which in 1840 still carried on this tradition.

85. Fodéré, *Essai historique et moral sur la pauvreté des nations*, Paris, 1825, p. 3.

86. Ibid., p. 23.

87. F. Leuret, 'Notice sur les indigents de la ville de Paris', *Annales d'hygiène publique et de médecine légale*, 1836.

88. A. Foville, *Des aliénés*, Paris, 1853, p. 79.

89. Cf. especially A. J. P. Parent-Duchatelet, *Hygiène publique*, Paris, 1836; *De la prostitution dans la ville de Paris*, Paris, 1836; Villermé, *Tableau de l'état physique et moral des ouvriers*, Paris, 1842. The enquiries into the workers by Villermé may doubtless have constituted the basis for an immense programme of 'social work', but they were also completely detached from any medical reference.

90. Cabanis, *Du degré de certitude*, p. 147.
91. Ibid., p. 141.
92. Renaudin, *Commentaires médico-administratifs*, pp. 20–1.
93. De Gerando, *De la bienfaisance publique*, p. 212.
94. Renaudin, *Commentaires*, p. 251.
95. De Gerando, *De la bienfaisance publique*, p. 75.
96. Ibid., p. 76.
97. Ibid., p. 43.
98. Renaudin, *Commentaires*, p. 23.
99. Cf. Foucault, *Surveiller et punir*; also H. Gaillac, *Les maisons de correction*, Paris, 1971.
100. G. Ferrus, *Des Prisonniers et de l'emprisonnement*, Paris, 1850.
101. Ferrus, *Des aliénés*.
102. Moreau-Christophe, 'De l'influence du régime pénitentiaire en général et de l'emprisonnement individuel en particulier', *Annales médico-psychologiques*, 1843, p. 430.
103. E. Durkheim, *Le Suicide*, Paris, 1912.
104. De Gerando, *De la bienfaisance publique*, vol. II, p. 287.

4 Providential Experts

1. E. Freidson, *Professional Dominance*, New York, 1970.
2. E. Freidson, *Profession of Medicine: A Study in the Applied Sociology of Knowledge*, New York, 1970, p. 205.
3. T. Szasz, *The Ideology of Insanity*, New York, 1970, p. 75.
4. It will perhaps be objected that the very definition of expertise implies that it is someone else who decides, for instance, the members of a jury, 'in soul and conscience', basing themselves on the medico-legal report of the psychiatrist, etc. Even within the framework of the law of 1838 (see above, chapter 5), it was not the certificate given by the doctor of the institution that decided on placement of the patient, but either the order of the prefect (mandatory placement, article 18), or the certificate of a doctor with no connection with the institution (voluntary placement, article 8). But we shall see exactly how the current 'drift' in the notion of expertise subverted these strictly legalist requirements. Renaudin had already pointed it out: every psychiatric diagnosis is a 'medico-legal act' (*Commentaires médico-administratifs*, p. 23), because it directly or indirectly involves the fate of a person. For example, when a children's judge decides upon placing a child in a closed environment, he essentially endorses a prognosis of the psychological development of the one concerned, and of the more or less pathogenic character of the family environment, etc.

5. A. T. Scull, 'From madness to mental illness', *Archives européennes de Sociologie*, 1975.
6. On all these points, cf. the impressive work of Imbert, *Le droit hospitalier*.
7. Cf. Camus, *Rapport au conseil général des hospices de Paris*, Fructidor, Year XI. On the situation during the first third of the nineteenth century, cf. also Pastoret, *Rapport au conseil général des hospices de 1804 à 1814*, Paris, 1816; Desportes, *Compte rendu du service des aliénés*, Paris, 1826; A. Bigorre, *L'admission du malade mental dans les hôpitaux de soin de 1789 à 1838*, Thesis, Dijon, 1967; G. Bolotte and A. Bigorre, 'L'assistance aux malades mentaux de 1789 à 1838', *Annales médico-psychologiques*, 1966, vol. II.
8. Cf. Desportes, *Compte rendu*.
9. J. E. D. Esquirol, 'Des établissements consacrés aux aliénés en France et des moyens de les améliorer', in: *Des maladies mentales*, Paris, 1838, vol. II, p. 400.
10. About a particular episode in the vicissitudes of this power take-over, cf. G. Bléandonu and G. Le Gaufey, 'Naissance des asiles d'aliénés, Auxerre-Paris', *Annales*, 1975, no. 1.
11. Cf. Esquirol, 'Des maisons d'aliénés, revision of the article in the *Dictionnaire des sciences médicales*, for the 1838 edition of *Maladies mentales*, to be compared with his 1818 memoir.
12. Ferrus, *Des aliénés*.
13. Esquirol, 'Des maisons d'aliénés', in *Des maladies mentales*, vol. II, p. 528.
14. Falret, *Des aliénés et des asiles d'aliénés*, p. 582.
15. Scipion Pinel, *Traité complet du régime des aliénés*, Paris, 1836, p. 42.
16. Renaudin, *Commentaires médico-administratifs*, p. 162.
17. E. Renaudin, 'Administration des aliénés', *Annales médico-psychologiques*, 1845, vol. V, p. 74.
18. Ibid., vol. VI, p. 230.
19. Dr Bouchet, 'Surveillant, infirmiers et gardiens', *Annales médico-psychologiques*, vol. III, 1844, p. 54.
20. Goffman, *Asiles*.
21. Constans, Lunier and Dumesnil, *Rapport sur le service des aliénés en 1874*, Paris, 1878, p. 160.
22. A. Linas, *Le passé, le présent et l'avenir de la médecine mentale en France*, Paris, 1863, p. 27.
23. Tenon, *Mémoire sur les hôpitaux*.
24. Pinel, *Traité médico-philosophique*, p. 70.
25. Renaudin, *Commentaires*, p. 73.
26. J. B. M. Parchappe, *Des principes à suivre dans la fondation et la construction des asiles d'aliénés*, Paris, 1851, p. 8.

27. Esquirol, 'Mémoires sur l'isolement des aliénés' (1832) in: *Des Maladies mentales*, vol. II, pp. 743–4.
28. Ibid., p. 785.
29. *Législation sur les aliénés et les enfants assistés*, vol. I, p. 12.
30. Bibliothèque de l'Assistance Publique, Mn EI 13, quoted by J. Lemoine, *Le régime des aliénés et la liberté individuelle*, Paris, 1934, p. 30.
31. Archives Nationales, F 131933, quoted by Lemoine, *Le régime*, p. 32.
32. Cf. Desportes, *Compte rendu*.
33. Cf. Lemoine, *Le régime*, p. 31.
34. The same proliferation of private institutions for the insane, run for profit, is to be observed at the same period in England. Cf. Scull, 'From madness to mental illness'. It is certainly from the beginnings of triumphant capitalism that must be dated the birth of a 'market' for madness.
35. Circular extensively quoted by Lemoine, *Le régime*.
36. Bigorre, *L'admission des malades mentaux*. The same situation exists in the Nord department.
37. Scipion Pinel, *Traité complet*, p. 303.
38. Esquirol, 'Examen du projet de loi sur les aliénés', in *Des maladies mentales*, p. 789.
39. Ferrus, *Des aliénés*, pp. 285, 290.
40. One can, however, detect signs of opposition to the mental health movement before the passing of the 1838 law. An anonymous work published in Marseilles denounced the pretentions of the doctor, who 'set himself up as supreme judge' and 'the disguised and genteel inquisition, much more terrible for a free people than that of Spain, for in those kinds of health establishments, it is exercised not only about matters of religion, but for every kind of thing.' (*Considerations sur le projet de loi présenté à la Chambre des députés sur les aliénés*, Marseilles, 1837, pp. 9–10. The expression 'Pinelières' ('Pinel's "looney bins"') had, it seems, even passed into everyday language from the 1820s onwards to designate institutions that had already become discredited: 'I thought I had seen the various kinds of prison that exist in this town and I was boasting about it to a distinguished doctor. You do not know the most curious ones, he said to me, those that are called institutions for the insane, which the public call "Pinelières" ' (*Supplément du Voyage en France de M. Leign*, Paris, 1826, p. 1). To pinpoint these hostile tendencies, cf. in the next chapter the analysis of the Parliamentary discussions on the 1838 law.
41. Georget, *De la folie*, p. 20.
42. Pinel, *Traité médico-philosophique*, p. 102.
43. 'I was not a little surprised to see several of the insane who at no time gave any indication of any defect of understanding, and who were

dominated by a kind of instinctive fury, as if the affective faculties had been damaged' (ibid., p. 156).

44. Ibid., p. 102.

45. Hoffbauer, *Traité de médecine légale*, Fr. trans., Paris, 1827. Through this translation, made by Chambeyron, Esquirol's disciple, and annotated by his master, this German treatise occupied a central position in the discussions on legal medicine in France.

46. Esquirol, 'Monomania', *Dictionnaire des sciences médicales*, Vol. XXXIV, reprinted in *Des maladies mentales*, vol. II, p. 98.

47. Ibid., p. 100.

48. E. Regnault, *Du degré de compétence des médecins dans les questions judiciaires relatives aux aliénations mentales*, Paris, 1828.

49. E. G. Georget, *Considérations médico-legales sur la folie et sur la liberté morale*, Paris, 1825, p. 24.

50. Esquirol, 'Mémoire sur la monomanie homicide', in *Des maladies mentales*, vol. II, p. 796.

51. C. C. H. Marc, *De la folie considérée dans ses rapports avec les questions médico-judiciaires*, Paris, 1840, p. 244.

52. J. P. Falret, 'De la non-existence de la monomanie homicide', *Archives générales de médecine*, August 1854.

53. Cf. the reports of these discussions in the *Annales médico-psychologiques*, 1854, vol. VI (nine sessions) and 1866, vol. II (three sessions).

54. Falret, 'De la non-existence de la monomanie homicide', p. 524.

55. Cf. a material intervention of this kind after the condemnation of P. Rivière in M. Foucault *et al.*, *Moi, Pierre Rivière, ayant égorgé ma mère, ma soeur et mon frère*, Paris, 1973.

56. Esquirol, 'Mémoire sur la monomanie homicide', in *Des maladies mentales*, vol. II, p. 842.

57. C. C. H. Marc, *De la Folie*, Paris, 1840, p. 29.

58. E. G. Georget, *Discussion médico-légale sur la folie et l'aliénation mentale, suivie de l'examen du procès criminel d'H. Cormier et de plusieurs autres procès*, Paris, 1829, p. 51.

59. F. Lelut, 'Revue médicale des journaux judiciaires', in *Annales médico-psychologiques*, vol. I, January 1843, p. 64.

60. The reporting of these cases repeatedly occurs in the psychiatric literature of the time, and they act as paradigms for the elaboration of the concept of monomania. Cf., for example, Georget, *Discussion médico-legale*; Esquirol, 'Monomanie homocide'; Marc, *De la Folie*.

61. H. Aubanel, 'Rapports judiciaires et considérations médico-légales sur quelques cas de folie homocide', *Annales médico-psychologiques*, 1845, vol. II, p. 383.

62. Ibid., p. 384.

63. L. Lunier, 'Revue médicale des journaux judiciaires', *Annales médico-psychologiques*, 1846, vol. VIII, p. 259.
64. J. Falret, *Des aliénés dangereux et des asiles spéciaux pour aliénés*, Paris, 1869, p. 53.
65. J. Moreau de Tours, 'Revue médicale des journaux judiciaires', *Annales médico-psychologiques*, 1845, vol. V, p. 118.
66. Sérieux and Libert, *Les lettres de cachet, 'prisonniers de famille' et 'placements volontaires'*, p. 12.
67. Esquirol, 'Mémoire sur la monomanie homicide', in *Des maladies mentales*, vol. II, p. 793.

5   Psychiatry as Political Science

1. On 'micro-powers' cf. Foucault, *Surveiller et punir*, particularly vol. IV, ch. 2.
2. *Législation concernant les aliénés et les enfants assistés*, vol. I, p. 4–5.
3. Cf. Constans, Lunier et Dumesnil, *Rapport général*, p. 22.
4. Archives Nationales, F15 444.
5. *Législation concernant les aliénés*, vol. I, pp. 10–11.
6. G. Bollote, 'Les projets d'assistance aux malades mentaux avant la loi de 1838', *Information psychiatrique*, June 1965. Bollote has already attributed the authorship of the note of 1813 to Lafont de Ladebat. But the original manuscript in the Archives Nationales is not signed.
7. Cited in G. Bollote, 'Les projets d'assistance aux malades mentaux sous la Restauration', *Annales médico-psychologiques*, vol. I, no. 3, 1966; cf. also Bollote and Bigorre, 'L'assistance aux malades mentaux de 1789 à 1838'.
8. *Législation concernant les aliénés*, vol. I, p. 8.
9. Esquirol, 'Des maison d'aliénés', in *Des maladies mentales*.
10. Archives Nationales, F15 444.
11. Cf. Scull, 'From madness to mental illness'.
12. Ferrus, *Des aliénés*.
13. *Législation concernant les aliénés*, vol. I, p. 18.
14. Ibid., vol. II, p. 14.
15. Ibid., vol. II, p. 211.
16. Unless it be to note that, as compared with the first half of the nineteenth century, the encroachment of administrative power upon the power of the judiciary is increasingly more and more tolerated. Thus the practice of administrative internment came into favour once more in 1939 for those individuals 'dangerous for national defence or public security' (decree-law of November 18), made worse under the Vichy regime for certain foreigners, Jews, prostitutes, etc., and renewed at

the Liberation for other categories (ordinance of 4 October 1944), broadly applied during the Algerian war (law of 27 July 1957 and ordinance of 7 October 1968). (Cf. Colliard, *Les libertés publiques*, 3rd edition, Paris, 1968.) The next work will deal with the connection between the collapse of legalism and the rise of miniature control mechanisms of the medical and psychological kind.

17. *Législation sur les aliénés*, vol. II, p. 92.
18. Esquirol, 'Mémoire sur l'isolement des aliénés', 1832, in *Des maladies mentales*, vol. II, p. 413.
19. Falret, *Observations sur le projet de loi relatif aux aliénés*, Paris, 1837, p. 6.
20. *Législation sur les aliénés*, vol. II, p. 315–316.
21. Casimir Pinel, 'De l'isolement des aliénés', *Journal de médecine mentale*, vol. I, 1861, p. 181.
22. Scipion Pinel, *Traité complet du régime sanitaire des aliénés*, p. 223.
23. Which does not at all signify that the mental health specialists were politically on the Right, as are those among present-day psychiatrists who follow their tradition (and who are today the only ones who have a clear conscience about it). A living psychiatry is the expression of a will to reform. It is therefore, at least in the beginning, more or less 'progressive'. This overall position of the profession in the division of labour in society can change as a function of a modification occurring in the historical conjuncture. It can also be associated with a fairly wide range of 'political' and personal attitudes. At the extreme, it is the 'contradiction' of Ulysse Trélat that was presented in the Preface.
24. Esquirol, 'Des établissements consacrés aux aliénés en France', in *Des maladies mentales*, vol. II, p. 413.
25. *Législation concernant les aliénés*, vol. II, p. 9.
26. Cf. C. Pauthas, *Guizot pendant la Restauration*, Paris, 1949.
27. Quoted by Pauthas, *Guizot*, p. 48.
28. Cf. C. Dupin, *Eloge du duc de La Rochefoucault-Liancourt*, Institut royal de France, 1827.
29. L. de Guizart, *Rapport sur les travaux de la Société de morale chrétienne pendant l'année 1823–1824*, p. 22–3.
30. Pauthas, *Guizot*.
31. J. Tissot (Brother Hilarion), *Le manuel de l'hospitalier et de l'infirmier*, Paris, 1829.
32. Cf. Bollote, 'Les châteaux de Frère Hilarion'.
33. This tendency began with Pinel, who saw in mystic exaltation the source of those states of delirium least amenable to treatment and who recommended that the insane be kept away from religious influences. If certain of his successors were less hostile, they placed very strict conditions upon the intervention of religion. 'In an institution designed for the treatment of insanity, experience shows that religion must in

some respect be reduced to a specialism.' (H. Girard, 'De l'organisation et de l'administration des établissements d'aliénés', *Annales médico-psychologiques*, 1843, vol. II, p. 257).

34. *Législation concernant les aliénés et les enfants assistés*, vol. III, p. 133. Brother Hilarion (Jean Tissot) would intervene in the debate about the law of 1838 through a minor publication, *Mémoire en faveur des aliénés*, Lyon, 1838: 'The law proposed would be disastrous; already it is causing disturbance in every institution for the insane, and desolation in the families of these wretched people' (p. 5), its adoption would be 'a veritable public calamity' (p. 15). Having been beaten, Tissot would adopt an increasingly violent position opposing the official system. In a work appearing in 1850, *Etat déplorable des aliénés*, he spoke of 'butcheries' in the asylums and inveighed against the 'mental health doctors' who, 'through blindness, error and cupidity, assassinate and maltreat patients every day' (p. 179). He doubtless gave the first coherent formulation to certain anti-psychiatric attitudes: antiprofessionalism, a mystical conception of the nature of madness, a practical plan for the destruction of the asylum: he set up an 'information office, for moral direction and free consultation so as to bring about the curing of the insane in their own homes'. He likewise proposed the constitution of small therapeutic groups of some ten persons in which the distinction between those treating the illness and those being treated was not sharply drawn. This is an illustration of the fact that there can be an antipsychiatry of the Right. This tendency, in which antiprofessionalism, irrationality and the struggle against state intervention take the place of a programme, has been maintained to the present day. For example, in the US a few years ago, the John Birch Society launched a campaign against psychiatry, and certain of these tendencies are not alien to the thinking of Thomas Szasz.

35. Such a statement does not, moreover, imply that kind of ecological myth that tends to prevail at the present time. Doubtless the madman never enjoyed a happy existence. So far as one can judge, he has always been controlled, mocked at, used, and, if one likes, 'repressed'. The scandal of the madman shut away, or exploited in the family or through local connivence, can indeed be set against that of 'arbitrary detentions'. As for the insane who were shut up in prisons before the setting up of the psychiatric system, their situation can arouse no nostalgic feelings.

36. Esquirol, *Examen du projet de loi sur les aliénés*, Paris, 1837; Falret, *Observations sur le projet de loi relative aux aliénés*, A. Faivre, *Examen critique du projet de loi sur la séquestration des aliénés*, Lyon, 1837.

37. *Législation sur les aliénés*, p. 11.

38. Ibid., vol. II, p. 9.

39. Certain opponents have very clearly identified what is at stake in the problem: 'I do not intend here to discuss the medical question: we are occupied with legislation, not medicine . . . Legislatively, we do not know what medical system we should adopt, what discoveries science will be able to make. I therefore ask that the government be left free to fix the conditions appropriate for ensuring good order and for reconciling this with individual liberty' (ibid., vol. II, p. 504).

40. Based on the dual procedure of 'compulsory placement' (upon the initiative of the administration) and 'voluntary placement' (upon the initiative of the family or persons close to it, backed up by a medical certificate), to which we shall return in the next chapter.

41. M. Dayrac, *Réformes à introduire dans la loi de 1838*, Paris, 1883, p. 250.

42. Esquirol, 'Mémoire sur l'isolement des aliénés', in: *Des maladies mentales*, vol. II, p. 745.

43. Falret, *Observation sur le projet de loi relatif aux aliénés*, p. 29.

44. Renaudin, *Commentaires médico-administratifs*, p. 65.

45. It will perhaps be objected that, according to the law of 1838, it was not the duty doctor admitting the insane person who made out the detention certificate. Yet this must be looked at more closely. In the case of what is termed 'voluntary' placement, in other words requested by the family, the certificate of the outside doctor, who was rarely a psychiatrist, was endorsed, or not endorsed by the '24 hour certificate', then the 'fortnight certificate', made out by the mental health specialist. For compulsory placement, it is true that the administrative authority only intervened to detain a person deemed 'dangerous to himself or to others'. But the sorting of the insane from the sane was always carried out at a certain time in accordance with medical criteria (in Paris, at the special infirmary of the prison, elsewhere through the 24 hour or fortnight certificate). It was moreover envisaged in the law that the prefect's orders must give reasons (article 18) and that if the doctor deemed a person compulsorily detained not to be ill or to be cured, the prefect had to issue a fresh decision without delay (article 20). But the most significant point is this: the complexity of these procedures should have entailed a host of conflicts between doctors and representatives of the administration. Now, at least up to recently, they have been exceptional. It is proof that the administrative authority could have confidence in its 'special doctors' and that the latter have fulfilled their social mandate well as guardians of public order.

46. This, moreover, is untrue: we have seen both that interdiction was rarely pronounced, and that, when it was, it was almost always after sequestration. But here Dufaure states what was strictly the law before 1838: all sequestrations without interdiction were in law illegal, even if they were already covered by a kind of *de facto* medical legality, which

now becomes legal *de jure*. This is an example of the transition of a 'normative fact', as Gurvitch would have termed it, to its legal endorsement.

47. *Législation sur les aliénés*, vol. II, p. 287.
48. Renaudin, *Commentaires*, p. 71.
49. *Législation sur les aliénés*, vol. II, p. 518.
50. G. Delasiauve, 'La responsabilité des médecins aliénistes', *Journal de médecine mentale*, 1868, no. VIII, p. 69.
51. *Législation sur les aliénés*, p. 149.
52. Ibid., vol. II, p. 103.
53. Ibid., vol. II, p. 136.
54. Ibid., vol. II, p. 498-9.
55. Ibid., vol. III, p. 192-3.
56. Cf. G. Delagrange, *De la condition des aliénés en droit romain et en droit français*, Paris, 1876.
57. C. Demolombe, *Traité de la minorité*, Paris, 1888, vol. II, p. 549.
58. *Législation sur les aliénés*, vol. II, p. 127.
59. L. Bonnafé and G. Daumezon, 'L'internement, conduite primitive de la Société devant le malade mental', *Documents de l'information psychiatrique*, vol. I, 1946, p. 83.
60. Ibid., vol. II, p. 315.
61. Ibid., vol. III, p. 102.

6   Law and Order

1. Dr Berthier, 'Excursions scientifiques dans les asiles d'aliénés' *Journal de médecine mentale*, 1861, no. I, p. 320.
2. Renaudin, *Commentaires médico-administratifs*, p. 15.
3. Ibid., p. 20.
4. *Législation sur les aliénés*, vol. I, p. 61. This repeats advice already insistently given in the first circular of 28 July 1838, one month after the passing of the law. Cf. ibid., vol. I, p. 48.
5. Constans, Lunier and Dumsesnil, *Rapport*, pp. 54-62.
6. Ibid., pp. 63-4.
7. Survey in T. Roussel, *Rapport au Sénat de la commission relative à la révision de la loi du 30 juin 1838*, Paris, 1884, p. 5. In 1872 Roussel put the numbers at 51,004 insane living at home (of whom 20,020 'madmen proper', and 30,984 'idiots and cretins') as against 36,964 insane in the asylum (of whom 32,815 'madmen proper' and 4,149 'idiots and cretins').
8. H. Aubanel, 'Rapports judiciaires et considerations médico-légales sur quelques cas de folie homicide', *Annales médico-psychologiques*, 1846, vol. VII, p. 240.

9. Circular of August 5, 1839, repeated also, although in a more nuanced fashion, on August 14, 1840; cf. *Législation sur les aliénés*, vol. I, p. 46 and p. 97.

10. Cf. A. Brière de Boismont, 'Appréciation médico-légale du régime actuel des aliénés en France', *Annales médico-psychologiques*, 1865.

11. A. Pain, *Des divers modes de l'Assistance publique appliquée aux aliénés*, Paris, 1865, p. 15.

12. Cf. M. Henne, 'Introduction à l'étude des questions administratives', *Information psychiatrique*, January 1960.

13. B. Haussmann, *Mémoires*, vol. I, Paris, 1890, p. 464. It deals with the time when Baron Haussmann was Prefect of Auxerre, where he collaborated closely with Girard de Cailleux, the mental health specialist, whom he had appointed as Inspector General for the Service for the Insane when he came to Paris, refurbishing with him the Service in the Seine department; cf. Biéandonu and Le Gaufrey, 'Naissance de l'asile, Auxerre-Paris.

14. Martin-Doisy, 'Aliénés', *Dictionnaire d'économie charitable*, Paris, 1855.

15. Renaudin, *Commentaires*, Préambule, p. 1.

16. Ibid., p. 391.

17. Ibid., p. 391.

18. Falret, *Des aliénés*, p. 713.

19. Daumezon, 'Méthode pour rédiger une nouvelle loi sur les aliénés'.

20. H. Girard, 'De l'organisation et de l'administration des établissements d'aliénés', *Annales médico-psychologiques*, 1843, vol. II, p. 243.

21. C. Lasègue and A. Morel, 'Etudes historiques sur l'aliénation mentale', *Annales médico-psychologiques*, 1844, vol. II, p. 243.

22. H. Girard, 'De l'organisation et de l'administration des établissements d'aliénés', *Annales médico-psychologiques*, 1843, vol. II, p. 245.

23. A caricature of this tendency was still to be found in 1831 in M. Pierquin, *De l'Arithmétique de la folie*, Paris. It is also very apparent in Fodéré, *Essai médico-legal*. I have referred very little to this tendency, which might be termed the 'pre-mental-health' period. It represents the direct application of Locke's philosophy to the theory of insanity, which likewise influenced Pinel, and afterwards his successors. But with Pinel, the acuteness of his clinical perception in part made up for this philosophical pre-judgement, in the sense that he brought his attention to bear upon those manifestations of madness that, from the intellectualist conception, were the most disconcerting. On this hesitation on the part of Pinel, see the texts cited in the discussion upon monomania in chapter 4. Likewise the young Esquirol, in his first conception of the moral aetiology of madness ('Dissertation sur les passions considerées comme causes, symptômes et moyens curatifs de l'aliénation mentale'), at first visualized it as a mere excess of the

passions. Finally, let us point out that the importance and the lengthiness of the discussions on the theme of madness and civilization are partly explained by this question: it arises from the scandal provoked in noting a growth in pathological disturbances that runs parallel to a progress in knowledge. It is understandable that the explanation that mental health specialists tend to adopt is of a Rousseauist type: the 'denaturizing' of man linked to the artificiality of civilized life, etc.

24. Falret, *Des aliénés*, p. 73. From this gulf between madness and reason Falret deduced directly the need for isolation, since his text continued as follows: 'Without neglecting these means, above all one must resort to diversion. To distract the feelings and morbid ideas is not to fight them by means of a precise logic or impassioned language, it is quite simply to remove those external impressions that foment disturbances of the understanding, and then to call attention to other objects.'

25. Pinel, *Traité médico-philosophique*, p. 218.

26. Constans, Dumesnil and Lunier, *Rapport*, p. 186.

27. Naturally there can be in this a symbolic use of cultural signs, that come into play also as features that promote distance from, and at the margin, the exclusion of, those who are deprived of them. On this point see the works of P. Bourdieu and J. C. Passeron, and in particular the theory of symbolic violence in *La Reproduction*, Paris, 1971. Yet, in the case of the institution of the school, it is the positive nature of the gains made from the accumulation of learning that marks out negatively those that are bereft of them. In transposing this into the psychiatric mould, it is the subject as person who is stigmatized, strengthening on the other hand the positive representation of themselves held by those outside the asylum. On the symbolic functioning of repressive institutions, cf. also J. Donzelot, 'Le troisième âge de la répression', *Topique*, no. 6, 1972.

28. In certain towns – Auxerre, for example – the two buildings faced one another, like two sacrificial columns of a temple of virtue.

29. *Législation sur les aliénés*, vol. II, p. 250.

30. This is also the interpretation that jurists have given to the law. Cf. Demolombe, *Traité*, vol. I, 540 ff.; A. Valette, *Attributions du préfet d'après la loi de 1838 sur les aliénés*, Paris, 1898'; also *Recueil Dalloz*, V, 'Aliénés', section III, article 2, no. 136.

31. A. Lisle, *Examen médical et administratif de la loi du 30 juin 1838 sur les aliénés*, Paris, 1847, p. 60.

32. T. Roussel, *Rapport au Sénat de la commission relative à la révision de la loi du 30 juin 1838*, Paris, 1884, p. 337.

33. We shall tackle in our next work this general displacement of the problem of control, what it implies as a transformation of the tech-

niques of power, and what it particularly owes to mental health medicine. Cf. also Donzelot, *La police des familles*.

34. *Législation sur les aliénés*, vol. II, p. 523.
35. J. Beaudoin and P. Raynier, *Assistance psychiatrique française*, Paris, 1965, vol. V, p. 200.
36. See for example, in the mental health specialist who was the most sensitive to the relationships between madness and the family, Trélat, *La folie lucide*, to what extent these limits were a hindrance: Trélat can only give advice, whereas he is burning to intervene.
37. *Législation sur les aliénés*, vol. II, p. 513.
38. Ibid., p. 513.
39. G. Daumezon, 'Méthode pour rédiger une nouvelle loi sur les malades mentaux', *Annales médico-psychologiques*, 1946, vol. II, p. 218.
40. *Législation sur les aliénés*, vol. I, p. 68.
41. Dr Berthier, 'Le surveillant d'aliénés', *Journal de médecine mentale*, 1863, no. III, p. 49.
42. M. Parchappe, *Des principes à suivre dans la construction des asiles d'aliénés*, Paris, 1851.
43. Goffman, *Asiles*.
44. Foville, *Des aliénés*, p. 199.
45. Dr Berthier, 'Du travail comme élément de thérapeutique mentale', *Journal de médecine mentale*, 1863, no. III, p. 119.
46. Haussmann, *Mémoires*, p. 229.
47. E. Renaudin, *Etudes médico-psychologiques sur l'aliénation mentale*, Paris, 1854, p. 8.
48. '*Young, Attractive, Rich, Verbal, Intelligent, Sophisticated*'. YARVIS is an acronym used in North America to denote the ideal client for psychoanalysis, the exact opposite type from the asylum patient.
49. Freud had been clear-minded enough to see in this a market to be exploited, and the honesty to recognize a motivation for 'inventing' psychoanalysis. Cf. the beginning of *Ma vie et la psychanalyse*.
50. Renaudin recommended three classes of paying inmates in the public asylums and described briefly their characteristics: *Commentaires*, pp. 327–8.
51. Constans, Lunier and Dumesnil, *Rapport*, p. 153.
52. Ibid., p. 154.
53. C. Pinel, 'De l'isolement des aliénés sous le rapport hygiénique, pathologique et légale', *Journal de médecine mentale*, Paris 1861, no. I, p. 221.
54. Cf., under the heading 'Variétés' in the *Journal de médecine mentale*, 1863, no. III, p. 398–9, the list of private clinics, with the names of the directors, that 'in the capital or the suburbs, offer a refuge for paying inmates of the upper classes'. Thus we note that three institutions were in the name of the family Brière de Boismont.

55. Since documents of the time are lacking, let us quote a recent opinion, but an authorized one, concerning a situation traces of which are still to be found today, particularly in the provinces:

> [The psychiatrist] spreads to a certain extent his psychiatric knowledge, and he generally delegates it to the various notables whom he normally meets in the exercise of his own functions as a notable in the department. In particular, he is at the same time usually director of the departmental asylum; by virtue of this, he has contacts with the departmental councillors, who are also mayors, in order to discuss the hospital budget. Likewise the various heads of the departmental services are in contact with him; the education officer talks to him about the woman primary teacher who presents signs of mental disturbance, the mayors talk to him, etc.

G. Daumezon, in *Histoire de la psychiatrie du secteur, Recherches*, no. 17, March 1975, p. 22.
56. C. Pinel, 'De l'isolement des aliénés', p. 221.
57. Pinel, *Traité médico-philosophique*, p. 227.
58. Ibid., p. 374–5.
59. Cf. G. Lanteri-Laura, 'La chronicité dans la psychiatrie française moderne', *Annales*, 1972, vol. III. With the historians of psychiatry, Lanteri-Laura tends, however, to accentuate the contrast between a first form of psychiatry, following Esquirol, humanist and liberal, and its degradation, as revealed in the great asylums of the end of the nineteenth century, when organicism led doctors to resign themselves to the incurability of patients. This evolution is not inconsiderable (see next chapter), but the essential characteristics of mental health practices (and above all others, the authoritarianism of the doctor and the mass treatment of the sick) are accepted from the outset, from Pinel onwards.
60. C. Loiseau, 'Eloge de Mitivié', *Annales médico-psychologiques*, March 1872, p. 124.
61. C. Pinel, 'De l'isolement des aliénés', p. 224.
62. Falret, *Des aliénés*, p. 682.
63. Ibid., p. 686.
64. Ibid., p. 699.
65. Ibid., p. 707.
66. A characteristic that has been too little noticed modifies the functioning, according to class, of psychiatry, but only for those patients that are the most seriously ill, and then to their detriment. The longer and more seriously ill a person is, the more he loses his class privileges. The family grows weary of consulting eminent doctors and of paying prohibitive sums for boarding, to no effect. The insane person of a good family can therefore find himself a permanent inmate, but after a slower and less necessary downward course than the indigent.

7 The Transition

1. Discussion at the Medico-psychological Society, in *Annales médico-psychologiques*, 1865, p. 248.
2. M. Proust, 'Rapport sur la législation relative aux aliénés criminels', *Bulletin de la Société générale des prisons*, December 1879, p. 882.
3. Cf. H. Desruelles, 'Histoire des projets de révision de la loi de 1838', *Annales médico-psychologiques*, 1938, p. 585 ff.
4. Cf. C. Pinel, 'Quelques mots sur les asiles d'aliénés et la loi de 1838 à propos d'une pétition au Sénat', *Journal de médecine mentale*, 1864, no. IV.
5. Cf. T. Roussel, *Rapport au Sénat de la commission relative à la révision de la loi du 30 juin 1838*.
6. The mental health specialists were very mocking of this proposal to set up a board including laymen. Yet it is the procedure that has prevailed in every state in the US; cf. B. Ennis and L. Siegel, *The Rights of Mental Patients*, New York, 1973.
7. Quoted in T. Roussel, *Rapport*, p. 298–9.
8. Falret, *Des aliénés*, p. 713.
9. A. Motet, 'Des aliénés et de la responsabilite médicale', speech made at the Paris Société de Médecine, *Journal de médecine mentale*, 1870, no. X, p. 87.
10. Garsonnet, senior lecturer at the Ecole Normale, made two stays in Charenton, after, as he says, 'momentary disturbances'. He had the feeling that he would have stayed there for life without friendly interventions made on his behalf because of his social position. He represents, as does later J. Lemoine, the author of an eloquent pamphlet against the law of 1838 (*Le régime des aliénés et la liberté individuelle*), those 'privileged ones' who have gone through the psychiatric machine and who have succeeded in extricating themselves thanks to their connections: they are also almost the only ones among the victims of the system whose testimony has gone beyond the asylum walls. The tone and level of their criticisms are very different from those of the professionals and administrators. Garsonnet, in particular, voices all the elements of criticism to be found in the most modern polemics regarding psychiatry. If the originality of anti-psychiatry has effectively been, not in the difference of its technical criticisms, but in denouncing this new type of power relationship that medicine brings into play behind the sensible relationships of therapeutic rationalizations, Garsonnet is indeed, without anachronism, an anti-psychiatrist who denounces at every level of mental health practice 'that exorbitant medico-legal authority, that unlimited despotism

which exceeds that of the plantation-owner over the negro' (*La loi des aliénés, nécessité d'une réforme*, Paris, 1869, p. 27). But the most significant fact is that such criticisms remained buried for a century, rejected by the complicity of an indifferent public and a body of professionals clinging to the defence of its privileges.

11. M. Garsonnet, La loi des aliénés, pp. 41, 43.

12. This question will be dealt with in a future work.

13. The Medico-Psychological Society included the principal mental health specialists. It met every month to discuss topical questions, generally on the basis of a paper read by one of its members or by a correspondent from the provinces or from abroad. Certain discussions on burning issues (monomania, the influence of civilization upon madness, degenerescence, the different modes of assistance for the insane, etc.) took up several meetings, and recurred on several occasions. The proceedings of these sessions are found in the *Annales médico-psychologiques*, and constitute one of the best sources for a detailed analysis of the evolution of the climate. The review has appeared without interruption from 1834 onwards, and the Society still holds its meetings. But after 1945 it set about bringing together the most conservative tendencies in the profession. The *Journal de médecine mentale*, directed by Delasiauve, is likewise a valuable source, but it only appeared for ten years (1860–70).

14. *Annales médico-psychologiques*, 1862, p. 15.

15. Ibid., p. 28.

16. Ibid., p. 31.

17. *Annales médico-psychologiques*, 1864, pp. 137, 143.

18. Ibid., p. 291.

19. G. Mundy, *Sur les divers modes d'assistance publique appliqués aux aliénés*, Paris, 1865.

20. L. Turck, *L'école aliéniste français, l'isolement des fous dans les asiles, l'influence détestable de ceux-ci*, Paris, 1864.

21. Discussion at the Medico-psychological Society, *Annales médico-psychologiques*, 1865, p. 249.

22. J. Moreau de Tours, 'Lettres médicales sur la colonie d'aliénés de Gheel', *Annales médico-psychologiques*, 1865, vol. VI, p. 265.

23. A. Linas, *Le passé, le présent et l'avenir de la médecine mentale en France*, Paris, 1863, p. 44.

24. C. Lasègue, 'Du délire de persécution', *Archives générales de médecine*, 1852.

25. Cf. *Bulletin de l'Académie de médecine*, 1854, vol. LXIX. Cf. also J. P. Falret, *Leçons cliniques de médecine mentale*, Paris, 1854, p. 249.

26. C. Lasègue, 'Morel, sa vie médicale et ses oeuvres', *Archives générales de médecine*, May 1873, p. 8.

27. Account in: *Annales médico-psychologiques*, 1860, vol. VI, p. 613.
28. Ibid., p. 616.
29. For the contribution to this debate of research on general paralysis, see chapter 3.
30. E. Marcé, *Traité pratique des maladies mentales*, Paris 1862, p. 34. Marcé, dead by the age of 36, two years after the publication of his *Traité*, did not have the time to bring his ideas, which tended towards organicism to fruition: 'This way of visualizing mental health medicine, which does not exclude the study of the moral element, but which examines it less in itself than in its relation to the organism, is that which governs me in writing this book (*Traité*, p. 36). But, among others, he influenced Magnan, who was his intern (cf. P. Sérieux, *V. Magnan, sa vie et son oeuvre*, Paris, 1921).
31. G. Ballet *et al., Traité de pathologie mentale*, Paris, 1903, Introduction, p. VI–VII.
32. B. Morel, *Traité des dégenerescences physiques, intellectuelles et morales de l'espèce humaine*, Paris, 1857, Introduction, p. XII.
33. B. Morel, *Le no-restreint* [sic], Paris, 1860, p. 93.
34. Morel, *Traité*, p. 691.
35. Ibid., p. 690.
36. Ibid., p. 76–7.
37. Ibid., p. 687.
38. Letter reproduced in *Le no-restreint*, p. 102–3. It is not without interest to make clear that Morel represents the most liberal tendency among the mental health specialists, being a partisan of 'no restraint', namely, the greatest possible limitation in the use of coercive means on the insane.
39. Ibid., p. 78.
39a.Ibid., p. 78.
40. Cf. G. Caplan, *Principles of Preventive Psychiatry*.
41. B. Morel, *Considérations sur les causes du goître et du crétinisme endémique à Rosières-aux-Salines*, Paris, 1850.
42. Morel, *Traité*, p. 685.
43. Not even the quasi-monopoly of mental health specialists over all problems of mental health medicine. If their authority remained undisputed in the asylum, their prestige outside it seems to begin to wane roughly about this time, although this is a fact that it is difficult to date with certainty. In any case by 1877 B. Ball, the university-based doctor, was preferred to Magnan, the mental health specialist, to take up the chair of mental illnesses at the Faculty of Medicine. We shall study later this conflict between the mental health specialists and the university-based ones, and the increasingly important part that the faculty took in comparison with the asylums, at least as a centre of innovation.

44. Cf. G. Daumezon, 'Essai historique critique de l'appareil d'assistance aux malades mentaux dans le département de la Seine depuis le début du XIXè siècle', *Information psychiatrique*, January 1960.

45. Cf. *Rapport de la commission instituée pour la réforme et l'amélioration des services d'aliénés du département de la Seine*, Paris, 1860. The report envisages a central asylum in Paris (Sainte-Anne) for recent cases of insanity and clinical teaching, to which is added an admission service for the allocation of the insane, a belt of asylums round Paris, and special asylums for epileptics.

46. P. Sérieux, *Rapport sur l'assistance des aliénés en France, en Allemagne, en Italie et en Suisse*, Paris, 1903. Sérieux frankly admitted the backwardness of France, and recommended a very differentiated system: asylum-colonies, psychiatric clinics, urban hospitals, sanatoriums for the 'neurotic', special asylums for the criminally insane, alcoholics and epileptics.

47. See the polemics aroused by the opening in 1922 of the Service Henri Rousselle at Sainte-Anne, reported in *L'aliéniste français*, particularly the years 1932 and 1933.

48. Reply of Dr Gouriou to 'Une enquête sur les services ouverts', an enquiry entrusted to E. Toulouse by the Minister of Public Health, November 1932, p. 563.

49. D. Rothman, in *The Discovery of the Asylum*, New York, 1971, has attempted to account for the implantation of the asylum system in the US through the characteristics of post-colonial society. However, what is most striking in this study is the presence – with a certain time-lag for their appearance – of the same elements that characterize the situation in Europe. In the same way the strategies through which English psychiatrists imposed their monopoly on the treatment of the insane about 1820 (cf. Scull, 'From Madness to Mental Illness') are analogous to those identified here.

Index